T0361191

INTERNATIONAL ENVIRONMENTAL GOVERNANCE

Volume 13

Futile Progress
Technology's empty promise

Full list of titles in the set
INTERNATIONAL ENVIRONMENTAL GOVERNANCE

Futile Progress
Technology's empty promise

Ernest Braun

publishing for a sustainable future

London • Sterling, VA

First published in 1995

This edition first published in 2009 by Earthscan

ISBN 978-1-84971-000-8 (Volume 13)
ISBN 978-1-84407-984-1 (International Environmental Governance set)
ISBN 978-1-84407-930-8 (Earthscan Library Collection)

For a full list of publications please contact:

Earthscan
Dunstan House
14a St Cross Street
London EC1N 8XA, UK
Tel: +44 (0)20 7841 1930
Fax: +44 (0)20 7242 1474
Email: earthinfo@earthscan.co.uk
Web: **www.earthscan.co.uk**

22883 Quicksilver Drive, Sterling, VA 20166-2012, USA

Earthscan publishes in association with the International Institute for Environment and Development

A catalogue record for this book is available from the British Library

Library of Congress Cataloging-in-Publication Data has been applied for

Publisher's note
The publisher has made every effort to ensure the quality of this reprint, but points out that some imperfections in the original copies may be apparent.

At Earthscan we strive to minimize our environmental impacts and carbon footprint through reducing waste, recycling and offsetting our CO_2 emissions, including those created through publication of this book. For more details of our environmental policy, see www.earthscan.co.uk.

This book was printed in the UK by CPI Antony Rowe.
The paper used is FSC certified.

Futile Progress

Futile Progress

Technology's Empty Promise

Ernest Braun

Earthscan Publications Ltd, London

For Dorothea

First published in 1995 by
Earthscan Publications Limited
120 Pentonville Road, London N1 9JN

A catalogue record for this book is available from the British Library

ISBN: 1 85383 243 X

Typesetting and figures by PCS Mapping & DTP,
Newcastle upon Tyne

Earthscan Publications Limited is an editorially independent
subsidiary of Kogan Page Limited and publishes in association with
the International Institute for Environment and Development and
the World Wide Fund for Nature.

CONTENTS

◆

INTRODUCTION

◆

The quest for progress is the most characteristic feature of our time; indeed, progress is at the pinnacle of our collective desire. Yet there is no consensus on the *aims* of progress, except in the narrow sense of general approval for technological progress. Thus technological progress has come to stand for progress in general; a society with greater technological prowess appears to us to be a better society. But has the relentless pursuit of technological progress led to a general social advance? Has it eliminated the blight of poverty, of inequality, of discrimination, of crime and of wars? Has more advanced technology increased the happiness of people and led to individual fulfilment and social harmony? It is possible that technological innovation has a positive effect on economic growth. But even if this is so, it is doubtful whether all technological innovation is equally desirable and whether the fastest possible rate of technological innovation is of the greatest economic benefit. The theme of this book is the analysis of these questions.

The first chapter defines the various concepts of progress and presents a brief analysis of these; the rest of the book describes the mechanisms by which technology advances and the effects of technology upon society, and deepens the analysis of the relationship between the progress of technology and sustainable social advance.

In order to investigate the role of technological innovation in human affairs we need to understand how technological innovation comes about. Why do firms innovate, why do governments help them in their endeavours, what are the mechanisms of the innovation process? These questions form the topic of the second chapter.

The third chapter investigates how public policy affects technological developments. It shows that technology policy has two faces in that it endeavours both to support and to control technology. The chapter gives a few contemporary examples – in the technology policies of various governments and the European Community.

The fourth chapter describes one of the main problems faced by humans as a result of the indiscriminate and thoughtless use of technology: the problem of environmental degradation. The point is made that market forces are unable to avoid environmental damage and that it is an inescapable task of public policy to take measures for safeguarding the long-term survival of the earth as a habitat for humans and the rest of nature.

Chapter 5 analyses and describes environmental policies. Effective environmental policies include technology policies applied to environmental problems, but usually need to include measures from other spheres of public policy.

Chapter 6 consists of a brief summary of the main arguments of the book and concludes that government policies ought to support only those technologies that are needed by society and yet cannot be sustained by market forces. The main candidates for public support are technologies designed to prevent further environmental degradation and to reverse some of the damage already done to the natural environment. Socially less important technological innovation may safely be left to markets, provided an adequate framework of regulation exists to safeguard society from a range of hazards posed by technology.

It is hoped that the book will be useful to students of technology management and technology policy, as well as to readers generally interested in the role of technology in society and the problems society faces as a consequence of the application of technology.

The book essentially consists of a critique of our present ways of fostering and regulating technological innovation and makes recommendations for improvements in technology policy. It is also critical of some prevalent social and political arrangements, but its recommendations and analysis are confined to technology policy. It is my fervent hope that the book will make a positive contribution both to the understanding of the role of technology and to improved social control of technology, and thus to sustainable advance for society.

Finally, I wish to thank my many past and present colleagues who have helped me to clarify my ideas by critical discussion and by drawing my attention to a great deal of information. I regret that I was unable to include even more information and argument.

Ernest Braun
1995

CHAPTER ONE

THE AIMS OF PROGRESS

◆

General Definitions

We generally define progress as the development of one state towards another state which is judged to be higher, better or more advanced in some way, albeit sometimes only temporally. Most progress depends upon human action, and it is this deliberate progress which is the concern of this book. Progress towards a better, or higher, state implies that some person or organization desires the achievement of a different state, and sees in progress a desirable movement towards a better future. Progress towards a goal can be seen as when a person, or an organization, is striving towards a different state and is coming closer to it. Progress, in this view, is change towards a temporally distant state and carries with it the connotation of improvement. Progress indicates movement with a time dimension, and hence with a velocity, so we speak of slow or fast progress. It is movement towards a distant goal, and any closer proximity to the goal, even without achieving it, is progress. In many cases the distant goal is vague and ill-defined, often not achievable, not uncommonly a moving target; yet any movement in the direction of the goal is deemed to be progress.

Progress can be of many different kinds, depending on the subject of progress. We need to distinguish between social progress, including the state of society, politics, economic activity, culture, and so forth; and scientific-technical progress. Although the main thrust of this book is technical progress, the reader who expects enthusiastic technical descriptions, such as those in 'Tomorrow's World' on BBC television or in technical journals, will be disappointed. The book's interest in technical progress stems from the relationship between technical and social progress. It views technological progress as a social activity with social aims and social controls, not as technical advance for its own sake, devoid of a social dimension. It discusses technical progress because technology is a social activity and technical progress finds almost universal acclaim, not so much as its own reward – leaving aside unadulterated technical enthusiasm – but because of the belief that it leads to economic and social well-being. It discusses technical progress because of its influence upon our lives and the state of society, and because technical progress is a deliberate and highly organized social activity.

This inevitably introduces two complex issues. One is the indeterminate nature of desires and thus the impossibility of describing desirable progress in any single deterministic and universally accepted way. The other is the self-interest of individuals or groups – and thus the inevitability of not just disagreement over goals but downright conflict between goals. The definition of desirable progress varies from person to person and from group to group, according to their different self-interests and sets of values. There is no such thing as a commonly and universally agreed aim towards which everyone wishes to progress, although there are some aims on which wide consensus exists, at least within relatively homogeneous social groups.

Before turning to the central issue of the book, technological progress, we need to consider the forms of social progress as the book's interest in technological progress is determined by its relationship to social progress.

Social Progress

It is impossible to avoid value-laden statements in any attempt to define or discuss social progress. Social progress is one of the central themes of politics and cannot be discussed in neat, objective, value-free scientific terms. Instead of beating about the bush and hiding a system of values behind long words of Greek origin and convoluted grammatical constructions, I shall attempt to describe explicitly what I regard as desirable objectives for a future social and political state, and thus define my own set of measures against which to judge progress from any given present state.

A desirable social state is, in my system of values, a state of social harmony. This requires the fulfilment of a number of conditions, such as: a reasonably narrow distribution of income and wide spread of wealth, where the word reasonably implies an absence of severely underprivileged and alienated groups in society as well as an absence of enormous ostentatious wealth. Herman Daly goes as far as to suggest that for the achievement of a steady-state economy – and, when all is said and done, this is the only possible economy in the long run – it is essential to have a lower limit on income and desirable to have an upper limit as well (Daly 1991: 54).

My list of requirements for a state of social harmony further includes:

- plenty of and equal opportunities for employment;
- freedom of expression;
- freedom of conscience and of beliefs;
- equal and ample opportunities for everybody to achieve an educational standard appropriate to their abilities and interests;
- good social security, medical provision and retirement benefits;
- equality of sexes, races, and other groupings;
- good housing, public transport, and leisure amenities;
- good provision for cultural pursuits of all kinds;
- high regard for the natural environment in word and in deed;
- clean and aesthetically pleasing urban environments.

One of the main results of such a state should be the virtual absence of criminality and a considerable sense of cooperation. Indeed, there would be very much more stress on cooperation than on competition, on equal opportunity rather than on privilege, on true achievement rather than on status.

It may be helpful to add a few political and economic criteria to the above sketchy description of social circumstances which appear to me desirable, as political institutions must be geared to achieving the above social objectives.

- There is no doubt that this ideal state presupposes some advanced form of democracy and requires adequate wealth to provide everybody with the necessities of life and with some of its niceties and luxuries although permanent economic growth need not be a precondition.
- Democracy and universal franchise is a condition *sine qua non*; the only political view that must be banned is one that wishes to abolish equality, freedom of speech, and universal franchise, and substitute dictatorship for democracy.
- All the freedoms and equalities outlined above, including freedom of information, must be safeguarded by suitable legal provisions, thus incitement to group hatred would be banned, as would be excessive state secrecy, and the natural environment would be protected by comprehensive legislation, backed by suitable institutional arrangements.
- Competition in commercial life should exist where appropriate, but should be sufficiently regulated to ensure high standards of honesty and fairness.

- Last, but not least, access to justice must be simple and affordable, as legal protection is of no avail if it is beyond the reach of individual citizens and small organizations.

On a more abstract level, we might say that the ideal state for society consists of:

- maximum personal freedom, compatible with minimum interference with other people's freedom;
- minimum constraint, compatible with maximum security;
- maximum equality, compatible with a necessary minimum of rewards and incentives for achievement;
- maximum compassion and cooperation, compatible with a necessary minimum of competition;
- maximum personal commitment to the welfare of society, compatible with maximum freedom of personal expression and fulfilment;
- lack of privileges by virtue of birth, compatible with the desire of free people to bestow benefits on their offspring.

In a recent television programme, Eduardo Galeano described the political compromises in East and West somewhat as follows: communism sacrificed freedom for the sake of justice; capitalism sacrifices justice for the sake of freedom ('Rear Window', Channel Four TV, 19 May 1992). In my view, satisfactory compromises between freedom and justice can and must be reached. This means some form of capitalism with a human face or, what amounts to the same thing, socialism with a human face. It is the human face that matters.

The ideas described above, alas abridged to the form of slogans, are by no means new. Indeed, the two great concerns of all so-called radical thinkers on political theory, from Greek times to the present day, have always been freedom and equality. For example, John Stuart Mill in his famous essay *On Liberty* writes:

> *The object of this essay is to assert one very simple principle,*
> *as entitled to govern absolutely the dealings of society with*
> *the individual in the way of compulsion and control, whether*
> *the means used be physical force in the form of legal*
> *penalties or the moral coercion of public opinion. That*
> *principle is that the sole end for which mankind are*
> *warranted, individually or collectively, in interfering with the*
> *liberty of action of any of their number is self-protection.*
> *That the only purpose for which power can be rightfully*
> *exercised over any member of a civilized community, against*
> *his will, is to prevent harm to others. His own good, either*
> *physical or moral, is not a sufficient warrant. He cannot*
> *rightfully be compelled to do or forbear because it will be*

better for him to do so, because it will make him happier,
because, in the opinion of others, to do so would be wise or
even right (Mill 1985: 68).

On equality it is more difficult to find a single representative quotation, but R H Tawney writes:

Hence, when liberty is construed, or implying, not merely a
minimum of civil and political rights, but securities that the
economically weak will not be at the mercy of the economically
strong, and that the control of those aspects of economic life by
which all are affected will be amenable, in the last resort, to
the will of all, a large measure of equality, so far from being
inimical to liberty, is essential to it (Tawney 1964: 168).

The equality which all these thinkers emphasize as desirable
is not equality of capacity or attainment, but of circum-
stances, institutions, and manner of life. The inequality which
they deplore is not inequality of personal gifts, but of the
social and economic environment... Their view, in short, is
that, because men are men, social institutions – property
rights and the organisation of industry, and the system of
public health and education – should be planned, as far as is
possible, to emphasize and strengthen, not the class
differences which divide, but the common humanity which
unites, them (Tawney 1964: 48–9).

Or, coming from a very different tradition, Karl Popper asserts regarding equality:

Our time has established it as an article of faith, even as
morally self-evident, that no one must go hungry as long as
there is food enough for all (Popper 1992: 216).

And on liberty he says:

We ought to be proud that we do not have one idea but many
ideas, good ones and bad ones; that we do not have a single
belief, not one religion but many; good ones and bad ones
(Popper 1992: 210).

Serious doubt must be cast upon the current fashion of regarding untrammelled competition as a means to social progress and indeed as a worthy end in itself. The currently confessed faith in the almost miraculously beneficial powers of competition is a dubious credo indeed. I agree with Hazel Henderson when she says 'we overvalue competitive activities and undervalue cooperation and social cohesion' (Henderson 1980: 79). Competition is a double-edged sword. On the one hand, it undoubtedly spurs people on to greater achievement. The will to win, to get ahead of the pack, to be better at whatever it might be than the next person, is a strong incentive toward greater effort. On the other hand, for every winner there are many losers and although the meek acceptance of being a permanent loser is regarded as a social virtue, it is in reality a disincentive to constructive action and a likely cause of social alienation with all its dreadful consequences. Competition looks much more desirable from the vantage point of the winner than from that of the loser. Competition is a form of licensed aggression, and as such is likely to bring out the worst in people, although it may also motivate them to creative effort. Thus unbridled competition is likely to do more harm than good, yet a measure of competition may be beneficial. cooperation, on the other hand, so little spoken of these days, is a prerequisite for much human achievement and a far less dangerous weapon than competition.

Competition, almost by definition, cannot protect the weak. Indeed competition is the enemy of compassion, and yet only a compassionate society can live in harmony. Civilization is concerned with providing a secure and reasonably comfortable life for all members of society, not only the strong, or lucky, winners. Competitive society emphasizes that there must be winners and losers, yet harmonious society is one without severe losers, and hence without outstanding winners. In an harmonious society, everybody is at least a moderate winner.

Competition on the economic/commercial level is, as at the personal level, a mixed blessing. The ostensible reason for safeguarding and fostering competition and a free market is the belief that a great variety of goods and services, to satisfy most human needs, can thus be supplied at the lowest possible price. If barriers to market entry are low, suppliers may enter the market with offers of goods and services and these offers will be sustained up to the point when all needs are satisfied. If consumers are fully aware of the quality and price of the various offers available, they are able to choose the product or service that satisfies their need best at the most advantageous price. Thus value for money and a great variety of choice are guaranteed in a perfect market. Unhappily, such perfect markets do not exist and many of the disadvantages associated with market competition are rooted in inevitable market imperfections. Other disadvantages – and these form the main topic of this book – are associated with a forced pace of technological change which causes a sub-optimum utilization of human and material resources. Known imperfections of markets are:

- barriers to entry;
- imperfect knowledge of available offers; and
- the tendency towards monopolies or oligopolies which are in a position to raise prices and thus extract unjustifiable profits and to raise entry barriers for would-be competitors.

Imperfect markets cannot guarantee that needs will be best satisfied, either in terms of the availability of a wide choice of products and services or of ensuring the best possible value for money to the customer. On the other hand, it is very difficult to eradicate market imperfections, and currently the high cost of technological innovation is proving an important factor in enhancing monopolistic tendencies.

Alas, even perfect markets cannot guarantee the best of all possible worlds. Competition imposes costs that must be borne by the consumers. The first cost is duplication and loss of economies of scale, such as they are. As each potential and actual supplier must do everything necessary to supply the market with whatever goods or services we care to name, there are normally more competitors than the market can actually support and many of them work under capacity, or are inefficient because they are too small, or fail altogether. The second cost is the cost of such failures. All the effort that goes into products that fail on the market must be written off. The third cost is that of competition itself: advertising and sales promotions; extravagant packaging; creating meaningless variations, gimmicks and brand-names. Finally, competition forces the pace of innovation and that, as will be described later, also imposes considerable costs.

Commercial competition plays a significant role in setting the overall tone of society and if it becomes too severe, social values become distorted away from the benign towards the aggressive. This is why governments have to ensure that competition is sufficient to promote good value and an adequate supply of goods while remaining honest and decent. The task is to set the rules under which competition is to take place and to ensure that these rules are adhered to. The legal framework under which competitive activity can take place and its supervision and enforcement are vital if commercial competition and a free market are not to deteriorate into a free-for-all. There is a fine line between legitimate dealing and dishonesty, between proper banking and usury, and between honest commerce and exploitation. All aspects of work and of property are, and indeed must be, governed by laws; and laws are only as good as their enforcement:

> The whole effort to treat laissez-faire as a principle of public policy, and then to determine what should be governed by law and what should not be, was based on so obvious an error that it seems grotesque. The error was in thinking that any aspect of work or of property is ever unregulated by law (Lippmann 1943: 186; see also Matzner: 231–60, in Matzner and Streeck 1991).

Social progress is progress towards an ideal state of adequate and fair competition, without any of its excesses or any unnecessary monopolies, though recognizing the possibility that some monopolies under public control may act in the best interest of society.

Competition forces manufacturers and other participants in the market to try to get ahead of their competitors. This can be done by lowering prices and improving quality – two entirely laudable goals. It can be done, however by lowering prices and reducing quality – a less laudable goal which frequently leads to commercial success. Because the customer is usually inadequately informed about the goods or services on offer, yet can judge the price very easily, the danger of obtaining poor value for money, albeit at a low price, is ever present. One victim of severe price competition and widespread efforts to reduce costs of personnel tends to be service to the customer, an intangible but most valuable aspect of commerce. It is also possible to compete by raising the price and moving the product 'up market'. Customers find it very difficult to judge whether they are getting value for money, as the qualities of modern products of technology are hard to assess. This is why the creation of an image, by means of advertising, external design and a sales ambience are so important. The faster the rate of change, both technically and commercially, the greater the danger of an ill-informed purchase.

It is the strong who win in commercial competition, as much as in personal competition. Yet being strong does not necessarily imply being good at doing the job in hand, or indeed in any other sense of the word. It may simply be the result of past accumulation or – worse still – of clever manipulations of the system. Thus the strongest firms or individuals in the economy are not necessarily those who produce the best quality products or services with the highest efficiency, but often those who operate monopolies, or near monopolies, or those who own scarce natural resources, or those who are best at manipulating the markets and the rules in their own favour. The ultimate logic of competition, in many branches of manufacturing industry and service provision, is the creation of large monopolistic, or oligopolistic, firms, surrounded by dependent suppliers and dealers. Rapid technological change enhances the trend toward oligopolies and governments are often unwilling to take effective counter-action:

> At this global level, the crisis of industrialism in market-
> oriented, mixed and socialistic economies involves an instant
> paradox: advancing levels of technological complexity
> systematically destroy free market conditions and render
> laissez-faire policies all but impossible; while, on the other
> hand, we humans have clearly not yet learned how to plan
> such societies (Henderson 1980: 195–6).

Perhaps the greatest failing of competition as the sole principle of organization for an economy is its inevitable failure to protect common goods, such as the natural environment. Competition means that each participant in the economy attempts to obtain the greatest benefit to himself or herself. Considerations of self-interest prevail over considerations of community interests. Altruism, or even enlightened self-interest, stand in stark and irreconcilable contradiction to pure economic competition. Hence governments, as guardians of the public interest, must regulate the economy in such ways as to safeguard those values and objects that unadulterated market forces cannot protect. Public health, the interests of future generations, and the natural environment are obvious examples. Compromise between these tasks of protection and guardianship and the wish to keep competition unhampered is always uneasy, but it is safest to err on the side of protection. Where there is doubt, those who cannot protect themselves should be protected: unborn generations and nature are high on this list.

The method of competition which is of the greatest interest is that of offering new goods or services, or goods and services with considerably enhanced qualities. This is achieved mainly by technological innovation. If competition forces the pace of innovation, ie innovation is undertaken faster and faster in order to sustain a competitive edge, this has several, largely undesirable, consequences.

1. The cost of research and development (R&D) soars as it becomes more and more expensive to achieve new or technically improved products. Technologies that are already developed to a high pitch can only be further improved by ever costlier small steps. This is one of the many instances where the law of diminishing returns imposes limits on human endeavour. Thus the customer may obtain technically novel products, yet his or her wants are satisfied at a higher than necessary cost.
2. Production processes run at sub-optimum efficiency because the pressure of innovation does not allow time to learn and finely hone the process. Users of technical installations often are unable to make best use of them because of the pace of change.
3. To make matters worse, manufacturers and businesses are forced to write off equipment which is perfectly serviceable on its own terms but needs to be disposed off under the relentless pressure to acquire new, supposedly better, equipment.
4. Finally, organizations and individuals are out of equilibrium most of the time; they have to adjust continually to new technologies and, because of the speed of change, they are not only permanently out of kilter but also have to spend an inordinate amount of effort on learning and adaptation. Nonetheless, governments feel obliged to do all they can to accelerate the pace of innovation, yet they do little to influence its direction toward those goals that need public support.

Individuals feel happiest and most secure in familiar surroundings. The sense of belonging, of being at home, of knowing one's way around, are important aspects of a person's sense of well-being. In a rapidly changing society this sense is lost and alienating disorientation is the frequent result. Thus a high rate of innovation carries high social, as well as economic, costs. Many people now believe that very rapid change in all spheres is a good thing, progressive, a sign of forward thinking. Yet change without a positive direction, change at a fast and thoughtless pace, can do nothing but destabilise society and disorientate its members. Rapid and universal change causes people to become strangers in their own countries, in their own cities, and in their own jobs (if they are lucky enough to have one). Change should not be regarded as a value in its own right; change is valuable only if it is well thought out and, preferably by consensus, it is change for the better.

As a result of over-investment in innovation, opportunities are lost for spending scarce financial resources on other, possibly more beneficial, things. These so-called opportunity costs can be very important, although they are difficult to quantify. The great effort made by governments to accelerate innovation carries the penalty of heavy opportunity costs. If, instead of supporting socially irrelevant innovation, governments spent the same amount of money on improving public services, protecting the poor and the sick, providing development aid, protecting the natural environment, would not the world be a happier place?

If social progress is defined as movement in the direction of an ideal state in the future, then it is clear that progress has been patchy and that in the course of history movement away from the ideal has been almost as frequent as that towards the ideal. It should be emphasized that the ideal state cannot be defined in absolute terms; it is merely an expression of personal preferences which may or may not be shared by large numbers of people. Considering my own set of preferences as stated above, it seems that in some countries, though regrettably by no means in all, major progress has been made over the centuries, albeit not in a monotonous fashion but with many backwards, forwards and sideways movements. Major landmarks on the path of social and political progress are the abolition of slavery, the creation of functioning parliamentary democracies, the abolition (or reduction) of racial and religious discrimination, social welfare provisions, the Charter of the United Nations, and many more. Yet a large number of countries are governed by ruthless dictatorships; drug abuse is rife; and the gap between rich and poor countries is widening.

That social and political progress is not unidirectional should not take us by surprise. Countries go through good phases and bad, depending on which groups and interests prevail in the inevitable struggle for political power, and what the vagaries of economic circumstances bring with them. Because ideals cannot be universally agreed, and because ideals are coloured by self-interest, it cannot be expected that progress toward a single set of ideals should prevail at all times. As groups holding different views come to power, so the deliberate march toward an ideal future changes direction. Add to these deliberate changes errors of policy and mismanagement, both leading inadvertently away from given objectives, and the tortuous path of social progress becomes the rule rather than the exception.

Indeed even the rosy view that by and large social progress has been made over the centuries must sometimes be doubted. Has not the present century seen some of the most barbarous regimes ever witnessed by humankind? Has it not witnessed two major and innumerable minor wars? Are not people being imprisoned, tortured, murdered, and impoverished on a massive scale? Are not civil wars raging in Europe and elsewhere? Are not drug abuse and crime on the increase? Is not our natural environment being destroyed on a massive, and possibly fatal, scale? If we wish to retain a reasonably sanguine view of social progress, we must be careful in our selection of periods of history and geographic regions. Alternatively, we may seek solace in the fact that what Karl Popper calls the Open Society, ie a society in which individuals have some choice and take some responsibility for their own actions and in which rational argument, rather than unquestionable taboos, form the basis for decisions, was first mooted in Greece, roughly speaking with Socrates, and hence its development is still relatively recent and uncertain (Popper 1966, vol 1, ch 10).

Be this as it may, social and political progress cannot move in a single direction because there is no consensus about the goals of such progress. History – even contemporary history – shows a tortuous path of social change, although over a long period optimistic idealists can discern some positive change. Sceptics, on the other hand, find little in the course of history to cause them to abandon their stance.

Economic Growth

The concepts of economic growth and of social progress on the one hand, and of technological progress and economic growth on the other, are inextricably intertwined. For many years now, economic growth has been a dominant aim of governments, and technological innovation has been regarded as one of the major determinants of such growth. It is not hard to understand why governments seek growth. Growth puts more money in people's pockets, even if some pockets are filled considerably more than others and some empty ones get emptier still. Growth also fills government coffers without the need for increased rates of taxation and thus allows flexibility in policies and permits expenditure on priority projects. It is much easier to achieve change in a time of growth than to juggle limited resources. In a world in which happiness is measured by material possessions and a healthy bank balance, economic growth is the best guarantor of a satisfied population. Altruism, or even enlightened self-interest, are no longer political forces to be reckoned with; unadulterated perceived economic self-interest is the order of the day. Governments under whose aegis the bank balances of a sufficient number of voters have grown tend to be re-elected (Galbraith 1992).

Economic growth is determined by many factors, such as:

- the rates of capital formation and of investment,
- interest rates and inflation,
- the external balance of trade and of payments,
- the structure of the economy,
- demographic factors,
- labour relations,
- availability of a well-qualified workforce,
- managerial efficiency,
- the quality of the infrastructure,
- the state of the world economy.

All these factors are decisive in positioning any one economy in the world economic fabric and thus allowing economic growth without running into insurmountable barriers, such as balance of payment or inflationary crises. The one decisive competitive factor that we shall concentrate on is technological and industrial prowess. Notwithstanding all the talk about an information society, dominated by the handling and trading of information rather than by the production of goods, the wealthiest nations of the world are those whose industry is best able to achieve large shares of world markets. It is very much easier to obtain a balance, or even a surplus, in external trade if domestic industry is able to satisfy a high proportion of domestic needs and is able to achieve a high rate of exports. Countries with weak industry need to import a great deal and fail to export. Thus, unless they happen to be desert kingdoms with huge oil reserves, they can balance their trade only with the aid of exports of services. To achieve large surpluses in this domain is, however, very difficult.

Britain provides a sad illustration for the fact that a country with a weakened industrial base cannot sustain a consumer spending spree without running into severe balance of payments deficits and inflationary pressures. Only a strong industrial base, or exceptionally favourable local conditions, such as great natural wealth or excellent conditions for tourism, can secure, in the long term, a healthy balance of payments.

A strong service sector is, unless exceptional local conditions prevail, largely dependent on strong industrial activity. Indeed the service sector of any economy consists to a not inconsiderable degree of services rendered directly to, or in connection with, industrial activities. Banking, financial services, insurance and information services need a domestic industrial base to become internationally competitive. Many services, such as R&D or design, can exist only in close symbiosis with local industry. Tourism may be the one exception to the rule, but tourism depends on special geographic and natural conditions and on a developed infrastructure. Although not wishing to argue that the service sector does not produce real wealth, I do argue that in a competitive world a country finds it very hard to balance its trade without a strong industrial sector. Tables 1.1 and 1.2 illustrate the malaise of some economies that suffer from a weakening manufacturing base, and compares these with truly strong economies, based on a healthy manufacturing industry.

To achieve and maintain a strong industrial base in the face of worldwide competition inevitably requires continuous technological innovation. The reason for this is twofold. First, industrial productivity must keep ahead of, or at least abreast with, the competitors and this requires continuous improvements in process technology, ie in the way goods are produced. If productivity falls too far behind, the products will fail in world markets on their price, unless exchange rates are particularly favourable or social conditions are such that low wages can be paid. Currently, Britain is trying to follow the low wage path in seeking competitiveness. Secondly, new markets must be opened and old ones maintained by a continuous stream of new or improved products. These may be truly new, aimed at the satisfaction of new wants or the better satisfaction of old wants; or they may be somewhat modified so as to create new demand by rendering the predecessor models obsolete.

The argument, stated here in its simplest terms, is unassailable. But life is not that simple and neither is the world economy. If the cost of innovation rises more than can be recouped from additional sales or, in the case of process innovation, from increased productivity, then the economy as a whole will not benefit from the innovation. Economists puzzle a great deal about what they regard as a paradox: the fact that despite all efforts at technological innovation, the rate of growth in overall productivity of the advanced economies has decreased. Any number of explanations has been put forward, none entirely convincing (OECD 1989). It is possible that an excessive rate of innovation, at too high a cost, may provide an explanation. The cosy assumption that innovation must lead to growth in overall productivity, and hence contribute to economic growth, does not seem to hold any longer, just as economic growth has ceased to guarantee full employment. The apparent enigma becomes explicable if we consider the overall costs involved in technological innovation, which may be higher than the gains achieved from it. In particular, the cost of prematurely writing off equipment and replacing it with the latest models, the cost of introducing ever-changing generations of information technology, and the cost of reorganizing and relearning all the time, without the benefit of ever reaching the optimum point on the learning curve, may be important explanatory factors which will be considered in more detail later.

A short digression on the measurement of economic activity and, hence, economic growth may be necessary. The only overall measure we have is GNP or GDP (gross national product or gross domestic

Table 1.1 Employment in manufacturing industry and in services in selected countries and balance of trade (exports less imports)

	Manufacturing industry %				% change	Services %				% change	Balance of trade 1988/90 Monthly averages $m
	1981	1984	1987	1990*		1981	1984	1987	1990*		
Germany	33.54	31.26	31.66	31.49*	-6.11	50.84	53.98	55.52	56.13*	9.42	5,824
Japan	24.82	24.94	24.11	24.08	-2.98	54.51	55.93	57.54	58.22	6.37	5,379
United Kingdom	25.98	22.93	21.33	20.07	-22.75	60.65	64.27	66.58	68.1	10.94	-3,577
United States	21.73	19.99	18.62	17.97	-17.30	66.19	68.02	69.63	70.7	6.38	-9,157

Sources: ILO (1991) Yearbook of Labour Statistics, ILO, Geneva; OECD (January 1992) Main Economic Indicators, OECD, Paris
* 1989 figure

Table 1.2 Balance of payments for 1987 and 1988 in selected countries, excluding capital transfers and other adjustments

Millions of US$	Germany		Japan		United Kingdom		United States	
	1987	1988	1987	1988	1987	1988	1987	1988
Merchandise: export	278,090	3,081,890	224,620	259,770	130,322	143,836	250,280	319,250
Merchandise: imports	208,220	228,780	128,200	164,770	148,248	180,812	409,770	446,460
Other goods, services and income: credit	82,060	86,910	70,660	117,780	124,210	150,677	195,850	210,530
Other goods, services and income: debit	89,600	97,810	85,380	123	108,108	134,003	165,880	195,230
Balance of payments, excl capital movements and other adjustments	62,330	2,842,210	81,700	212,657	-1,824	-20,302	-129,520	-111,910

Source: UNO (1990) Statistical Yearbook 1987, UNO, New York

product). By common consent this is an accurate measure of all commercial economic transactions of items of final consumption in an economy, but a highly unsatisfactory measure of the well-being of the population. Not only does it beg the question of the relationship between wealth and happiness; it includes only transactions that are officially recorded; it excludes all non-remunerated services (eg bringing up children and maintaining a household) and includes all 'defensive' expenditure. For example, the cost of all precautions against crime and the cost of medical and police services to deal with the consequences of accidents count as positive economic activities. If goods are shoddily made and have to be replaced, the expenditure for the original purchase and the involuntary replacement count in GNP, while durable goods count only once. 'In summary, all we can say about GNP is that it is a measure of the volume of trading going on in a country which has no necessary relation to the quality of life' (Douthwaite 1992:17).

The creation of new demand by new technology is generally regarded as a major cause of economic growth. The capture of a large share of this new demand is a major cause of the growth of individual firms or individual countries. One of the ways of maintaining high consumption in wealthy countries is to offer a never-ending stream of novel goods, so that even those who have everything always find something new to spend their money on. Markets for durable goods tend to saturate and only the creation of new or improved products, or built-in obsolescence, can counter this saturation. The rich do, of course, always find ways of spending money on so-called positional goods: masterpieces of art, houses with unique views, holidays in exclusive and exotic resorts. The supply of such goods is inherently limited, and increasing their price merely ensures that exclusivity remains the privilege of the rich, without causing real economic growth (Hirsch 1977).

The argument that markets are saturated may sound extraordinary in view of the sickening poverty which prevails in most of the world. It is a fact, however, regrettable as it is, that demand for goods without the backing of sufficient purchasing power is ineffectual. Indeed even the developed countries currently suffer from a lack of effective demand caused, in part, by unemployment (a classical vicious circle) and low wages. Such is the order of the world that even surplus manufacturing capacities cannot be utilized to satisfy the demands of the poor. Wealth does not trickle down. Without the necessary political will it does not even spread from the rich to the poor in a single country, and it certainly does not spread from the rich countries to the poor ones. The dice in the economic game are loaded in favour of the wealthy. The natural tendency of wealth is to concentrate; not to trickle down. The following tables and graphs illustrate how economic growth can take place without benefit to the underprivileged members of society. Between the years 1978 and 1990 the real household dispos-

17

able income per head in the UK rose by approximately 45 per cent (Central Statistical Office 1992: 89). Yet the benefits were not shared by all. For example, the share of post-tax incomes going to the top fifth of households rose from 37 per cent in 1978 to 44 per cent in 1988, whereas the share of the bottom fifth dropped from 10 per cent to 7 per cent in the same period, even after considering all transfer payments (op cit: 100). If we further consider the impact of a substantial shift from direct to indirect taxation, with its strongly regressive effect, the growing iniquities become much more blatant than tables of income and direct taxation can possibly show.

Table 1.3 and Figure 1.1 provide an illustration of the dramatic divergence between the fortunes of the rich and the poor. The equally dramatic increase in the absolute numbers of families living in stark poverty can be gauged from the fact that while in 1979 22 per cent of UK households lived at, or close to, the generally recognized standard of poverty, this proportion had risen to 34.3 per cent by 1987 (Townsend 1991: 32). (For an explanation of how the standard of poverty is defined see Townsend 1979: 241–7).

Table 1.3 *Average annual disposable income of richest and poorest UK households (£)*

Year	Poorest 20% At 1989 prices	% Change 1979=100	Richest 20% At 1989 prices	% Change 1979=100
1983	3,315	105.4	21,223	105.4
1984	3,197	92.9	21,442	106.5
1985	3,156	91.7	22,847	113.5
1986	3,245	94.3	25,010	124.2
1987	3,272	95.1	26,802	133.1
1988	3,304	96	28,472	141.4
1989	3,282	95.4	28,124	139.7

Source: Townsend 1991: 11,13

Wealth and economic success can be combined with a variety of social systems; indeed economic success is compatible with social systems corresponding to quite different sets of values. Yet not all social systems are compatible with economic success. When the so-called command economies of the recent past in Eastern Europe are considered, it is obvious that these systems were too inflexible, permitted too little initiative and gave too few incentives for technological innovation, efficient production, effective provision of services and, hence, economic success. It is remarkable, and probably no accident, that all rich industrial nations have more or less democratic regimes. The range of freedoms may differ, the distribution of wealth and the degree of social welfare may differ, but all of them are democracies of sorts. It would appear that economic success in the modern industrial

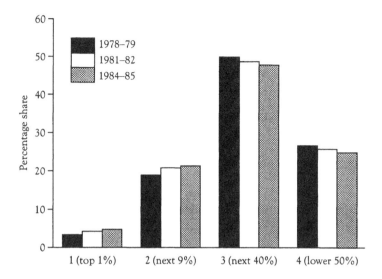

Source: Central Statistical Office (1988) *Social Trends 18*, HMSO, London

Figure 1.1 *Distributions of income after income tax, 1978–79 to 1984–85 (no other taxation considered)*

world depends on allowing sufficient freedom of economic action, unhampered by too much supervision, state planning, and fear. What is sufficient may be arguable, but the freedom required goes well beyond that offered by any dictatorial system. Nobody innovates if failure might be construed as sabotage; nobody finds niches of market demand if bureaucratic rules either forbid the process or make it too arduous. Nobody can succeed in economic activities if each and every step needs lengthy approvals by ignorant outsiders. No economy can thrive if too much effort goes on the sterile production of arms. This argument must not be taken to an extreme, as government intervention in economic life is quite vital and a complete free-for-all can never lead to a socially desirable state. As will be argued at some length later, there can be no doubt that modern technologies require a considerable degree of regulation by the state lest they inflict great harm to the population, the natural environment, and social structures. The present argument merely implies that a modicum of freedom is a necessary condition for economic success. The corollary is that a modicum of economic success is a necessary condition for any desirable social state within the framework of modern Western thinking. Wealth alone, however, cannot suffice for a pleasant life either for the individual or for society at large and some argue, possibly rightly, that true happiness is not compatible with a relentless quest for more worldly goods.

To sustain full employment and a high quality of life in the modern world it is necessary to lend public support to public services, to infrastructural facilities, and to the protection of the natural environment. Whether this support is achieved by a suitable legal and contractual framework or by direct state intervention is immaterial; the fact remains that without state support public services and parts of the infrastructure will decay, and the natural environment will be sacrificed to human greed.

Virtually all societies strive for economic progress, and technological progress is regarded as one of the chief means of achieving it. Technological innovation is a major input into economic growth, because it opens up new avenues of consumption and because it tends to increase overall productivity. Technological prowess has become the touchstone of international competitiveness. Most advanced countries aim to accelerate technological progress as much as possible and the main thrust of this book is to doubt the wisdom of such policies, especially if no attempt is made to influence the direction of technological advance toward a sustainable economy. The fastest possible technological innovation involves high costs and inefficiencies and is unlikely to achieve the best possible economic or social results. To force the pace of progress is futile, as it is unlikely to achieve either the high rate of economic growth expected from it, or social harmony and a high quality of life. Technological progress, carried out merely for economic purposes, is causing untold damage to the natural environment. Progress ought to be directed toward social utility, including the preservation and restoration of nature.

Technological Progress

While social progress is convoluted and shows movement in many directions and towards many goals, technological progress is somewhat more unidirectional. In view of the enormous variety of technologies and the virtually infinite number of technological changes that have taken place and are taking place, this statement may seem strangely naive. To avoid misunderstanding, let me stress immediately that I do not believe that technological progress can or should be equated with progress toward a better life or a better society. Nor do I believe that technological progress constitutes movement towards a fixed, albeit distant, goal:

> Neither the historical record nor our understanding of the current role of technology in society justifies a return to the idea that a causal connection exists between advances in technology and the overall betterment of the human race (Basalla 1988: 218).

Nevertheless, it is true that each generation of technological products is, in a real sense, more advanced than its predecessors, even though sometimes this advance is bought at an unjustifiably high cost, either in terms of money or of losses to nature or to people. Whereas social progress is not a monotonous function of time – social and political conditions get worse with time as often as they get better – technological progress is a monotonous function of time. This statement should not be taken to imply unconditional approval of technological progress: it merely indicates that technology does not, in its own terms of reference, ever move from a 'higher' to a 'lower' state.

The direction in which technology progresses is determined only in part by its internal logic; another, not insignificant, determinant is the system of values and the institutional settings of the society applying the technology. In a Darwinian analogy, technological inventions may be regarded in the same light as spontaneous mutations of species. Inventions become successful innovations if society selects them, much in the same way as mutations lead to the development of species by a process of natural selection (see eg Basalla 1988 and Nelson and Winter 1982). The successful artefacts of technology are chosen by a social selection environment, whereas the success of living organisms is determined by a biological selection environment. The analogy breaks down in so far as technological inventions do not appear spontaneously, nor are they even entirely a product of the internal logic and workings of science and technology. Inventions themselves are, to a not inconsiderable degree, an outcome of social direction of inventive effort.

Technology is a social construct and the ways and social mechanisms by which technology evolves are the subject of considerable debate (see eg Street 1992: 23–45). The evolutionary view proposed here does not regard the development of technology as a kind of Greek tragedy with its inevitable and immutable outcome (Hill 1988: 23). It is simply suggested that researchers and others put forward ideas for technological innovations, based on their perception of what is technically possible and what might find a market. I do not wish to dispute that these ideas are influenced by the general beliefs of the people concerned and by the agendas of the day. My description of the development of technology is not incompatible with the so-called interest approach which argues that 'knowledge claims made by scientists will embody or be informed by certain social, sometimes political interests' (Webster 1991: 16). By a series of selection processes the ideas put forward for innovations are sifted and, when finally an innovation emerges, this undergoes a further selection process in the marketplace. In all these mechanisms, both for ideas put forward and, even more so, in the selection of successful innovations, social and political power play decisive roles. Only those technologies will be selected that can make money in the marketplace. In the case of process technologies, the selection mechanism is dominated by the ability of the technology to increase productivity, improve the competitive position, and increase profits for its owner.

Generally speaking, it may be said that technology moves in two dimensions: towards higher performance and towards the satisfaction of an ever increasing range of potential human wants. The second dimension means that technology endeavours to take over more and more tasks previously carried out by humans, and that it extends human capabilities. Examples of the former are washing machines, mechanical diggers, automation, or the present trend to motorize everything; examples of the latter are telecommunications, aircraft, submarines, microscopes, video cameras, and computers. Technology enables humans to do things they never knew they wanted to do. Humans equipped with technology become gargantuan in their accomplishments and in their requirements: they can move huge quantities of earth in the shortest possible time, they can travel at enormous speeds, and they consume vast amounts of energy, space and materials. It is as if each person, in the developed world at least, had turned into a voracious giant.

Technological performance can be described by some composite 'figure of performance', which is made up of the main performance characteristics of the technology in question. Generally, technical progress can be seen as moving in the direction of higher performance, meaning greater speed; larger capacity; higher cost-effectiveness; higher efficiency; increasing reliability; reduced effort required from human labour, indeed substitution of machine effort for human effort; more autonomously acting machines, ie a higher degree of automation; and so forth. The performance of a technological product is often measured against the best available products, representing the state of the art (SOA), although there is a considerable degree of arbitrariness in defining what constitutes the figure of performance (Dodson 1985). One of the many problems of measurement of technological progress is the fact that each product represents a different compromise between available design parameters, and thus different products may be good for a particular purpose and less good for another. The designer can often improve one performance characteristic only at the expense of another. The art of design is the reconciliation of incompatible demands. Success in the marketplace is achieved by those designs which most closely approximate to the compromises the purchasers are willing to strike. Technological progress occurs along some abstract 'tradeoff surface', meaning that overall the performance improves, although different characteristics improve at different rates in different designs (Martino 1985).

An example of increasing performance, and its simple description, is furnished by computers. The National Science Foundation (quoted in OECD 1988, Table 1.2) compiled an index of performance for computers, composed of a weighted average of measures of their speed (kilo-operations per second), their cost, and their capacity. Between 1951 and 1978 the speed changed from 0.27 kops/sec to 19,019 kops/sec; the cost from 7 kops/$ to 65,932 kops/$ and the capacity from 8 kbyte to 16,384 kbyte. The computed index of performance thus changed from 0.011 to 72.675.

Generally, a range of standard products evolves to fit the main applications of a given technology, although often specialized models emerge in addition to fulfil the requirements of niche markets. The best of these products are said to have reached the state of the art, and the performance of new market contenders is measured against this SOA. The SOA improves continually, until such time as the technology in question meets a challenge from a radically different technology. The SOA may then improve rapidly in an effort to fight off the challenge, but often this proves merely the last fling of the given technology before it is relegated to obsolescence or to niche markets. At this point a new series of development starts for the usurper technology. An example of this process is the obsolescence of gas lighting, which eventually had to give way to various forms of electric lighting of ever-increasing sophistication and quality.

As technological devices develop, they tend to become easier and more comfortable to use, although this may sound unbelievable to the thousands of people involved in desperate struggles with their recalcitrant computers. Machines tend to become cleaner, less noisy, and smarter in both appearance and capabilities. Despite all the insurmountable problems of measuring technological progress in any meaningful, accurate, and practical way, and the impossibility of defining the direction of progress with any precision, its general direction is clear and relatively unchanging over reasonable periods of time. Such change as there is, is caused mostly by the fact that each period has a different dominant technology, although some changes in the selection environment, with societies in different periods setting different priorities and making different demands on their technology, do also occur. Currently, information technology is the dominant technology and one of the most characteristic features of our time. It is somewhat difficult to compare its progress directly with the progress of, say, transport technology or chemical engineering, but the general feature of movement towards higher performance is common to all technologies.

The second dimension of technological progress is the expanding range of human wants that can be satisfied by technology. The fact that these wants mostly arise only as a result of the possibility of their satisfaction, and are stimulated by sales techniques, does not alter the fact that ever more actions and activities can be undertaken with the aid of ever new technological artefacts (see eg Braun 1984a, ch 6 and 7).

Let us consider technological progress in transport as an example. The fastest possible, and most convenient, movement of goods and people, at reasonable cost, has been the implied aim of transport systems for a very long time. The need for transport changes with the size and density of population, the range and extent of economic activity, the terrain, and other factors. In most places, a dual system of animals carrying loads and people, and of animals pulling wheeled vehicles, evolved. Interestingly, the wheel did not evolve in all cultures, a fact which has lent additional force to the argument that technologies evolve in relation to perceived needs and are not simply a result of technical capabilities (Basalla 1988:7–14). When the need arose during the industrial revolution to carry bulk loads over long distances, the transport system was augmented by canals, which are particularly cost effective, although they require large capital investment. The availability of investment capital was, of course, one of the enabling factors of the industrial revolution. The move from animal to ship provided little or no advance in speed, but it did provide a large increase in carrying capacity. The canal system was soon supplemented, and eventually largely supplanted, by the railway system, characterized by the capacity to carry bulk loads, or large numbers of people, at higher and increasing speeds. The railway system was also better able to overcome topographical barriers.

The next important development came from the substitution of the internal combustion engine for the animal in wheeled road transport. In the course of time, engines became more powerful and efficient, vehicles became faster and goods carrying vehicles became larger. The variety of specialized vehicles increased, the whole transport system became capable of handling all types of loads and moving them at high speed over long distances. In the early days of the horseless carriage it was hailed as the saviour of cities that were drowning in the excrements of increasing numbers of horses, catering for rising populations with rising demands for mobility and supplies. The fact that automobiles were lauded for their cleanliness may now strike us as bizarre, but the polluting nature of automobiles was not recognized until a later stage, when scientific knowledge had increased. It is noteworthy that while most modes of transport have evolved – as is the wont of technology – to become extremely labour saving, the currently dominant form of transport for people, the car, is extremely labour intensive. Presumably owner-drivers do not regard their own efforts as work. Although the performance of the individual motor vehicle has become very high in its own terms, the transport system based mainly on roads is rather ineffectual and highly resistant to improvement. The contradiction between flexible individual vehicles and the movement of large numbers of people and large amounts of goods has not been resolved. This is not so much a case of technological failure as of social failure. The technical efficiency of motor vehicles may be high; their environmental and social efficiency is abysmal. Social selection mechanisms do not always work in the best interest of society as a whole.

Transport by sea evolved similarly, with the size, variety, speed, and reliability of ships increasing as sailing ships and rowing boats were replaced by steam and diesel-engined ships, and timber gave way to steel as the material for construction. In ships the trend toward smaller crews and less hard work, as well as the trend toward huge size, have been particularly extreme.

The final step – ignoring space travel – in the story of transport is the conquest of the air. Although flight has been mankind's dream through the ages, its realization had to wait for the development of aluminium alloys as a suitable material for the fabrication of light and strong structures, and for considerable advances in internal combustion engines (including gas turbines) before it achieved its present status as the major mode for long distance travel for people and an important link in the long-distance goods-haulage system. The same features of technological development can be seen yet again, as each successive generation of aircraft became larger, faster, more reliable, and more cost effective. A small number of standard designs has emerged and these are either modified for specialized tasks or supplemented by specialist craft, such as small planes for hobby pilots and, on a more sinister note, military aircraft. It is interesting that supersonic passenger transport, although an obvious extension of aircraft capabilities in the direction of speed has, to date, been a commercial failure. The reasons are the unacceptable supersonic boom on the one hand, and, on the other hand, very poor fuel efficiency and cost-effectiveness. The wide-bodied jet, which comprises a different compromise of design features, was selected by the social environment in preference to the supersonic aircraft. In military aircraft, operating in a different selection environment, the story is quite a different one.

Apart from illustrating how technology develops along a path towards higher performance and towards an extension of human capabilities, there are several more lessons to be learned from the history of transport. Perhaps the most important one is that technologies – and transport technologies are an outstanding example – tend to form clusters which operate as systems: a ship, an aircraft, a car, are all but links in a chain which constitutes the system and are quite useless in isolation. Other essential links are the supply of fuel, manufacturing facilities, repair and service facilities, harbours, airports, roads, booking systems, navigation systems, legal regulation, training facilities – to name but some of the more important of the dozens of items and sub-systems necessary for the functioning of transport systems.

The second lesson is that initial progress after a major technological change is usually very fast, but increasingly more effort is required to achieve further improvements, until almost infinite effort is required to achieve infinitesimal improvements. If we look at the car during the first 20 years of its life, improvements were substantial in almost all aspects of its performance, and yet they were brought about by a large number of sometimes quite small craft-based manufacturers. But if we look at the last 20 years, improvements are anything but spectacular and development costs have risen dramatically, so that they can now be sustained only by a very small number of very large manufacturers. Transport technologies provide some excellent examples of the operation of the law of diminishing returns.

The third, and least happy, lesson that can be learned is that people are willing to accept high casualties if that is the price to be paid for a theoretically fast and convenient system of transport, despite the fact that in reality it suffers from severe deficiencies. The fact that about half a million people die each year on the world's roads has not caused any significant reduction in permitted (and even less in actual) speeds travelled, nor has it led to a very great effort to increase the overall safety of the transportation system. While enormous and highly publicized development effort goes into increasing the power and efficiency of engines, or to obtain marginal improvements in the creature comforts provided by cars, the few modest efforts at increasing safety have until very recently been the exclusive domain of a very small band of elite manufacturers. Safety as a feature worthy of mention in sales literature and in journalists' appraisals of mass-market cars is a very recent – and highly welcome – development. It would appear that very large numbers of people care more for speed than for safety, and this shows that systems of values, embodied in the social selection environment, matter not only for social progress, but also matter greatly for the direction of technological progress.

While speed and load carrying capacity, as well as price, safety, reliability and labour intensity, are clearly the most significant parameters for transport technologies, descriptors for other technologies are somewhat different, although they fall into the same generic categories. Speed is a highly significant descriptor for a large number of technologies, including information technology. The speed of processing signals and the speed of access to stored data are important in computers. The speed of establishing a communication link matters in telecommunications; indeed, the speed of transmitting information across the globe distinguishes present-day communications from those of old. Load-carrying capacity similarly appears in somewhat modified form in information technology: the band-width of a communication channel determines how much information can be transmitted per unit time; the amount of data that can be processed in a computer per unit time characterizes its power; the number of logic units on a chip determines either its storage capacity or its processing power, depending on whether it is a memory or a logic chip.

Similar categories for describing technical progress hold for other, quite disparate, technologies. Textile machinery now moves at very much higher speeds and can thus weave or spin much larger quantities of material per unit time than in the past. The assembly of cars now requires far less manual effort, as robots and automated machinery have largely taken over tasks such as welding, paint spraying, insertion of windows (see eg Womack et al 1990). Modern cameras can take sharper pictures under worse conditions than earlier models and are virtually fully automatic – ie foolproof. Modern recording and music reproduction systems have reached an unprecedented pitch of perfection and ease of handling. Music reproduced from compact discs not only sounds very nearly as a real concert, but discs are also easy to use and can be programmed in all sorts of, mostly unnecessary, ways. Even building technology, perhaps the least automated and most labour intensive of all technologies, is dominated by computers in the design office, huge cranes on the building site, fast-assembled scaffolding, huge concrete mixing machines, prefabricated windows and so on.

The same characteristics of bigger, faster, more efficient, less labour intensive, more automatic, more convenient, closer to ideal performance, apply to all examples of technology that come to mind. Never in the history of technology have humans reverted to the use of an inferior technology when a superior one had become available. The latter statement has to be interpreted with some care, as not all new technologies have been accepted. It means that all things considered, the winning new technologies always have a higher figure of performance than their predecessors; or else they cater for wants that were not previously catered for. Some new technologies are not successful either because their performance at the given price is not judged good value; or because the potential want they aim to satisfy cannot be kindled; or because a rival technology, aiming at the same market, is successful in capturing it.

The fact that unemployment has risen inexorably in the last decade or more has not made any difference to the social selection of labour-saving technologies by manufacturers. Although the theoretical concept of 'appropriate technology' (Schumacher 1974) is unassailable, it is inconceivable that manufacturers in advanced countries should deliberately decide in favour of higher labour intensity. They see their task as increasing efficiency, securing profits, and advancing technology. If people become unemployed in the process this is hard luck, but you cannot, manufacturers argue, stop progress: '...new technologies made people redundant without the economy having anything else equivalent for them to do, just as Ned Ludd feared was happening in 1812' (Douthwaite 1992: 81).

Most of the basic needs of humans in the developed world have long been satisfied with the aid of technology. These are basic food, protection from inclement weather (shelter and clothing), clean water and adequate hygiene. All the above real needs can now be fulfilled at a luxurious level for most (albeit not all) people in the rich countries of the world. In addition, health care has advanced greatly beyond rudimentary needs and many lesser wants can be catered for, such as the need for play with the plethora of technological toys available; or the need for autarky with the availability of home entertainment, home freezers, and DIY equipment (Braun 1984a: 170–1).

It is easy to quote examples of an expanding range of technologies designed to fulfil an ever-widening range of latent human wants. Some of the above examples can be used to illustrate the point. Starting with information technologies, the early telephone had great difficulty in establishing itself. Most people could not see why they should need a telephone and, to compound the problem, a telephone is only useful if many people have it – ie it is useful only when it is already established. By now, most people in the developed world cannot imagine life without a telephone and indeed they now need answering and fax machines, mobile phones, data links, video links, and a variety of so-called value added services, such as home banking, on-line databases, and electronic mail. Computers are another good example. While most people formerly were content to keep card-indices or address books, they now need a computer database. While most people were happy to write with a pen or, later, with a typewriter, they now need a computer with a word-processing programme. Even the dot matrix printer used in conjunction with wordprocessors now looks distinctly jaded in comparison with the luxurious laser printer or its cheaper cousin, the inkjet printer. Children were once content to play with sticks and, later, with more and more sophisticated toys. Now they need a computer to play games with.

When the transistor was first announced in 1948, people regarded it as a rather specialized replacement for the ubiquitous electronic valve ('tube' in American parlance). Yet the use of the transistor expanded and it became much more than a replacement for the tube; in its later form of an integrated circuit (a 'chip'), it became the foundation of all modern information technology and it is now difficult to envisage a household in an advanced country which does not contain dozens of chips of various types (see eg Braun and Macdonald 1982). Chips are found in watches and clocks, in home computers, pocket calculators, telephones, central heating controls, controls for other domestic machinery, television, video recorders, stereo equipment, burglar alarms, and many other devices, none of which were needed until recently. To paraphrase one of Parkinson's famous laws: needs expand to meet technological possibilities.

We have asserted that technology develops in what might be seen as monotonous movement in the direction of higher performance and of satisfying an ever wider range of wants. Whereas social progress has been described as an irregular movement with worsening of social conditions as frequent as their betterment, technology advances monotonously despite the fact that it is a social construct. This apparent contradiction calls for some explanation:

■ First, there is an inner logic to technology. It is self-evident to the technologist that any technological artefact should be improved so that it will work more reliably, more accurately, faster, more comfortably; in other words, better. Having climbed one pinnacle, the challenge of the next one comes into sight. It is also self-evident to the technologist that if anything can be done by a technological device it should be done; thus technologists are in constant search for new wants that might be kindled and satisfied by new technology. It is a quest without end.

28

- Second, notwithstanding some dissent, society concurs with this view of technology. For process technology it is obvious that it is in the manufacturer's interest to obtain ever faster, more reliable, more automated, more cost-effective machinery because this is one way of increasing profitability and competitiveness. The workforce, on the other hand, either sees itself as sharing some of these interests or else it is forced, bribed or talked into accepting the new machinery. The unemployed and under-employed have, by and large, no say in the matter. Whether by persuasion, by education, or for whatever reason, the fact is that the dominant social view of technological progress is in congruence with the view of relentless improvement. The constant search by entrepreneurs for new wants that they might kindle and satisfy at a profit is one of the most fundamental properties of the capitalist system. The search for new business opportunities is a never-ending quest, and what better ally than technology, with its endless stream of new devices to satisfy potential wants!
- Third, as much innovative effort is concentrated on what is euphemistically called defence technologies, and measures of progress in these technologies are only too painfully obvious, the general direction of technological progress receives further endorsement. Greater range, greater power, greater accuracy, greater reliability, higher speed, ease of use under adverse conditions, all these criteria for progress apply with deadly intent to defence technologies.

Thus technological progress appears largely autonomous because it is deeply rooted in the industrial system of production and in the general culture, or ambience, of the age. Technological progress has come to stand for progress in general. One of the aims of this book is to question this identification.

For the present, however, we shall turn our attention away from the progress of technology toward scientific progress, which has become so closely associated with technological progress.

Scientific Progress

Natural science aims at observing and understanding nature. This means that by observation and experiment, aided by scientific instruments, facts are established and theories are constructed with the aim of obtaining laws which relate, explain, and predict results of further observations. Thus we seek factual information as well as a theoretical framework which orders such information into as simple and as comprehensive a set of laws as can be managed. Theories are judged both on their explanatory power for existing facts and on their predictive power for future observations. Theories are altered, or even discarded and replaced, if conflicts arise between theoretical predictions and actual observations (Popper 1969). It is immaterial, in the present context, whether we believe that in this way we are gradually approaching the truth – ie are discovering the laws and mechanisms which actually govern the behaviour of nature and its parts – or whether we believe that we are merely achieving a human construct which enables us to relate and predict, and thus understand, observed natural phenomena. In either case, our knowledge increases, our theories become better in the above sense, the range of phenomena we know and understand increases. Thus scientific progress is unidirectional: from fewer to more observations, from theories with little explanatory and predictive power to theories with greater power.

Saying that science progresses unidirectionally does not necessarily imply any kind of approval of either the aims of science, or the objects of scientific study, or indeed the types of theories that science constructs. Nor is it denying the undeniable fact that the aims of science are set by humans. It is merely saying that science progresses in a single direction on its own terms and within the framework of its own objectives. Occasionally errors are made and occasionally theories maintain their hold longer than they should be tenable, but by and large science progresses to achieve more factual knowledge and better understanding. It succeeds in solving more puzzles of its own choosing (Kuhn 1970).

The puzzles selected for investigation are not always natural phenomena as such, but are often posed by technology. The investigation of the fundamental properties of engineering materials, for example, is a perfectly acceptable scientific problem. This is only one of the many bonds that now exist between science and engineering. Indeed although science and technology have different historical roots and, in the abstract, different basic aims, they have now become very close and interdependent (Braun 1984b).

Science often discovers new phenomena or new principles which may be used as a foundation for an engineering development. In the course of this development, science is used extensively to investigate and overcome problems on the path of obtaining a practical engineering device. Indeed, we now usually speak of research and development as the source of technological innovation, ie the invention and development of new products or processes to be offered on the market. We do not ask whether it is scientific or engineering research, nor do we draw very exact boundaries between research and development. This is not because of intellectual laziness, but because the boundaries between all these activities have become blurred in modern practice. Science has lost much of its original mission of a quest for knowledge for its own sake and has become one of the most potent instruments for the generation of wealth. We no longer seek primarily enlightenment: our search is for the means to become rich and richer. Cooperation between science and engineering in the development of new technologies forms a bond between them and thus technological and scientific progress are inextricably joined in a common endeavour.

One class of technological artefacts are scientific instruments. They are usually based on scientific discoveries and are then further developed by engineering methods and in cooperation between science and engineering. Scientific instruments play a vital role in science, as without their assistance observation and experiment would be very rudimentary. Scientific instruments also play a vital role in technology. Not only are they technological products in their own right, they are also used extensively in engineering practice, in development, and in other technological products. Just as biology cannot be conceived without a microscope, or civil engineering without a theodolite or its modern equivalents, so no car without a speedometer or petrol gauge can be imagined. Advances in scientific instruments are an essential part of advances in science as well as of advances in technology. Here scientific and technological progress can be seen to be closely coupled and moving together in a single direction. As instruments advance, so a greater range of phenomena become measurable or observable. As developments progress, instruments become more accurate, easier to use, and generally smarter.

Progress of science and engineering is monotonous, yet this does not mean that it is deterministic in the sense that science and engineering progress autonomously in a predetermined direction. Although they do possess a degree of autonomy and do, to some extent, progress according to an inner logic, this is moderated by economic constraints and the setting of agendas by society (for a detailed discussion of the 'autonomous' view see eg Winner 1977). Both scientific and engineering activities are not only human activities in the sense that they are carried out by humans; they are also social activities as they are the result of cooperation between many humans, are highly organized, and are financed by society at large. Science and technology do not simply march along in their own right; they are a social activity, and a highly organized one at that. Two questions arise immediately: why does society support and organize these activities, and how can and does society control the direction they take?

One part of the answer is that science has made itself indispensable by its involvement in technological progress. If society desires technological progress it must, under contemporary circumstances, support the science which is so intimately associated with it. Numerous examples can be found to support this statement. Modern electronics owes its existence to science; modern biotechnology was born out of science; modern agriculture uses science extensively; modern medicine is heavily laced with science. Science is regarded as an integral part of the technological endeavour and owes much of its support to this fact.

The association between science and technology has, of course, boosted scientific research, but it has also taken away much of its independence. Scientific research must now be largely justified on grounds of technological expediency; long-term curiosity-driven research has suffered greatly. What has suffered even more is criticism. Although Popper is undoubtedly right in suggesting that rational debate is the only way towards intellectual progress in general and scientific progress in particular (see also Collingridge 1987), criticism dies when the researcher is reduced to short-term funding. Any criticism, however indirect, might lead to loss of the next contract, and thus the researcher becomes subservient to the interests and aims of those who hold the purse-strings – he who pays the piper calls the tune. Yet unfettered critical thought and its expression are the true stuff of positive progress. Particularly in the social sciences, but even in natural science and technology, the newly bred subservience of scientists spells the death knell to the open society. Without a spirit of critical enquiry no worthwhile progress can be made.

Some support is still given to so-called pure science, which is undertaken without much hope for technological applications – even if a remote hope always exists. Pure science is supported simply as part of our culture, as an enterprise designed to satisfy our curiosity about who we are and where we live. Astronomy is a good example of this type of research. Although astronomy is useful for navigation and, more recently, for space travel with civilian and military applications, the main thrust of astronomy is to answer questions about the structure and the origin of the universe. Similarly, the physics of elementary particles, which swallows large amounts of taxpayers' money, aims almost exclusively to answer fundamental questions about the structure of matter. The chance of yielding technologically and economically useful results is very remote, although it is sometimes argued that the development of the very sophisticated machinery and instrumentation needed for this type of research brings valuable engineering advances. There are cheaper ways of achieving such practical results. In recent years curiosity-driven research has been relegated to an existence under sufferance – and indeed the gigantic costs of some basic research in 'big science' seem entirely unjustifiable.

The usual argument in justification of public funding for basic research is its role as provider of ideas and fundamental knowledge for technological innovation. Technology cannot thrive without constant replenishment of the well of scientific knowledge. If the argument in favour of supporting science as a cultural enterprise ceases to carry weight, we are in danger of viewing all science as a provider of technological progress rather than as one of humankind's great intellectual quests.

The Pursuit of Happiness

When all is said and done, progress, including and especially technological progress, is supposed to increase human happiness. Hence we must discuss, albeit briefly, the question of the relationship, if any, between technological progress and happiness.

Although the task of defining happiness is well beyond the scope of this book and beyond the ability of its author, we can nevertheless agree, even in the absence of a proper definition, that the pursuit of happiness is something all humans engage in, to a greater or lesser degree, throughout their lives. Jeremy Bentham (1748–1832) suggested that all human actions are determined by either the pursuit of pleasure or the avoidance of pain:

> *Nature has placed mankind under the governance of two*
> *sovereign masters, pain and pleasure. It is for them alone to*
> *point out what we ought to do, as well as to determine what*
> *we shall do* (Bentham 1970: 11).

Bentham regarded the greatest possible increase of happiness as the utility of all actions and, as such, as the source of moral justification for actions, including, in particular, the activities of the state. His guiding principle, the Principle of Utility, is defined as:

> *...that principle which approves or disapproves of every action*
> *whatsoever according to the tendency which it appears to have*
> *to augment or diminish the happiness of the party whose*
> *interest is in question: or, what is the same thing in other*
> *words, to promote or to oppose that happiness* (op cit: 12).

Society at large consists, in his view, of the individuals in it and the interest of society consists of the sum of individual interests:

> *An action then may be said to be conformable to the*
> *principle of utility...when the tendency it has to augment the*
> *happiness of the community is greater than any it has to*
> *diminish it* (op cit: 12–13).

To Bentham the measure of correctness and moral justification of all actions is whether they increase the sum total of happiness, where any decrease in pain is equivalent to an increase in happiness. The most profound difficulty of this type of theory is that it recommends, unexceptionably, the maximization of an immeasurable quantity. Who is to say that one type of happiness is greater than another, or that the small pain of many is worse than the great pain of a few? Although it is not possible to derive precise guidance to action from Bentham's theory, the principle of causing the greatest possible happiness to the greatest possible number does attribute great weight to compassion and equality as measures for the utility of practical action, and thus comes close to the underlying values of the social state that was described above as desirable.

The attempt to create a better world is a continuous activity of humankind. Our actions and artefacts are the results of our desires and dreams, although sometimes they may be selfish and even evil dreams. We can, to some limited extent, foresee the consequences of our actions and thus shape the future consciously and deliberately. But Popper warns of over-optimism:

> *We are right to believe that we can and should contribute to*
> *the improvement of our world. But we must not imagine that*
> *we can foresee the consequences of our plans and actions...*
> *In any case, one part of our search for a better world must*
> *consist in the search for a world in which others are not*
> *forced to sacrifice their lives for the sake of an idea* (Popper
> 1992: 28).

It seems to me that this issue is crucial to the question of happiness: none of us should ever imagine we have the sole key to happiness and thus feel duty-bound to force this particular view upon others. On the other hand, I believe that Popper is too pessimistic with regard to our ability to foresee the results of our actions. If we try to foresee at all times, if we use our ingenuity and learn from our experiences, if we keep an open mind and do not succumb to dogma, then we can improve the world we live in. The concept of technology assessment demands that we should apply those ideals whenever we introduce new technologies.

In wealthy technological societies it is rare for people to act purely out of the necessity to maintain life; for most people in these societies the activities connected with the maintenance of life are combined with the gratification of other desires, ie with the active pursuit of pleasure. Most of us eat not just to live, but also to derive pleasure from eating food we enjoy; most of us do not shelter in hovels but derive pleasure from living in nice comfortable homes; most of us do not wear clothes merely for protection from inclement weather or in conformity with religious and social taboos, but as ornaments, as expressions of our personalities, as sources of pleasure. In Great Britain, however, at the time of writing, more than one person in six lives in dire poverty and finds mere survival the only task left to him/her (Meacher, *The Guardian*, 21 January 1992). In the USA the situation is very similar and when we speak of rich technologically advanced nations we ignore a substantial minority of deprived citizens who live in the rich countries.

Actions necessary to maintain life are, in modern technological society, almost entirely divorced from the very direct actions of primitive societies. In the dim past, most of those who wanted to eat had to hunt, gather, or plant. With the increased division of labour and the increased use of technology, the link between necessity and its gratification has become tenuous and is maintained almost entirely via the universal means of exchange, money. The process of producing the necessities of life, and that of producing goods and services far beyond the necessities of life, is a social process and most members of society participate in it via some form of employment, and in return obtain wages which they can spend on the necessities of life and on all kinds of pleasurable consumption. Thus obtaining the means for the maintenance of life – and for indulgent consumption – is mostly linked to employment. It is immaterial whether this employment is via an employer or by self-employment; in all cases the individual and his or her dependants are linked to the social production and distribution system via employment. The more deplorable is the state of those without employment, as their link to society is severed. They can live only by virtue of a system of support, given the more grudgingly the more society moves away from the social state in which compassion and notions of equality play a large role, towards a state dominated by the idea that unbridled competition is the only arbiter of utility.

Gainful employment not only provides the essential link between people and their society, which gives them the feeling of being part of the social fabric; it also prevents one of the worst diseases of our time: boredom.

> *Work, therefore, is desirable, first and foremost, as a*
> *preventive of boredom, for the boredom that a man feels*
> *when he is doing necessary though uninteresting work is as*
> *nothing in comparison with the boredom that he feels when*
> *he has nothing to do with his days* (Russell 1961: 134–5).

People who are not driven by necessity, whose timetable is not governed by external forces, often find it very hard to fill their time with activities they regard as important or at least pleasurable.

The pursuit of happiness has many facets. Many of them are almost unrelated to technology and involve categories such as love, sexual gratification, harmonious human relations, parental pride, social recognition, intellectual and aesthetic pleasure, creativity, wonderment, elation. This incomplete but spiritually oriented list is not as free of technological inferences as might appear at first sight. Even wonderment can be induced by technical marvels and human relations are strongly influenced by material circumstances.

Bentham discusses the sources and kinds of pleasure and pain at some considerable length. In his list of pleasures, mostly of a mental, social, sensual or spiritual kind, the pleasures of wealth occupy a very small part:

> *By the pleasures of wealth may be meant those pleasures*
> *which a man is apt to derive from the consciousness of*
> *possessing any article or articles which stand in the list of*
> *instruments of enjoyment or security, and more particularly at*

the time of his first acquiring them; at which time the pleasure
may be styled a pleasure of gain or a pleasure of acquisition:
at other times a pleasure of possession (Bentham 1970: 43).

Technology and Happiness

Technology reduces drudgery and hence increases happiness by decreasing suffering. Technology has also made the dominant contribution to increasing life expectancy, decreasing infant mortality, decreasing the incidence of a variety of plagues, and providing basic food, shelter and other necessities of life to a greatly expanded population of the advanced countries. Technology has not, however, solved the problem of poverty in rich countries or the much greater problem of extreme poverty associated with underdevelopment.

If happiness is the avoidance of pain, then technology plays an important role in freeing people from the pain of hard physical labour. The avoidance of much sweat and blood in construction, mining, manufacture, agriculture, and housework undoubtedly contributes to the sum total of happiness. (Even though sometimes one doubts this statement when watching people inflicting on themselves a great deal of voluntary pain in their sporting and keep-fit activities!) The easing of human toil has always been a prime cause of technological development, although, as is the wont of prime causes, it no longer plays a primary role in technological innovation. On the other hand, the easing of toil has now gone much beyond sheer physical effort to include the taking over by machines of easy repetitive tasks, such as washing the dishes or doing sums. However the question of where the relief from pain stops and the painful side-effects of automated technological devices start, is the subject of much argument.

The second, and much more questionable, role of technology in the pursuit of happiness consists of turning it into a quest for products of technology, in the futile belief that happiness can be embodied in possessions. Technology does not just satisfy needs, it attempts to create demand by offering ever new, or ever changing, products. The pursuit of happiness by consumption has become the dominant, alas elusive, mode of seeking the good life. It is a moot point whether the acquisition and possession of goods can be a major component of happiness, although it certainly can be a source of pleasure and satisfaction and a major contributor to our creature comforts. The advertising industry conjures up images of immense happiness to be obtained by purchasing whatever it is they are trying to sell, yet these unrealistic expectations are bound to be disappointed. Because of the rapid obsolescence of products of technology, purchasers are constantly disappointed, as their latest proud acquisition is rapidly put in the shadow by a later model. Thus the spiral of aroused want, its gratification, and immediate new want turns ever faster.

Happiness in most of its forms is not just determined by the makeup of the individual and the circumstances he or she lives in, but is also considerably affected by the culture the individual is part of. What makes people happy depends on their expectations and thus on the patterns of behaviour, thought, beliefs and values they are surrounded by. Even the most intimately human aspects of happiness depend on culturally determined expectations. What we expect from marriage, from children, from friends and relations, all depends on the culture we live in. Happiness depends on whether our expectations are fulfilled or disappointed, on whether reality is compatible with our dreams or bears no resemblance to them.

In highly developed societies – meaning societies that use a great deal of technology and whose wealth far exceeds that necessary for mere subsistence – our pattern of expectations involves the ownership of a large quantity of technological artefacts. More generally, we expect to own a good deal of wealth and, beyond ownership, to have at our disposal a well-functioning technological infrastructure. We expect long holidays with the possibility to travel, a short working week, good housing with all comforts, such as central heating, bathrooms, well-equipped kitchens. We expect clean running water, good medical provision if we need it, good educational facilities, sports facilities, cultural provisions in the sense of music, theatre and art. We expect a functioning public administration, a high degree of security, a functioning legal system, a banking and insurance system, good communications services, mains electricity, sewage, good public transport. Above all else we expect to be able to acquire goods of every description in a wide variety of choice at prices we can afford. To own a colour television set, a video recorder, stereo equipment, a refrigerator and a freezer, as well as a car are regarded as perfectly normal expectations. We could extend the list almost indefinitely, but that is not the point. The point is to show two things: first, that our culture is such as to gear individual expectations to very considerable and increasing consumption; and secondly, that virtually all the goods and most of the services consumed are produced, or supported, with the aid of technology. Anybody who cannot acquire a good part of these conveniences feels deprived and suffers from relative poverty, even if his/her biological existence is not deprived to the extent of facing hunger or exposure to the elements.

One aspect of our acquisitiveness is related to restlessness and the constant quest for improvement. We constantly seek out weak links, things in our homes and our lives that could be improved. A chair that is a bit shabby, a corner of the garden that is not quite up to scratch, a bathroom that could do with better tiles. Or, perhaps, a new sporting activity that we could take up and equip ourselves for, or a new game we could play at home. All in all, we find it hard to sit still, to contemplate what we have with quiet contentment and without the need for active change. But our restlessness does not come from within; it forms part of our acquisitive culture. Our desires are related to the offerings of the market. We are constantly battered by images of all the beautiful possessions we might have; advertising, magazines, television, shop windows, all ram home the same message: look at what you could have, compare with what you actually have – buy, buy, buy! And those who can, buy, while those who can't, borrow to buy, and those who cannot borrow feel deprived and unhappy. Many desires and dreams are related to the offerings of the market; our creative wishes to improve our situation find outlets in ways determined by the market and the manipulators of our wishes in their various guises as sales managers, engineers, designers, advertisers or journalists.

The measurement of happiness, or the quality of life, or contentment, is notoriously difficult. The answers obtained in surveys depend critically upon the questions asked. Besides, most people are aware of their state of contentment only when they are either ecstatically happy or dismally unhappy. Despite these difficulties and inconsistencies of evidence, we shall quote one result which seems intuitively correct and is empirically reasonably well documented. Simply stated, it seems that, cases of absolute poverty apart, it is the relative position within one's own society that matters more than the general affluence of the society.

Elemér Hankiss found that 'while per capita personal income grew about 40 per cent, the proportion of Americans describing themselves as "very happy" declined by 20 to 30 per cent' (Szalai and Andrews 1980: 48). The conclusion is that there is only a very loose, if any, connection between the *general* level of income and general happiness. On the other hand, there is a correlation, albeit not a very well documented one, between the *relative* income of a person and his/her state of happiness. In the early '70s in the USA only 20 per cent of those with incomes under $1,000 were very happy, as opposed to 53 per cent of those with incomes of $15,000 or above.

> ...economic growth may entail a decline in the general
> satisfaction or happiness level of the population – at least,
> this is what happened in the USA in the last three
> decades...at a given point in time and within a country, the
> higher the living standard of a social class or group, the
> higher will be its satisfaction level! This relationship is,
> however, relatively weak (op cit: 49–51).

The nature of acquisitive society was aptly described by R H Tawney:

> Such societies may be called Acquisitive Societies because
> their whole tendency and interest and preoccupation is to
> promote the acquisition of wealth...The secret of its triumph
> is obvious. It is an invitation to men to use the powers with

which they have been endowed by nature or society, by skill or energy or relentless egotism or mere good fortune, without enquiring whether there is any principle by which their exercise should be limited...By fixing men's minds, not upon the discharge of social obligations, which restricts their energy, because it defines the goal to which it should be directed, but upon the exercise of the right to pursue their own self-interest, it offers unlimited scope for the acquisition of riches, and therefore gives free play to one of the most powerful of human instincts. To the strong it promises unfettered freedom for the exercise of their strength; to the weak the hope that they too one day may be strong. Before the eyes of both it suspends a golden prize, which not all can attain, but for which each may strive, the enchanting vision of infinite expansion (Tawney 1924: 32–3).

The spectre that disturbed Tawney was the absence of social conscience or social obligation, the idea that nothing was allowed to stand in the way of sheer greed. It is one of the tragedies of contemporary society that the carefully nurtured expectations of wealth are, albeit incompletely, fulfilled for only a proportion of the population of the rich countries. This proportion depends upon the total wealth available, but more markedly upon the social and political ambience, the degree of social conscience and compassion that prevail at any given time. The expectations of wealth and consumption are not fulfilled at all for the populations of the poorer countries, which means that the vast majority of humankind can only observe the rich from a distance and without a glimmer of hope of being able to emulate them. They stand in the cold and look in through the proverbial window – provided, symbolically and aptly, by television.

Tawney did not condemn profligate consumption as such; this is a worry of a later period. His worry was ownership by the rich, unfettered by social obligation. He was not worried about the inability of the natural environment to withstand the onslaught of rapidly expanding populations and even more rapidly expanding consumption. Tawney saw clearly that society may not be happy without some constraints upon greed and some considerations of human welfare; he did not see that society may spiral into irredeemable decline if the environment is stretched beyond its capacity to withstand the terrible havoc wreaked upon it by humans armed with ever more potent technology.

Consumption as an active path to happiness is, even in the absence of gross social inequalities, a doubtful key to a joyful life. The good consumer must constantly require more; he or she can never be satisfied; each small pleasure of acquisition must soon be followed by the next dose of this stimulant. The purpose of salesmanship is to arouse desires; a satisfied and satiated citizen is of no value to the salesperson. And the faster the pace of technological innovation, the more futile the quest for contentment through the acquisition of products of technology becomes. It is a race towards a moving target. Although this is not to deny that a degree of satisfaction can be obtained from the use of the products of technology, particularly if the emphasis is on use, rather than on the constant quest for more acquisitions. The achievement of true happiness, however, depends not so much on having technological products as on living in harmony with friends and family, doing satisfactory work, enjoying elating cultural experiences, feeling comfortable in society, and living in harmony with nature.

We owe our conspicuous consumption to three factors:

1. Our agriculture is extremely efficient and can produce more than enough food with a minimum input of labour:
2. Industrial production is almost equally efficient and is able to produce a huge array of goods with a labour input of only between 20 and 30 percent of the workforce:
3. We disregard the needs of the natural environment, of future generations, of the poor in our own countries, not to mention those in the poor countries, and shamelessly indulge in our own consumption without much regard, or even thought, for all these distasteful considerations.

Whatever our income and wealth might be, the offerings of the market are such that there are always things we cannot afford. Whatever satisfaction we obtain from purchasing and ownership, we always feel dissatisfaction with the inability to purchase or to own:

> We are constantly bombarded by the idea that people who own things are happier than those who don't...It is inevitable that we shall all meet our own limit. Frustration and dissatisfaction result because we have been conditioned to want more than we can have (Houston 1981: 18–19)... many of us sense that, by providing us with all these material benefits, our society has created a new sense of loss, of hollowness, and a dulled life experience (op cit: 2).

Yet there can be no doubt that many products of technology make life easier, more comfortable, and more pleasant. Although a daily shower or bath is not strictly necessary, it is very enjoyable, especially if water of the chosen temperature comes straight from the tap, without the slightest effort by the consumer. A well-kept lawn gives pleasure to its owner and evokes admiration from visitors. A power-driven mower reduces the physical effort involved in mowing it to a very minimum, and a range of fertilizers, weedkillers and power-tools make it easier to keep the lawn immaculate. To be able to hear one's favourite music, played almost to perfection, at the touch of a button is pleasing; to have ready-cooked meals in the freezer and be able to heat them in a matter of minutes is highly convenient; to do all the laundry without any drudgery and to have it bone-dry in no time even on rainy days, is nothing short of marvellous. If we feel that our sedentary occupation, travel to work by car, and lack of physical effort in the home and garden, do not provide sufficient exercise for our bodies, a technological remedy is at hand. We can buy exquisite modern machines to torture our flabby flesh, or, if torture in private is not to our liking, we can flog ourselves in public and under expert guidance in a fitness studio. Technology offers a remedy for (almost) every problem it causes.

I am not advocating a return to a technologically primitive existence; the argument is merely against the overwhelming predominance of possession and consumption as virtually the only mode of existence, tempered only by occasional lip-service to supernatural beliefs and religious ceremonial or mystical mumbo jumbo. It is an argument against an over-emphasis on material possessions as against simple pleasures: nature, food, good company, reflection. It also is an argument in favour of Culture writ large: good theatre, good literature, good music, good visual arts; all these provide enjoyments that are less destructive and go deeper than any gadgets can ever provide. Finally, it is an argument for putting human values before material possessions. Happiness without too many possessions is possible: happiness without good personal relations and compassion is not.

Marketing is the art of making people want what they do not need. Technological innovation is grist to the marketing mills. In fairness, this verdict applies to marketing of consumer goods only. Marketing of industrial goods is an entirely different matter. It is a far less one-sided affair, with advertisers having all the say and consumers merely dipping into their pockets. The industrial market is one of give and take, with industrial firms having real demands on their suppliers and often being able to negotiate the supply of goods to their own specifications. Not that industry is immune from ordinary sales pressures, but this pattern of marketing is not the dominant one in the industrial sphere. Generally, very clear distinctions must be made between the marketing of investment goods and that of consumer products, even though some of the items sold under either heading may be identical.

Returning to consumer markets, industry does not aim simply to satisfy consumer demands, let alone needs; it aims to create a continuous cycle of dissatisfaction with existing products, to be remedied by new products, which in their turn cause dissatisfaction to be remedied by even newer products. We may regard this as a natural progression in the sense that technology moves along a unidirectional development trajectory. The objectionable point is the speed of rotation, as it were, along the spiral. Far from being satisfied with modest movement along the spiral, allowing technologies to reach something

41

akin to an end of their natural life before they are replaced by newer, substantially better technologies, competitive pressures and the Zeitgeist demand that every conceivable effort should be made to accelerate the movement. Technologies must change more rapidly, new model must chase new model in ever faster succession. The recommended cure to economic stagnation is ever faster innovation. Yet ever faster innovation extracts its own heavy toll.

Technological progress can contribute to the sum total of happiness. The elimination of much physical hardship and much ill-health is an achievement of enormous benefit. Yet if progress becomes too fast, if all we own is obsolescent or even obsolete, if all we see around us is in constant rapid flux, if sales pressures are such as to make us buy things beyond our purchasing capacity, then technological change turns the dream of progress into a nightmare.

The fact that the computer has become the intermediary between people and their administrative tasks, and also between people and those who are supposed to serve them, exacerbates the sense of alienation many of us feel. The drive for ever higher productivity, made possible by computer technology, means that more and more customers must be processed by fewer and fewer staff and nobody has time to look after the customer as a person with needs, fears and quirks. All the hopes that were placed in computers as enablers of a genuinely participative democracy have proved elusive. An information society it may be, but not many people feel better informed.

One of the problems of modern information handling is, yet again, the excessive speed of change. No sooner has an operator become familiar with a computer system than he/she is told that the system is obsolete and must give way to a new one. No sooner has an organization been reorganized around an information system, than this is replaced and reorganization follows in the wake of a new system. Thus the optimum on the learning curve remains elusive, and people feel unfamiliar and uncomfortable with their tasks.

If information technology is to serve mass markets, we shall all have to consume ever more information. Not, alas, information of the expansive, contemplative type, as embodied in books, but information carried by electronic media. If we are to be good consumers, we shall have to watch one television programme while recording another and members of our family will do likewise with different programmes. While away from home, we shall watch television on a portable receiver, take films with a video camera, still pictures with the latest 'high-tech' electronic camera, and transmit our creations to our friends and relations on broad-band telecommunication lines. Both at home and away from home, we shall constantly listen to taped music on earphones while members of our family listen to a compact disc and simultaneously play several computer games. We shall have digital recording equipment for disc and tape and record extensively, yet use these recordings exclusively for our own private enjoyment.

The latest desk-top and lap-top computers with suitable printers are a must; how else could we do our household accounts or keep an address list for Christmas cards, not forgetting the aforementioned computer games? It goes without saying that we must have an electronic diary and a portable telephone, and that all our computers must be linked to a global information network, preferably an information super-highway. Will all this make us happy?

One result of the introduction of information technology (IT) into commercial life is the possibility – and hence the need – to have all kinds of information available instantly. Everything must be up-to-the-minute; yesterday's information is deemed to have no value. There is no time for reflection; information and action must be instant. Pressure on the worker increases, and the depth of analysis decreases. Everything is fast, everything skates on the surface. Instant comment, ephemeral texts, vivid images – these are the essential features of contemporary information. Most people suffer from an overload of information and have to struggle hard to separate the wheat from the chaff. While millions of people are out of work, those in employment have to work ever harder, ever faster. Is this the way to increased happiness, or even to increased efficiency and wealth?

One of the roles of technological innovation and of model changes, which often occur without much real technical change, is to whet the consumer's appetite continually for new purchases. Ever since the introduction of multi-channel colour television, people have tended to keep the same set for a long time and manufacturers have been trying to counteract this tendency by introducing a variety of frills: larger screens, stylistic changes, remote control, stereo sound. The big push for the replacement of virtually all current sets will come with the advent of high definition television (HDTV) in one form or another.

The change to HDTV is a major technological innovation. It involves not only very different receiving equipment, but also a whole new system of production and distribution of programmes. The change has required an enormous R&D effort and the outcome, either in technical or economic terms, is still far from clear. It now seems that HDTV might become just one aspect of digital television and this, in turn, might become an aspect of the information highway (Bruce and Buck 1994). It is not clear whether the tremendous R&D effort will ever be repaid in terms of additional revenue from sales of the new system. If we add the question of opportunity costs – ie what could have been done and remained undone – with the resources spent on development of HDTV, the answers become entirely a matter of personal conjecture. A great deal of public money is involved. In Europe, for example, the Commission of the European Communities is supporting R&D on HDTV, and even larger sums are dispensed under the auspices of the EUREKA intergovernmental research initiative.

Consumers of present-day television appear to be perfectly satisfied with the technical quality of their pictures. No voices have been heard in public, no outcry has become known, no pressure groups of disgruntled citizens have formed to demand higher quality TV images. Yet high definition television is around the corner and state and industry have formed an unholy alliance to produce such a system with all possible haste. It is all done in the name of satisfying consumer demand; yet consumers are not demanding a better picture and are happy with what they have. It is confidently expected that anybody who has seen HDTV will become instantly dissatisfied with the current technology and will rush out to buy the better picture. Thus a new spiral will start. Dissatisfaction with current technology by comparison with new technology; purchase of the new, and, in due course, dissatisfaction with that technology in comparison with the next technological innovation. Indeed the introduction of HDTV may follow such a path in several planned steps, with a precursor technology introduced first, to be improved on later, followed perhaps by a third step. It is possible that HDTV will offer scope for new artistic departures, but one wonders whether these will improve the quality of TV programmes. Although competition and choice have been introduced, they have so far only served to reduce the quality of programmes to the lowest common denominator.

One of the greatest enemies of humans in contemporary advanced societies is boredom, and although information super-highways will attempt to alleviate boredom by providing more entertainment, the introduction of more information technology into work processes will probably decrease employment and thus increase the sum total of boredom.

CHAPTER TWO

TECHNOLOGICAL INNOVATION

◆

Causes

The accumulation of private wealth and the promise of more wealth tomorrow is the dominant ideology of the day. Technological innovation is regarded as the mainspring of present and future wealth. The capacity for technological innovation is to us potential wealth, much as land, gold, or coal were to former generations. Current economic orthodoxy regards the potential and actual ability to create ever new technological artefacts as the mainspring of economic success. It is therefore regarded as incumbent upon governments to do all they can to increase the potential for innovation and to accelerate its pace as much as possible, although there is some disagreement among economists and politicians as to the degree of support that should be given and as to the means that should be adopted.

My own arguments are in some disagreement with such orthodoxy. Although I do not wish to deny the utility of, and need for, technological innovation, or even its important role in economic success, its pace ought not to be forced by political intervention. Indeed, I regard it as somewhat ironic that at a time when economic orthodoxy prescribes a minimum of government intervention in economic and social affairs, public support for technological innovation should be viewed as vital. My own arguments stand this position almost on its head: I regard some intervention in economic and social affairs as inevitable in order to safeguard minimum standards of infrastructural provision and of social equity, while at the same time arguing that the public good does not require much public intervention in technological innovation, except to direct adequate innovative effort toward safeguarding health, safety and the natural environment. Let commercially oriented innovation thrive at a pace determined by its own rhythm, rather than try to force its growth in a hothouse constructed at tax-payers' expense.

One of the main assumptions behind public support for technological innovation is the belief that rapid innovation in process technology – ie in methods of production – can continue to increase productivity and thus provide higher profitability and an impetus to growth and international competitive advantage. Some economists doubt whether this assumption is still justified.

> ...in a given historical context, the embodiment of technical progress in the production sphere made a period of high growth possible. But the impact of this new factor has gradually declined, until today it is negligible. In other words, technology has operated like any other factor of production employed in increasing quantities: after an extraordinarily successful period, later extended by the injection of science, it has recently reached a phase of declining returns... (Giarini and Loubergé 1978: 47).

That non-intervention and neglect of infrastructural measures leads to public squalor, private despair and social disease need not be argued here; the facts both in Britain and in the United States stare one in the face. Only those blinded by dogma can fail to see that public transport, housing for the poor and environmental care, among other things, have all reached a catastrophic state. It is equally obvious that millions live in relative and, often, absolute poverty; that crime rates have reached epidemic proportions, reducing everybody's quality of life; that health care for the less well off is, at best, rudimentary. Some public investment and intervention might have avoided the squalor and contributed substantially to the maintenance of a civilized quality of life, while public neglect has caused very obvious deterioration.

The advanced world experiences occasional riots, expressions of deeply felt alienation and frustration with a society that displays ostentatious wealth and extravagant life styles, while at the same time depriving a large proportion of its population of virtually all aspects of civilized existence. If two-thirds of the population live in relative affluence, nobody cares about one-third living in squalor (Galbraith: 1992). If the deprived third indulges in criminal activities and occasional riots, the state simply recruits more police, imposes tougher sentences and, as a last resort, sends in armed troops. The private citizen and private business invest in security systems of every description.

The currently orthodox economists, although by no means all

economists, prefer to ignore such little imperfections. They greatly admire a state that turns a blind eye to squalor and deprivation, neglects its duty to protect public goods such as the natural environment, but allows private profit motives a completely free hand in its speculative and manipulative activities. Some such economists cheer the government when it gives generous handouts to private enterprise for accelerating technological innovation, regardless of whether or not such innovations serve any purpose that might be regarded as useful to the public.

Public involvement in the fostering of technological innovation, on the other hand, has had no visible impact and has achieved no obvious results. It is a moot point, and will always remain unproven and controversial, whether the state of the British, or US, or any other economy would have been worse without public attempts to foster technological innovation.

My argument is not against all aspects of support for technological innovation; it is only against direct support of socially irrelevant technologies. It is not against support for technological innovation which is needed to protect the environment or to improve other public goods; neither is it against support for a good basic research system and, even more important, a good system of education and training. Only public support can secure these public domain goods, and hence adequate public support should be given to them. Technological innovation in the commercial domain, on the other hand, can be achieved by industry alone, and hence it should be industry's sole responsibility.

To avoid any searching questions being asked about the utility of innovation, economists build a large edifice of theory proclaiming that all innovations serve human needs; indeed, that the better satisfaction of people's needs is the only cause of innovation. In reality, innovations are an instrument of competition and firms work hard to produce them, and even harder to sell them to a reluctant public. At the same time, the really burning and glaring needs of humans throughout the so-called developing world remain unsatisfied and poverty in the developed world goes unchecked. One of the major strands of innovation is to produce labour saving processes, enabling firms to cut their workforce, which leads to even greater unemployment, unless sufficiently increased demand compensates for the job losses. Very few people believe that on present trends technological innovation can lead our economies back to full employment: they merely think that rapid innovation can achieve better results than technological innovation pursued at a slower rate. I believe that the trend towards accelerating innovation is wasteful of human and natural resources and a steadier rate of technological progress would lead, other things being equal, to greater welfare. Some economists share this view (see eg Henderson 1980; Daly 1991; and Douthwaite 1992).

At the level of the industrial firm there are several factors conspiring to push in the direction of accelerating technological change. One

47

is technology itself, because technology has a 'natural' tendency to move forward. As each technological solution is a compromise between the desirable and the possible, there is always hope for a better compromise, for the possible to come closer to the desirable. In addition, there is always the hope of stimulating new desires and of formulating old desires in new ways. Technology is never perfect; the last word is never said. Thus technologists have a tendency to go on forever producing new and better products. But technologists and scientists also have a tendency to try to safeguard their positions within firms. Established research organizations tend to get bigger. New organizations tend to become established not only in new firms, but also in new fields of scientific or technological developments. The pressure for continuity and growth comes both from the subject of R&D itself and from its practitioners, who act just like any other humans employed in organizations.

The numbers of researchers have reached significant proportions of the total workforce in some of the more science-based or high-technology industries. If we consider that these workers are among the most highly educated in the total workforce, and hence are very able to express their views and make their voices heard, it is not surprising that their influence is felt in their organizations and cannot be disregarded easily.

It is very difficult to imagine firms such as Rolls-Royce, General Electric, ICI, IBM, Hitachi, Ford, or any other of the large chemical, aerospace, information technology, electrical and electronics, or automobile firms, without major research laboratories. It is equally hard, or even harder, to imagine that these laboratories will say to their firms: 'Our latest product is so brilliant that there really is no need to improve it any further and we cannot think of any new products we might come up with, so why not simply send us all home and go on producing what you are producing now.' The contrary is much more likely to happen. Research departments are likely to say to their bosses: 'Look at our brilliant new product, but remember that, given more time and money, we can improve on that quite considerably. We also have very clever ideas for quite different new products that are likely to prove extremely profitable and will put our firm right ahead of the pack.'

Each firm in a particular industrial sector looks over its shoulder to see whether it is spending as high a proportion of its turnover on R&D as its competitors, and thus an upward pressure on the size of research budgets arises not just from within the firm, but also from without it.

This brings us to the most significant pressure of all: the pressure of competition. As long as the prime strategic objective of a firm is to survive and grow in the long term it must, among other things, keep its manufacturing technology and its products at an adequate level. Adequate in this context means several things: the cost/performance ratings of the products must be such as to maintain, or increase, their market share while providing sufficient profit for the firm, which means that the quality of the products, at the given price, must equal contemporary standards; it also means that the manufacturing technology must be good enough to guarantee a productivity which allows profitable sales and guarantees adequate quality. Those are minimum requirements. A large firm with a range of just adequate products and equipped with just adequate technology – other things being equal – is very vulnerable to fluctuating demand, fluctuating economic conditions and aggressive moves by the competition. A firm with many above-average performers in its portfolio of products and with some exceptionally good manufacturing technology will – other things being equal – stand up much better to the vagaries of external circumstances.

It is now commonly claimed that markets demand greater flexibility and put greater emphasis on non-price factors. Greater flexibility means many things, among them a greater demand on labour to show flexibility in the allocation of tasks (multi-skilled workers); in the hours worked (part-time workers and workers without security); and in systems of pay (Bessant 1991: 117). 'And although the flexible strategy may emphasize the importance of up-grading knowledge, "skills" and autonomy these may be seen by the worker not as enhancing flexibility but as increasing their workload and responsibilities' (Scarbrough and Corbett 1992: 41).

Flexibility also means that an apparently great variety of products is offered and that the numbers produced of each type can be varied quickly. The variety is obtained by relatively minor variations of the main product and modern, computer-controlled machinery is well suited to achieve this sort of flexibility. Markets are unlikely to demand anything unless manufacturers offer it to them, and flexibility is a case in point, despite the common argument that flexibility is demanded by customers. Among non-price factors quality looms large. However, quality in this sense merely means that each item is up to the design standard; not that the design is of outstanding quality, nor that the durability of the product is high.

That competitors look very closely at the products of their rivals can be seen even from trivial examples. No sooner has one automobile manufacturer introduced some new gimmick – say, central locking or electrically operated windows – then all manufacturers follow suit in a very short time. The same applies to more important advances, such as anti-blocking braking systems (ABS). In most cases manufacturers tend to offer these items for several years as optional extras on their basic models and as standard equipment on the more expensive ones. All manufacturers are constantly on the look-out for some such minor or major improvements, preferably ones which are easy to produce and highly visible, in order to increase the appeal of their particular product. This is a process of innovation which occurs under conditions of commercial competition and is not forced by government intervention. It is what we might call the natural pace of progress. Small innovations, sometimes beneficial, sometimes not, are the most frequent result of such innovative activity.

Many people will argue that even this pace of progress is too fast, because it causes the technical and commercial obsolescence of products before they are physically worn out. Nevertheless, I do not advocate removing competition altogether. The technological and commercial stagnation that results from lack of competition, and the deterioration in the quality of goods and services, which was so vividly demonstrated in the command economies in the recent past, provide sufficient argument in favour of some competition, albeit not at all cost and certainly not in all spheres of life.

The third pressure to innovate comes from the need to avoid saturating the markets. All the advanced countries operate under conditions of plenty and of surplus capacity, although occasional bottlenecks do occur and substantial numbers of the population are excluded from the bounty. Currently, for example, there are huge overcapacities in agriculture, the steel industry, the motor industry, textiles, armaments, and many more. The fact that at the same time the majority of the population of the world lives in dire poverty and often starves is quite a different matter and, unhappily, does not change the argument. In a very real sense the economies of the advanced countries form a closed system which, although it trades with the less developed world, maintains it own affluence irrespective of what happens elsewhere. Conditions of plenty imply that there is sufficient purchasing power in the population to ensure that most goods, including durable consumer products, will find large numbers of buyers; yet surplus capacity remains and further opportunities for expanding consumption are sought. This does not imply that all needs in these societies are satisfied; there are needs of the less well-off that remain unsatisfied because of their lack of purchasing power, and many more unsatisfied needs of a kind that cannot be satisfied by the private consumption of industrial goods.

With some products it is impossible to increase total consumption; thus the total amount of food bought is determined by the capacity of the population to eat. As countries become more affluent, food consumption shifts towards more expensive processed and exotic foods, but total consumption remains limited by total appetite. Both agriculture and, more particularly, the food processing industry and the large retailers try to innovate and increase the added value of their products. The choice of ready-cooked meals, for example, is increasing continually. The food industry also adapts to current fashions and health fads: thus, currently, more fibre, less animal fat, more vitamins and less sugar are the slogans of the day and these influence what is to be found on the shelves of supermarkets. In that sense market pull, albeit the pull of a manipulated market, does operate.

Manufacturing industry as a whole is in the happy position of not having to face an overall upper limit to total consumption. Apart from environmental concerns and restricted incomes, people can, in theory, consume ever more goods. Apart from limits on purchasing power imposed by macro-economic constraints beyond the scope of our discussion, the main obstacle to permanently and rapidly increasing consumption is seen in the durability of products and the consequent saturation of markets. Although manufacturing industry would not like to face a natural upper limit of consumption as the food industry does, it would like consumption of all goods to be as continuous as the consumption of food. The shorter the time-span between a purchase and hunger for further purchases, the better for industry. The faster the cycle from purchase to waste, the happier industry becomes.

From the point of view of nature this is, of course, a catastrophic point of view. As far as nature is concerned, the fewer raw materials and the less energy are consumed, and the less waste is produced, the better.

From the point of view of the consumer, durability should be a desirable attribute of all goods. Wealth should not be perceived as the ability to consume, but as the ability to have all useful goods at one's disposal. What matters is not how new the car is, but whether it operates reliably; not whether the sofa is new, but whether it is comfortable and aesthetically pleasing; and similarly for every kind of consumer durables and not so durables, such as electric light bulbs and such like.

There is a conflict, at least an apparent conflict, of interest between nature and consumers on the one hand and manufacturing industry and retailers on the other. Fortunately for industry, it has managed to use its collective salesmanship and advertising power to convince most consumers of the virtues of novelty and of the almost despicable nature of any remaining habits of trying to retain goods for as long as possible. Only the New Brand X is good, indeed superlative; its predecessor, old Brand X, is, by implication, pretty useless. Yesterday's proud purchaser of old Brand X must today hang his/her head in shame and sorrow, and rush out to buy New Brand X, even if a new loan may be required to finance this new purchase.

When a market is saturated and sales of a certain product decline, industry tries very hard to convince the consumer that the product is obsolete anyway and that a new purchase ought to be made. I have mentioned the example of television, an industry poised to break the barrier of stagnation with digital television and HDTV. In the same way, the long-playing record was replaced by the compact disc, the tape recorder will be replaced either by digital tape recorders and/or by recording compact disc players, the video recorder will be replaced by a digital video recorder, and so forth. The telephone dial has been replaced by a touch-button system and supplemented by a memory. The replacement of the analogue telephone by a digital one is in progress and the mobile telephone is making great strides. These are examples of the replacement of an item by one fulfilling similar functions, albeit at a more advanced level.

There are many examples of entirely new products, satisfying needs that nobody knew they had. In the realm of communications technology, one of the recent extraordinarily successful examples is the facsimile machine, or fax, which has spread very rapidly in the business world and is beginning to capture, albeit more slowly, the residential market. Interestingly, the current type of fax is already obsolescent, and the next, faster and better type of machine is already in the offing.

Micro-Economic Theories of Technological Innovation

Distinctions are made between product and process innovation, and between radical and incremental innovation. Many more criteria for differentiation have been suggested and are often helpful. Freeman and Perez have suggested a taxonomy of innovations according to both their technological intensity and their impact on the economy. They distinguish between:

1. incremental innovation, ie the process of continuous improvement and development of products and processes;
2. radical innovations, ie technological discontinuities which are usually the result of deliberate R&D;
3. changes of technology system, ie 'far-reaching changes in technology, affecting several branches of the economy, as well as giving rise to entirely new sectors';
4. changes in techno-economic paradigm (technological revolutions).

This type of technical change has pervasive repercussions throughout the economy and, once established as the dominant influence, becomes a 'technological regime' for several decades. (Freeman and Perez: 45–7, in Dosi et al 1988). The frequency of occurrence obviously decreases with the ranking of these types of innovation.

The introduction of new production processes into a firm, even if the processes themselves are not so new, has sometimes been called 'manufacturing innovation' (Braun 1984a: 39–43), but this term has now largely been subsumed under the title of 'management of technology', or 'management of change', implying that it has been widely realized that the introduction of new technology into a firm is important and complex, and needs careful attention from management.

The micro-economic theory of technological innovation has undergone considerable development during the period since World War II. While previously most economic theorists, with the notable exception of Schumpeter and a few others, ignored the question altogether, the post-war period saw the emergence of much thinking, with regard to both the role of technological innovation in the economy and to the actual process of innovation.

According to Rothwell (1992), the theory of the process of innovation has now reached its fifth generation. The first generation, of the immediate postwar period, took the so-called linear view of technological innovation. This theory assumes that scientific research discovers the feasibility of potentially useful new technologies. These ideas are then taken up by technologists and developed into prototypes of new products or processes. At this stage we have an invention. Investment then takes place into production facilities for the new products and attempts at marketing them are made. A product or process becomes an innovation when it is actually offered on the market. The new technology then begins to diffuse through the economy. In the lucky cases, this diffusion will be widespread and will yield profits to the innovator. Indeed at first the profits will be large, because the innovator holds a monopoly for the new product or process until such time as imitators appear on the market.

This linear view of technological innovation is now regarded as discredited, although it was shot down in the traditional way of dealing with other people's scientific theories: take a theory, distort and oversimplify it and then shoot it down in flames. It is easiest to discredit simplified beliefs that were not held by anybody in the first place. The linear theory is supposed to have committed the cardinal sin of ignoring the market, although few people ever believed in such crude oversimplification. The proponents of the linear theory were well aware that an innovation could only succeed if it found a market. Similarly, there was an awareness that not all technological innovations stem from scientific discoveries and an acknowledgement of the fact that much innovative activity results from gradual technological improvements which owe little or nothing to scientific research. The linear theory, in its simplest form, overemphasized the importance of science as a progenitor of technology and under-emphasized the role of economic and other factors. On the other hand, the belief that scientific discoveries can lead, with due regard to markets and economic considerations, to new products and processes is still held – witness the uncounted millions spent on scientific research by an uncounted number of industrial firms, aided and abetted by their respective governments.

The simplified linear theory of innovation has caused one fatal error in the planning of technological innovation in many business firms: it divorces scientific research and development too much from production and marketing activities. Science parks, ie small-scale industrial developments located near, and associated with, academic institutions, were an important and arguably only moderately successful policy response to the perceived need for increased innovative potential in the economy and, as argued by Massey et al, were based on the linear theory of innovation. 'At the core of the science-park phenomenon lies a view about how technologies are created. The view is that scientific activities are performed in academic laboratories isolated from other activities. The resulting discoveries and knowledge are potential inputs to technology' (Massey et al 1992: 56).

According to Rothwell, the first generation linear theory of innovation was based on the premise of technology-push, ie the view that a technology is developed in the hope of finding, or creating, a market, rather than in response to a known market demand. Although I believe that technology push is, and always has been, the main cause of all radical technological innovation, it is a little surprising that the roots of this view are to be found in World War II, when an unprecedented effort in pure and applied research and in technological development yielded undoubted results, such as radar, the nuclear bomb, and other marvels of human ingenuity that were first deployed in the barbarity of war. During the war, surely, more than at any other time, necessity was the mother of invention.

The second generation of innovation theory, although still linear, assumed that the impetus for the innovation emanated from the market. The market signals a need, this signal is picked up by scientific research and a new technology may emerge to satisfy the need. This model, known as market-pull or need-pull, is based on the belief that technology develops only, or mainly, in response to articulated human needs.

The so-called technology-push, ie the belief that a technological invention, whether based on science or not, lies at the heart of all innovation is the ingredient of the linear theory that has become discredited, as it flies in the face of the most favoured myth about technology, the myth that technology develops for no reason or purpose other than to satisfy known human needs.

It is widely claimed that research on technological innovation shows that innovations are based on findings about the needs of the market. This statement requires some critical examination. First and foremost, the truth or otherwise of the statement depends on the type of market under discussion. There can be little doubt that major capital goods, say aircraft, are never (in view of Concorde, we should say hardly ever), developed without detailed consultations with potential buyers, in this case the airlines. Similarly, any manufacturer of textile machinery will disregard the comments made about his machinery by textile manufacturers operating it to his peril. Of course the salesforce of such companies must be in touch with its customers and must listen to technical comments and the expression of wishes for improvements. In this category of goods the buyers know virtually as much about the equipment as the producers and are very well able to articulate their needs.

Even in such cases, truly radical innovations are brought about by the equipment manufacturers alone. When it comes to designing spinning, or weaving, or any other equipment based on truly novel principles, the manufacturer is forced to fall back on his own technical resources, his own inventiveness, his own hunch on what might provide a better answer than traditional concepts. When the small

Austrian manufacturer of spinning machinery, Fehrer, invented a new process which he thought would yield better results for the spinning of certain yarns, he undertook the development work at his own risk and without consultation with potential buyers. Obviously, he thought that the machines would sell; nobody is foolish enough to indulge in technology-push without at least guessing at, believing in, and hoping for a market for the new technology. After a long struggle, this particular innovator was proved right, but many are less fortunate and their innovations fail to gain acceptance.

It is perfectly possible for an invention, although probably not a radical one, to emanate from a textile manufacturer rather than from a manufacturer of textile machinery. In this case, some form of collaborative agreement might be made between the two types of manufacturer, which would ensure the pooling of their technical resources and the joint development of the new technology (Braun and Milla: 106, in Hübner 1986). Similarly, there is close cooperation between suppliers of production equipment and major producers of microelectronic circuits. The supplier knows what is needed, and the circuit manufacturer knows what is feasible. Many manufacturing operations consist of assembling parts or sub-systems that are bought in from outside suppliers. In these cases, the assembler specifies very precisely what is wanted and we may truly say that the customer demands certain products. This is a far cry, however, from saying that the end user has any major say in technological innovation.

Von Hippel describes a range of collaborations between suppliers of capital equipment and their clients, which illustrate that the technically knowledgeable operator has plenty of ideas about his equipment and that an alert supplier can learn a great deal about desirable technical developments from his clients (von Hippel: 105–16, in Roberts 1987). These are clearly instances of market pull, yet even in these customer–supplier relationships the great technological leap is normally made by the supplier alone, and almost wholly in the dark about likely market potential. Radical innovation is almost invariably driven by technology and by faith, not by market demand.

Computers may serve as an illustration. The initial push for computers was almost wholly based on speculative R&D, although a very limited military requirement was anticipated. Early computers represented the art of the technically possible, and not the desire to fulfil any needs, let alone articulated needs. Of course the early proponents of computers hoped that their brain children would find markets, but initial hopes were very modest indeed. It was widely held that a tiny number of machines would wholly saturate any possible market, which would be mainly military and scientific. As the capabilities of computers became greater, particularly through their unforeseen synergetic relationship with semiconductor devices, so more applications became possible and a wider market developed. The computer did not fulfil articulated needs, but by its technical prowess and effective marketing managed to create markets for itself. As the number of computers increased and knowledge about them developed, more of the users of computers became expert themselves and a dialogue between computer manufacturers and computer users began to develop. Further developments in large machines and in their software began to be driven by this dialogue, so that the market began to exert its influence. It seems, however, that in computers technology-push is the dominant force to this day, although the market exerts a strong modifying influence. The term 'technology-push moderated by market requirements' would describe the current situation better than the term market-pull. This regime becomes possible, however, only at a stage when the initial pure technology-push has succeeded in raising the technology beyond its infancy.

It is generally true that most innovations are the result of the innovator's opinion that a new technological possibility, whether arising out of a new scientific discovery or not, might kindle a human want that it can satisfy and thus find a market. In a relatively few cases the want is known with some accuracy in advance, and we may then truly speak of market-pull; in most cases it is merely an inspired guess, so we must speak of 'enlightened technology-push'. Once an innovation, particularly a radical innovation, has begun to carve out a market for itself, its further development is strongly guided by this encounter with the market, and we may speak of market-oriented diffusion and further development. We may also view the market as a selection environment which picks winners out of the many hopefuls emerging from technology-push. The market selects from the offerings of technology, and technologies are adjusted and modified by market signals and by further R&D during their course of diffusion through the economy.

Microelectronics may serve as a further illustration of these points. The ancestral device of modern microelectronics, the transistor, was a child of science. The science of solid state physics investigated the properties of semiconductors and it was clear to many of the investigators that it ought to be possible to emulate some of the properties of electronic valves in solids, obtaining savings in power and in volume, while increasing robustness. Thus discoveries in pure science led to applied research, in the hope of obtaining practical devices. The research was not in response to a known need, but was guided by a very general knowledge of what might be useful, of what might provide improvements in existing technology. There was no call for such devices from a market that knew nothing of the transistor's potential. When eventually the transistor was announced, it was greeted with indifference by the market, as the advantages over the established valve technology were slight and the disadvantages far outweighed them. The scientists and technologists were undeterred. They were convinced that a better device could be produced and that a market could be established, and they were determined to succeed. It was technology-push all the way, but informed by intelligent guesses of what the market might accept, if only the technology could achieve it.

Eventually, better devices were produced and small market niches were carved out. Hearing aids, where small size and small power consumption were important; portable radios, known to this day as transistor radios. The military became interested in these small and highly portable devices for mobile, air-borne and, eventually, space-borne applications. And, equally important, the synergetic relationship between semiconductors and computers became established, as the power consumption of valves put severe restrictions on the size and complexity of computers. By this stage of the development the enterprise had moved out of the research laboratory and had entered the market place. Although a great deal of further R&D took place and the most important breakthroughs, the integrated circuit, the semiconductor memory and the programmable chip (microprocessor) had yet to come, an infant new semiconductor industry had arisen and was chasing every possible opportunity of selling its wares. The market had become very important, but the major breakthroughs were still led by science, although now in a more confident expectation of market success. The pure technology-push had become market-oriented diffusion and further development. The early pioneers of what became known as microelectronics were the first to admit that the scale of both technical and commercial success was beyond their wildest dreams (Braun and Macdonald 1982).

We have seen how users of capital goods can influence their technological development. With goods that are bought by the public at large, the influence cannot be exerted by the customers themselves, but large retailers can act as some form of proxy for the customers. Large chains of supermarkets and similar outlets have tremendous power to decide what will and what will not reach the customer and what price will be paid. Some people might call this relationship between front-line customer and supplier market-pull, yet no real technological breakthroughs come about this way. The customer influences developments and gives the thumbs up or down to goods, but the true innovations come from manufacturers and are offered to the buyers. This is not to say that the manufacturer does not receive ideas from his marketing department which arise out of consultations with customers, but rarely, if ever, does radically novel technology arise in this way. Large retailers and their suppliers form a united front; they both wish to lure their customers into buying more of their wares. The end user can only choose between the items on offer.

Much knowledge about the innovation process comes from interviews and questionnaires. Questions about the importance of markets generally rank high on the list of queries. The innovator might have indulged in pure technology-push, but not without thinking about possible markets and believing that his/her invention might find favour with buyers and might be perceived as useful to them. The innovator is thus unlikely to say to the researcher that he/she disregarded markets and simply indulged in technological fantasies. The response is much more likely to be that markets played an important part in his/her considerations. Because the myth that technology merely fulfills needs rides high, most innovators will support this myth and will present themselves as benefactors of humankind. It is, after all, much nicer to be seen as a benefactor of humankind than as a self-indulgent technological freak.

It is not surprising that it has become customary to lay claims for market-pull on virtually all types of technological innovation, not merely on the rather specialized case of incremental innovation in capital goods. I would regard the evidence on which this theory is based as somewhat unreliable and, in legal parlance, unsafe and unsatisfactory.

One study of six cases of innovation, in which users of the new technology were involved, reaches the following general conclusion:

> *In cases that meet the preconditions, when the technology is advanced and complex, when it has wide applicability, and when both the producer and customer are technology driven, User/Innovator cooperation on product design and/or marketing is apt to be valuable for both parties* (Mantel Jr and Meredith: 36 Hübner 1986).

This cautious statement, showing very clearly the highly specialized nature of the direct involvement of users in the further development of an established technological innovation, is a far cry from the generalized theory of market-pull.

The market-pull versus technology-push debate has an ideological dimension. For those to whom the market is the embodiment of all wisdom and all virtue, there is great comfort to be derived from the thought that all innovation occurs merely in response to market demands. On the other hand, for those who believe strongly in the beneficial and liberating nature of science and engineering, there is comfort in thinking that new markets are created and that economies expand as a result of purely scientific/technical activities.

It is the constellation of a new scientific/technical possibility for a product or process, coupled with general knowledge about what the market might accept, which causes all radical and many smaller or improvement innovations. On the other hand, there are many cases of small innovations, or improvements to existing products, that are undertaken in direct response to information received from users and often undertaken in conjunction with selected users. The experience of early users often causes the further development and adaptation of radically new products. Creating a market involves a period of trial and error, of feedback from users and of modifications to make the product more acceptable. Often the final users are different from those envisaged early on and the product may need modification to meet the previously neglected requirements of the unexpected users.

The relative role of technology-push and market-pull, or market feedback, depends to a considerable degree on the stage of the development of the product and, of equal importance, on the branch of industry. It is as perilous for a firm to develop technology without due regard for potential or actual markets as it is to wait for signals from the market demanding new technologies. In the first case, a technically marvellous product may never find a market, whereas waiting for market demand for new products can be like waiting for Godot.

> Where R&D is strong and communication with the market poor, technical considerations may dominate the change process, frequently with disastrous results if the needs of the users are insufficiently appreciated. Conversely, where marketing is strong the technical departments can become subservient to an extent which eliminates their potential for originating innovative products. A meeting of minds between these two departments is only one, albeit often the most important, of the many linkages which can lead to ideas for change (Twiss and Goodridge 1989: 114).

Classical studies of innovation, such as project SAPPHO (described eg in Freeman 1974: 171–97), reach the conclusion that market awareness is a vital ingredient of successful innovations. That this should be so is so plausible and so well documented, that it would be foolhardy to dispute it. Yet saying that market considerations influence both the form and outcome of technological innovations is not equivalent to saying that innovation occurs in response to market needs. The very same studies have also shown that firms who maintain good communications with the scientific and technical communities are more likely to produce successful technological innovations than firms that have no sensors for the many signals emanating from the outside world. Technological innovation is not possible without awareness of technological possibilities; success in innovation is not achievable without awareness of market forces.

Technological innovation is a process fraught with problems and risks. One side of human nature always wants to improve, to change, to invent; another side seeks stability and prudent caution. These conflicts arise in any firm that is trying to innovate: the technical departments create new marvels, while the commercial departments seek to avoid risk and to manage prudently. Compromises have to be struck, as competitive pressures favour both sides. A firm that takes too many risks and presses ahead with too many ill-considered innovation projects is as likely to fail as one that takes too few risks and rests on its laurels for too long.

Because of the possible internal conflicts and the very difficult management tasks involved in innovation, the literature abounds with descriptions of the various tasks and problems that have to be faced by managers. Several major roles, most favoured among them the 'product champion', have been described which must be filled by enthusiastic and able people if the innovation project is to succeed. Other creatures that frequent the innovation literature are 'business innovators', 'internal entrepreneurs', 'change agents', 'administrative entrepreneurs', or even that fabled creature, the 'Maxwell demon or mutation selector' (Maidique: 49, in Roberts 1987). In essence, these are all people within the organization who cause, enable, and select technological innovation and change. Their importance lies in the fact that it takes dedicated champions to prevail in the conflicts and diffi-culties that are inevitably engendered by novelty.

Large developments, involving many actors, need careful co-ordination and tactfully nurtured cooperation between rival people, rival groups, rival traditions and rival ideas. Often the difficulties seem insurmountable, at other times the solution appears to be just around the corner and yet proves stubbornly elusive. It is as difficult to know when to stop a project as when to start it. While perseverance is a virtue, obstinacy is a sin; but who is to tell where perseverance ends and obstinacy begins?

To say that all purchases are made in response to needs is stretch-ing the meaning of the word 'need' beyond all reason. The fact is that most consumers in all the highly developed countries buy goods and services which far surpass what they need; they indulge in luxuries of every conceivable kind. The Culture of Contentment, as Galbraith calls the present situation and attitudes of the affluent societies, is based on relentless consumption by the contented rich and lack of hope for the discontented poor (Galbraith 1992). Modern societies do much more than satisfy needs; they create wants that can be satis-fied and proceed to satisfy them. Technologists work very hard to produce ever new products and the sales forces work equally hard to sell these products to a satiated public. It is a treadmill without escape, yet one that apparently leaves its participants contented; the non-par-ticipants are without a voice. The ultimate victim, nature, meanwhile drifts inexorably toward its doom.

Throughout the life of a technology, technologists attempt to improve its performance and to widen its appeal. When the ultimate limits of the given technology are reached, or even sooner, attempts are made to circumvent the limits by developing technologies that are not inherently limited in the same way. We speak of a technology pro-ceeding along its natural trajectory and, when a new trajectory is started, of radical innovation (Coombs et al 1987: 119).

Information and knowledge are the most important ingredients of innovation and the most important assets of a firm. Knowledge of the latest technological methods, knowledge of markets, knowledge of regulations, knowledge of opportunities and pitfalls, knowledge about the capabilities of competitors – all these are crucial ingredi-ents of success. Knowledge consists both of continuously gathered information and, more importantly, of the skills to use such information. Large firms spend a great deal of time and money on gathering, filtering and disseminating knowledge. They employ gate-keepers, information scientists, data banks, and a variety of devices designed to make sure that up-to-date relevant information is available to those members of the firm who might profit from it. Despite all the filtering and targeting of information, many managers, engineers and scientists feel overwhelmed by floods of information and find it difficult to assimilate it all. Ironically, perfect targeting of information reduces both the likelihood of overload and the likelihood of serendipity – the lucky chance encounter with information that triggers off a new cross-connection in a fertile mind. Small firms tend to be overwhelmed by the task of information gathering and are forced to ignore much of it. Their knowledge is obtained by haphazard and inadequate means.

Information and knowledge are the most highly valued factors of production, yet the rate of the production of information is such as to render much of it obsolete with terrifying rapidity. No sooner has somebody spent a great deal of time and effort to gather and assimilate information than it becomes outdated and of no value. Thus we constantly throw away that which we most value. The rapidity of change imposes very high costs in terms of obsolescence of information. In the extreme, the speed of obsolescence can exceed the speed of assimilation and render the whole process utterly futile. Outdated information is worthless, yet the faster information is produced the more of it becomes worthless even before it has a chance to be of any use. Thus the cost of information can exceed its benefits if the rate of innovation and change becomes too high.

After this extensive excursion, we return to the third generation of innovation theory: the coupling model according to Rothwell (1992). This took a more sophisticated approach and acknowledged that there are many different couplings and linkages in the innovation process. These include linkages between science and technology, as well as linkages between the external world and the innovating firm and between various stages of the innovation process.

All theories of innovation accept that the process is one that can be logically subdivided into several phases. The simplest models take these phases as temporal sequences, while the more sophisticated models realize that the logical sequence need not be a temporal one and that there is much coupling and much going backward and forward between the different phases. 'Innovation proceeds through several phases with complicated feedback between them. The phases describe a logical sequence, temporally they may overlap considerably (Braun 1984a: 50).

The phases of an innovation process vary with the kind of innovation that is to be described. For product innovation, for example, the phases that have been suggested are:

1. the idea or invention, which may or may not be derived from scientific research;
2. development, which may involve relatively simple trial and error or sophisticated R&D;
3. prototype, which should be the result of development but may go through several stages, and early marketing;
4. production, which may involve a great deal of investment and even development of new production processes;
5. marketing and diffusion.

It is not until this last phase that the success or failure of the innovation becomes apparent and the cash flow may become positive. Thinking about markets does not, of course, begin only in the phase of production and diffusion – in a sense it accompanies the whole process of innovation.

To show the need for a thorough appraisal of the firm's needs and possibilities, a 'know thyself' phase preceding all other phases of the innovation process, a zeroth phase of innovation has been suggested (Braun 1984a: 58). Other writers have used different terminology to describe the need for self-appraisal as part of the innovation process. It is mostly subsumed under terms such as innovation strategy, or strategic appraisal, and suchlike. Twiss and Goodridge, for example, suggest that management should ask the following questions before embarking upon a major product innovation: 'How can we utilize our technological competence to develop products for new market segments? How long can we expect to exploit existing products through incremental improvements? What is the optimum timing for introducing an entirely new product? What is happening to our market share?' (Twiss and Goodridge 1989: 62). These questions can be varied, and they should certainly include the key question: what are our technical and commercial capabilities?

Technology is now often described as a strategic asset of the firm and many large corporations have instituted a strategic corporate management function for technology. Technology means knowledge and the mastery of certain technologies gives the firm the capital of knowledge on which to draw for its competitive advantage. Whether the technologies are needed for new product development or for improvements in manufacturing processes, in all cases mastery of certain skills is vital to success. The fund of available knowledge determines the strategic options of the firm. Among other things, it influences the make or buy decisions for components and sub-systems and limits the possibilities of entering certain markets.

The attitude to technology by top management is the main ingredient in the general make-up of an industrial firm. A recent report highlights the differences in attitude to technology between British and German firms. While British firms are often content to acquire technologies through joint ventures or licensing agreements, German firms put much more emphasis on in-house development of core proprietary technologies. They believe that only the ownership of these technologies gives them the freedom they need to make the strategic choices (Leadbeater, *Financial Times*, 18 June 1991).

If by technology we mean the knowledge and skills necessary to use technologies, and also the ownership of exclusive rights over certain technologies, then there is no doubt that technologies are the most important strategic assets of manufacturing firms. When all is said and done, technology determines what the firm can manufacture, how well and efficiently it can manufacture it and, hence, at what price it can sell its products. And that, surely, is the very core of the enterprise. Of course, good management, and good marketing and financial prudence are important; but the essence of manufacturing is technology and the other factors are boundary conditions.

Having said that technology is a strategic asset, we have opened a Pandora's box in the sense that strategic investments cannot be costed by the normal methods of a pay-back period or by realistic cost-benefit analysis. The value of a strategic asset is pure guesswork, and hence strategic decisions on technology have a degree of financial arbitrariness that is worrying. German firms, in which technologists play an important role in top management, clearly value technology highly and their success in world markets amply justifies their valuation. British firms, heavily influenced by accountants and the search for short-term profit, tend to value technology less highly, and the decline of British industry over the past decades demonstrates starkly the failings of this attitude. The above is not to be taken as a complete analysis of the causes of the relative positions of German and British industry; their respective situation is the result of many factors, of which the attitude to technology is only one, albeit possibly an important one.

We return to the successive generations of theories of innovation. The fourth generation of innovation models was based largely on observations of the process of innovation in large Japanese companies, although their methods have since spread to Europe and the USA. The model extends the number of actors in the process of innovation well beyond the main innovating firm and describes the essential role of the main innovator in integrating and coordinating the various aspects of the innovation process. The model includes the many interactions between the innovating firm and its suppliers, its associates and its customers. For the first time, the theory began to consider alliances and R&D cooperation between rival firms, and the role of suppliers as producers of innovative sub-systems in their own right.

The fifth, contemporary, model of the process of technological innovation is known as the 'systems integration and networking' (SIN) model (Rothwell 1992: 74). The name is a jumble of all the current buzzwords and the model tries to show the current activities of major firms in their frantic efforts to increase the pace of technological innovation.

*It includes fully integrated parallel development; strong
linkages with leading edge customers; strategic integration
with primary suppliers, including co-development; strategic
alliances where appropriate; emphasis on corporate
flexibility and on development speed; and focus on quality
and other non-price features* (op cit: 74).

What does it all mean? It means that the cost of innovation has
become so great that firms have to try to share the costs and the risks
with their suppliers and often form strategic alliances with their competitors. Computer networks have become an important link in
commercial transactions of all kinds, including transactions involved
in R&D, design and supplies. Suppliers of components or sub-systems, for example, have to be linked to their customers by specified
computer links, involving the transmission of designs, orders and
funds. In major innovations the innovating network of firms tries to
form early linkages with major customers. This fifth generation model
is applicable only to innovations on a large scale and has an air of
major military campaigns about it. It all sounds rather frantic and
frightening. Parallel development – ie we do not take the time to await
the outcome of one step of development before embarking on the
next – adds greatly to the risks and costs of innovation. Collingridge
sees the space shuttle, the fast breeder reactor, and similar large-scale
innovation projects as examples of inflexible technologies, with decisions taken in too centralized a way, and lacking the adaptability to
learn from one step before the next step is taken. In his view, incrementalism is the only way to avoid costly mistakes in strategic
decisions on major innovation projects (Collingridge 1992); '...a technology that performs better is likely to be one which can be developed
in a series of small steps, with choices made in a decentralized way'
(Collingridge 1990: 181). Incrementalism, as advocated by Collingridge, does mean slowing down the process of innovation, but this
possible loss, if loss it is, is far outweighed by gains made through
avoiding costly mistakes and failures, and by obtaining better technologies in the end.

The Law of Diminishing Returns and R&D Cooperation

By now, after so much accumulated effort in all the industrially relevant sciences and in engineering, any small further progress has
become difficult and costly. The easy things have been done; experi-
mental equipment is extremely sophisticated and costly; the flood of
information that needs to be assimilated is overwhelming. In those
branches of engineering that are already very highly developed, any

further small improvement has to be bought with increasing effort. Only the more dynamic, newer branches of engineering still yield results in return for reasonable effort.

To take the first steps in an entirely new technology is comparatively easy and cheap. When Ted Hoff of Intel invented the first micro-processor in 1971, its design took only nine man-months (Braun and Macdonald 1982: 108). It was a brilliant idea, although the first device was, by present-day standards, quite crude. However, it worked sufficiently well to convince Intel, its customers, and its competitors that here was the beginning of a worthwhile new technology. In other words, a new technological trajectory had started, with generation of micro-processor following generation with great regularity. Less than ten years after the announcement of the first micro-processor, the design time for a new chip had risen to one hundred or more person-years, despite tremendous progress in computer-aided design (op cit: 119). While the first micro-processor chips contained only some 2300 individual transistors, 20 years later the most high-powered chips, again from Intel, contained 2.5 million transistors (*Financial Times*, 7 June 1991). Each successive generation of chip requires new production technologies, as advances in design are intimately linked to improved production processes. Costs have risen dramatically and it is estimated that by the turn of the century it will cost between $1.5bn and $2bn to build a plant capable of producing the most advanced chips. Under these circumstances it is not surprising that the US National Advisory Committee on Semiconductors suggests that the semiconductor industry, in collaboration with government, must forge close links.

> *The semiconductor industry is entering an era where no*
> *single company has the financial resources to develop all the*
> *manufacturing processes and equipment and build the*
> *factories needed to process chips at the end of the decade*
> *(Financial Times, 17 May 1991).*

The pooling of resources, necessitated by high R&D costs, sophisticated production equipment and short-lived products, has become common in the European semiconductor industry. SGS-Thomson, the Franco–Italian semiconductor group, is collaborating with GEC-Plessey, the UK group, in the development of semi-custom chips. These are chips that can be adapted by different users, such as telecommunications equipment manufacturers, for the design of their own circuits. It is estimated that the collaboration will halve the time required to bring new semi-custom chips to the market (*Financial Times*, 4 July 1991).

SGS-Thomson would like to go further and have suggested a merger of their semiconductor operations with those of the other two large European firms, Siemens and Philips. The three Europeans together accounted for only 8.1 per cent of the world semiconductor market in 1990, and it is reckoned that any one firm needs to obtain at least 5 per cent of world markets to ensure its long-term survival. All three European firms made losses on their semiconductor operations in 1990. Siemens and Philips are, for the time being, resisting the advances by SGS-Thomson (*Financial Times*, 11 June 1991). These examples show very clearly that the rising cost of innovation is an important factor in the trend towards oligopolies, if not monopolies, in key areas of technology.

Even in the US, with its severe anti-trust legislation, the rising costs of R&D have led to the formation of the controversial SEMA-TECH, a non-profit R&D consortium involving fourteen US semiconductor firms in a collective attempt to ward off Japanese competition. Initially, half of the $200m annual budget came from the Federal government. The above collective venture is taking place notwithstanding the fact that several US firms have close collaborative links with Japanese firms (Alic: 157, in Krieger-Mytelka 1991).

In the computer industry, which has been affected by the same difficulties of the high costs of R&D and the rapid obsolescence of products, mergers and take-overs have become the order of the day. The number of survivors is very small indeed and even among these collaboration and alliances appear to be likely. On the other hand, there remains a large number of relatively small assemblers of personal computers, which are sold widely as IBM clones or compatibles. The arch-rivals in personal computers, IBM and Apple, have formed a technology alliance, covering both hardware and software, which will enable users to mix Apple and IBM products in their networks. The goal of the agreement is to

> *create powerful new open system platforms for the 1990s*
> (*Financial Times*, 4 July 1991). *The combination of Apple's*
> *software and IBM's chip technology could set a new*
> *standard for the next generation of desktop computers,*
> *presenting a formidable challenge to competitors such as*
> *Compaq Computer and Digital Equipment, which recently*
> *announced plans to create compatible products* (*Financial*
> *Times*, 27 June 1991).

There are many such agreements between rival computer firms. For example, Bull, Siemens and ICL jointly sponsor an artificial intelligence research laboratory in Munich. In Cambridge, Olivetti and Digital Equipment have agreed to operate a joint research programme. 'The agreement is indicative of the cooperation computer companies are now proposing so as to check the spiralling costs of fundamental research and development' (*Financial Times*, 17 June 1991).

Matters are no different in the aerospace industry. The development of new jet engines is now so expensive that even the few remaining giant firms cannot afford to develop them without involving either government help or industrial partners, or both.

In 1984 a consortium, called International Aero Engines, consisting of Pratt & Whitney of the US, Rolls Royce of the UK, Japan's Aero Engines Corporation, MTU of Germany and Fiat Aviazione of Italy, was formed to produce what became known as the V2500 turbofan jet engine. The engine went into service on the Airbus A320 in 1989. Early in the project, the partners agreed to establish a private global communications network, the V2500NET, to exchange the huge amount of data involved in the operation. The network provides an example not only of cooperation in the manufacture of aero-engines, but also of the technical means necessary for such cooperation. Pratt & Whitney and Rolls -Royce are arch-rivals, yet it makes commercial and technical sense for them to cooperate in view of the enormous development costs and risks involved.

The GE-90, which is to become possibly the world's largest commercial jet engine, will cost between $1.2bn and $2bn to develop. The main US manufacturer, General Electric, a giant firm by any standards, is seeking to share the costs and risks with both European and Japanese partners. In Europe they have an established partnership with the French state-owned firm Snecma and are seeking cooperation with the German firm MTU. The new engine is supposed to develop 95,000lb of thrust and, it is claimed, should provide a 10 per cent improvement in fuel consumption compared with today's engines. The other two major aero-engine manufacturers, Pratt & Whitney of the US and Rolls-Royce in Britain, plan to compete against the new GE engine by producing stretched versions of their respective existing engines (*Financial Times*, 17 January 1990).

The cooperation between GE and MTU ended with an acrimonious divorce. GE sued MTU when the latter, a subsidiary of Daimler-Benz, negotiated a cooperation agreement with Pratt & Whitney. GE claimed that this infidelity would involve the disclosure of technical information that might help the new partnership to compete more successfully with the GE-90 engine. GE was seeking a ban on MTU to be involved in high-thrust engines, as it had at its disposal technical information from GE, which it took many years to develop (*Financial Times*, 6 April and 9 April 1990).

For smaller jet engines, with thrusts between 12,000lb and 22,000lb, Rolls-Royce has teamed up with the German car manufacturer BMW to build a new plant in the former East Germany at an estimated cost of $225m. The development cost of the new family of engines, to be produced in the plant, is estimated at about $850m. The joint venture has asked the German government for funding support (*Financial Times*, 15 June 1991).

In the aero-engine business most segments of the market have only two competing producers. The contest between them is fierce, but does not correspond to the characteristics of a normal free market. More normal competition exists among the thousands of suppliers and subcontractors of the major firms, although in recent years that market has become somewhat distorted as the major firms are attempting to shift some of the burdens of innovation on to the suppliers and tend to operate long-term, Japanese style, relationships with main suppliers.

It is said that the development cost of the Boeing 767 aircraft was nearly $3bn and the design definition phase took nearly six years. The older Boeing 727, on the other hand, was designed in two and a half years. If nothing else, the enormous costs of developing products in the aircraft industry represent an almost insurmountable barrier to entry (Mowery: 81–96, in Krieger-Mytelka 1991). That the Airbus succeeded in entering this market was undoubtedly owing to the very considerable help given by several European governments. Indeed, government help to the Airbus is still the subject of acrimonious conflict between the US and Europe.

Cooperation in the motor industry is equally common. Rover cooperates intimately with Honda, yet even so, Rover was finally bought by BMW as it proved to be too small to be viable. Renault and Volvo have signed cooperation agreements and exchanged share holdings, but an attempted full merger failed to obtain the approval of the Swedish shareholders. General Motors, Ford and Chrysler – the American big three – have agreed to the joint development of a new multiplexing system, which is supposed to replace the conventional electrical wiring harness in the car of the future. The big three have also agreed with the US government to spend $1bn over the next 12 years on a joint research and development programme on advanced batteries for electric vehicles (*Financial Times*,, 31 May 1991).

The costs of R&D and the investment needed for the production of a truly new model are staggering. Volvo spent $2.5bn between 1986 and 1991 on the development and production facilities for its 800 series car. Almost a third of this total went on developing a brand-new range of engines and on refurbishing the engine production plant. The development of a new six-cylinder high-performance engine for its top-of-the-range cars cost Volvo about $1bn (*Financial Times*, 21 August 1990). Annual R&D expenditure went up from about $500m in 1986 to about $800m in 1990. This means that in 1990 R&D costs had reached over 10 per cent of turnover (*Financial Times*, 14 June 1991). No wonder Volvo were seeking an alliance with a much larger manufacturer with a complementary range of products. VW spent $1.6bn in R&D and plant and equipment for the new Golf (*Financial Times*, 21 August 1991). Ford are reputed to have spent $6 billion in six years on the development of the Mondeo and its derivatives, such as the Contour for the US market, to serve as their new global car (*Financial Times*, 29 March 1994). Ford were criticized for the long development time, but say that this was caused by problems associated with producing a global car and that the next new global car will be developed much faster.

Japanese car-makers, who have managed to turn their cars into high-fashion products and are churning out so-called new models at an alarming rate, are greatly admired. The fact that the new models are almost identical to the previous ones seems to go unnoticed. Honda claim to have reduced the development time for a new model to three years (Bessant 1991: 29). Is there any reason to believe that such rapid model changes are beneficial to the consumer or, for that matter, to anybody at all?

The estimated mean R&D cost per approved new chemical entity (NCE) in the pharmaceutical industry, in the mid-1980s, was $231m in 1987 dollars. A study conducted less than ten years previously had put the cost at $100.7m, again in 1987 dollars. Thus the R&D costs in the pharmaceutical industry had risen by a factor of 2.3 in just under ten years.

> The costs required to discover and launch a new drug onto major world markets are accelerating significantly in real terms. In addition, product life cycles for new drugs are shortening as a result of fast followers, reduced patent exclusivity periods and greater competition in the post-patent period... Not all the current firms may be in the competition a decade from now (Grabowski 1991: 7).

And indeed take-overs are the order of the day.

The rate of the withdrawal of drugs from the market for safety reasons fell in the UK with the tightening of regulations. The number of NCEs withdrawn from the market within 15 years fell from an average of 33 per cent for NCEs introduced during the five years 1955–59, to an average of 12 per cent for those introduced between 1970 and 1974. The number of introductions decreased from an average of 44 in the first period, to an average of 19 in the second period (Steward and Wibberley 1991). Thus it seems that tighter regulations, combined with rising R&D costs, reduce both the number of introductions and the number of withdrawals of NCEs.

The average R&D expenditure of the top ten pharmaceutical firms is estimated as 10.6 per cent of turnover for the period 1987–88. In the telecommunications industry the top ten firms spent an average of 7.5 per cent of turnover in 1986, which represents an increase of 9.6 per cent over the previous year (Krieger-Mytelka 1991: 19).

All the data presented so far are no more than illustrative examples of the law of diminishing returns and some of its consequences. Hard measurements and data are difficult to come by. Two proxy measures are suggested, although both are flawed. One is the R&D expenditure per patent obtained, the other is the R&D expenditure per new product. The latter has been measured for the pharmaceutical industry, where new products are comparatively easily defined. For other industries there is a degree of arbitrariness in the definition of new products which makes a mockery of the term measurement.

Soete, Verspagen, Patel and Pavitt (OECD 1989) show that the number of patents per million $ spent on R&D (current R&D expenditure plotted against patents granted three years later) decreased dramatically between 1957 and the 1970s, while between the 1970s and 1982 the decrease was more gradual. If we take the Federal Republic of Germany as an example, $1 million spent on R&D in 1957 bought about 50 domestic patents; by 1982 the figure had dropped to 5. One of the many difficulties of this type of measurement is that the 'patent productivity' varies greatly between sectors, and thus the average figures do not mean a great deal and are distorted by sectorally different propensities to patent, as much as by sectorally different R&D costs. Patent productivity also varies greatly between countries, possibly because of a different sectoral composition, although perhaps because of national differences in the propensity to patent, or because of true differences in research productivity. Despite all the problems of measurement, the most plausible explanation of the rising cost of patents is that indeed returns on R&D investment are diminishing in real terms.

With the soaring cost of research and the ever-increasing pressure on firms to produce innovations, it has become fashionable to speak of pre-competitive research as an area in which competing firms can collaborate and thus share costs. Pre-competitive research can either be goal-oriented basic research or applied research. The condition that needs to be fulfilled is that the technical solutions should not be fully specified, so that each firm can seek its own competitive designs and solutions in the future, or even in parallel with the pre-competitive research.

There are two fundamental causes for the need for this new category of research. First and foremost, it is the relentless pressure to innovate and thus to carry out ever more research and development. As a result, firms are seeking means to collaborate with one another in order to share costs, but also in order to chart uncharted waters jointly with their main competitors. Competitive firms find it necessary to know the general direction in which technology and markets are moving, and it gives them reassurance if the general direction is generally agreed.

Competition between manufacturers is more subtle than the marketplace analogy might suggest. They do, of course, compete on price and on quality of products. They also compete in advertising. As the quality of products is very difficult to ascertain or compare, the advertisers step in and create, jointly with the designers, images that substitute for realistic assessments of the actual properties of the goods.

Time has become an important dimension in competition between manufacturers. If several manufacturers attempt to bring a very similar innovation to market, only those who can charge premium prices for the new product stand a chance of recouping the development costs. To be early on the market is thus a substantial ingredient of potential success. The attempt to be early brings with it the danger of coming to market too quickly, before all the difficulties with the new product are ironed out. In this way the name of the product may be ruined even before it is properly established; or the first manufacturer may have such high costs associated with teething troubles that in fact the second or third competitors will do better.

It is one of the many costs of fast innovation that immature and insufficiently developed products reach the market. The unfortunate purchasers of such products have to perform some of the tasks of the development engineer and discover weaknesses and malfunctions that should have been discovered before the product was released on to the market. For consumer products and small industrial equipment, this works entirely to the detriment of the buyer. With production equipment, this process is often carried out with the full knowledge and agreement of the purchasers; indeed, some privileged early buyers knowingly contribute to the development of the product or process in return for becoming early users and for being able to influence the design in accordance with their own needs.

Competition is, in some ways, akin to warfare. Just as warfare is barely possible without espionage and intelligence, so industrial competition is not possible without a great deal of knowledge about the nature and intentions of the competitors. Competing manufacturers need to know what their competitors are up to, in which direction technology is moving, what the production methods are, which markets and in what ways they are trying to tackle, what organizational changes are in train. Manufacturers also have many common interests – eg the regulatory conditions under which they all have to operate, financial markets, trading conditions, and, last but not least, the availability of government incentives for investment and R&D.

There is a second main reason for the invention of the term precompetitive research. It is the wish of governmental agencies, such as the Commission of the European Communities (CEC), to support joint R&D by consortia of firms. In Europe, this serves two purposes: it enhances cooperation and technology transfer between European firms and thus brings the European Union closer to economic reality. Secondly, it enables the CEC to support R&D in areas that it regards as important in the competitive battles between Europe, the USA and Japan. The theory of this support is that European firms, jointly though in competition with each other, will be able to bring new products and processes on to world markets in qualities, at prices, and with timing that should enable them to compete effectively with US and Japanese manufacturers. The concept of working in concert yet in competition is one that Japan has adopted with great success. Although manufacturers compete with each other, they join forces and coordinate their efforts when it comes to fostering, supporting and strengthening Japan Inc.

In a world in which knowledge has become a major ingredient of success and the creation of knowledge has become exceedingly expensive, the sharing of resources is often seen as the only way of remaining innovative and competitive. If going it alone is too expensive, too slow and too risky, joining forces with a competent rival, or even with Beelzebub, is often seen as the only option. The European aircraft industry, for example, was forced into cooperation by the enormous size of the task of developing and building modern commercial aircraft and by their confrontation with the two remaining giant American firms. As the cost of producing new knowledge and new technology increases inexorably, so firms are forced into alliances by the need to share the costs and risks of innovation.

Innovative pressures have increased enormously in recent years. While in the early Eighties only two-thirds of German manufacturing firms were engaged in any innovation, by 1987 75 per cent of all firms were innovating in some way (BMFT-Journal, June 1991).

To cope with rising costs, firms must try to achieve larger markets, possibly through amalgamations. The telecommunications equipment industry provides an excellent example of both these trends. It is estimated that the cost of developing the next generation of digital telephone exchanges (central office equipment in US parlance) will be $1.5bn to $2bn. The product lifetime, on the other hand, may only be five to ten years, whereas in the past such equipment was in service for about 30 years. In order to recoup the R&D investment, it is estimated that any one firm will have to have something between 10 and 15 per cent of the world market. Thus possibly fewer than eight firms will survive worldwide. 'The mergers, acquisitions and joint ventures taking place in this area of the industry are thus part of a shakeout, as firms attempt to stabilize an uncertain environment and position themselves strategically' (Jenkins: 169, in Krieger-Mytelka 1991).

Since the crisis of the early or mid-Seventies, when rising oil prices combined with market saturation for durable consumer products, with a slow-down in productivity gains and with increasing imports of standard products from low-wage countries, the advanced economies have been trying to shift production to high technology, ie to knowledge-intensive industries. The stability of the previous mass-production regime was shattered and global competition heightened the uncertainties. Floating exchange rates added further to the unpredictability of markets and thus further increased risks. Strategic alliances are one possible answer to spreading increased risks. Unfortunately, they do nothing to cure the underlying problems of excessively expensive innovation.

> Paradoxically, new strategies designed to cope with the slow
> growth in productivity and in demand have only added to
> the level of uncertainty. This was particularly true of
> strategies that promoted knowledge-intensive production in
> the guise of structural adjustment as these gave impetus to

72

*the process of innovation and accelerated the diffusion of
new technology* (Krieger-Mytelka 1991).

The pressure for innovation does not come from market demands,
it comes from the fear of market saturation. In that sense manufacturers, even rival manufacturers, and their retailers share a common
interest. If they can innovate more effectively by sharing costs, risks,
skills and tasks with their competitors, they will often do so. The pressure for innovation also comes from competition for market shares,
and in that sense manufacturers truly compete with each other. In many
instances of technological innovation the common interest prevails and
the number of agreements among competitors is truly astounding.

Between 1980 and 1985, for example, the number of agreements
involving European firms in R&D intensive industries rose from 15 to
149 (OECD 1992: 74). Specifically in information technology, the number of strategic links Philips was involved in rose from 40 in the period
1980–84, to 127 during 1985–89. The respective figures for Siemens
were 51 and 134, and for IBM 48 and 108 (op cit: 229). When the cooperation between almost independent firms reaches very high intensity
and complementarity, we speak of the networked firm as a novel form
of organization. We face a continuum of arrangements: from cooperation in limited fields between independent firms; to the networked
firm; to true mergers, such as the recent marriage of giant US aerospace
and defence contractors, Lockheed and Martin Marietta.

Both the need for cooperation and its feasibility are especially
high if parallel development is being undertaken. It is then easy to see
that one firm can pursue one path, while another firm pursues another, each within the sphere of their greatest competence.
Simultaneously, suppliers can develop the necessary components,
materials and sub-systems. In this way much time can be saved, but
the tasks of coordination and management are very complex indeed
and the scope for error and failure is substantial. There is also much
scope for conflict, as each participating firm might walk away with its
successes and leave the others in the lurch. Extremely delicate equilibria between secrecy and the sharing of information, and between
cooperation and going it alone, have to be maintained. Conflicts arise
out of questions of sharing and controlling the costs, questions of
whether all partners are pulling their weight, and questions of preferred technological designs. Technologists suffer from as many
idiosyncrasies and personal preferences in their ideas as anybody else.
The so-called inner logic of technology is not as compelling as outsiders might think; there is a great deal of leeway for personal and
institutional preferences.

The central problem of knowledge-intensive industries is that as
the product cycle shortens with the relentless pressure of innovation,
and the cost of producing new products increases with the operation
of the law of diminishing returns, so the chance of recouping the

investment in innovation and making a profit decreases. Hence it is necessary to concentrate the industry in order to obtain large enough markets to make a profit at least a realistic possibility. Industry is faced with an insoluble dilemma: invest ever more in new products, with only a remote chance of being able to recoup the investment; or do not invest and go to the wall with outmoded products and outmoded methods of production. The only two possible solutions are either concentration, leading to oligopolistic markets in which the pressure of competition is slightly eased and the size of the firms and their markets are large enough to allow expensive innovation; or reduce the pressure of competition, and hence the pace of innovation, by some other, as yet unknown, means. It seems likely that the first solution will dominate in the immediate future, as it has dominated in the past.

> ...the evolution of the computer and telecommunications
> industries since the late 1970s suggests that the process of
> concentration continues to play itself out in successive new
> knowledge-intensive industries as firms in these industries
> move beyond their initial innovative entry and into second
> and third generation products (Krieger-Mytelka 1991: 21).

The rising cost of producing new technology and the increasing internationalization of markets have increased the uncertainties for industry while, at the same time, increasing their need for investment capital. In the semiconductor industry, for example, the minimum investment required for a new production line is equivalent to the total value of its annual output (op cit: 21). Strategic alliances between firms are much in favour, as the total scope and capabilities, as well as the flexibility of the network as a whole, are considered vital competitive advantages for the partners in the network. '...the key factor to success is to be faster than the others. ..the global multinational can be called "instant" multinational on the model of "instant" coffee' (Michalet: 42, in Krieger-Mytelka 1991).

Alliances between firms are hailed as a means to achieve organizational learning and innovation. Indeed, to be effective, alliances force such learning upon their participants. 'Alliances are the institutional arrangement that allows firms to implement strategies for organizational learning and innovation more effectively' (Ciborra: 51, in Krieger-Mytelka 1991). The transaction costs of alliances are, however, high.

Japanese firms appear to be particularly adept in the art of collaboration. In the motor industry, for example, the supplier firms are tied in closely with the main manufacturer and are given tasks of developing whole new sub-systems for new models, rather than just components (Womack et al 1990). In key sectors, a very high proportion of firms are engaged in some form of R&D collaboration and the filing of joint patents has increased greatly (Levy and Samuels: 120, in KriegerMytelka 1991).

It is the deadly combination of rising R&D costs and shortening product life-cycles that makes it so difficult to recoup the investment into innovation. Everybody is trying to run faster and faster, yet the returns are more and more difficult to realize. We are paying, collectively, ever increasing costs of development for products that give us ever shorter periods of service. We pay more and get less. Firms form alliances in an attempt to escape from this treadmill, but the final consumers of goods cannot escape from paying the high price of the forced pace of progress.

The realization that the speed of innovation cannot be pushed up indefinitely and that a more sedate rate of innovation would yield more profitable results, is slowly beginning to dawn on some observers.

> *Japanese manufacturers are starting to abandon their time-honoured habit of throwing as many products as often as possible at the market. Fewer product changes, they reason, means reduced marketing costs and a smaller capital spending bill. Kleinwort Benson, a stockbroker, estimates that if, say, Hitachi were to reduce its R&D spending to 1988 levels as a proportion of sales (still double that of 1982) its pre-tax profits would rise by half (The Economist, 21 March 1992).*

One manufacturer of electronics components realizes the futility of introducing 'new' models in consumer electronics every few months, as 'there is a limit to how many variations of personal stereos or camcorders can be sold' (*The Economist*, 21 March 1992). The typical life-cycle of a TV set or a video-recorder was between 10 and 20 months in 1988, and a typical manufacturer would offer between 30 and 40, in some cases up to 70, model varieties (Bessant 1991:29).

Although the accumulation of knowledge might be expected to occur through purchases – as knowledge is a traded commodity – the markets for knowledge do not work very well. It is difficult to assess the right price for any given information and its purchase cannot be equated with its acquisition. An unread book is as useless as a patent which the purchaser cannot utilize for lack of the relevant skills. Thus it is difficult to bypass the problem of the rising cost of knowledge.

The ultimate logic of all these alliances, take-overs and mergers is a considerable reduction in the number of players and thus, ultimately, a removal of competition. It is unlikely that this ultimate logical end will be reached, but it is likely that competition in many advanced capital- and knowledge-intensive industries will become more and more oligopolistic. It is remarkable that this should be so at a time of economic neo-liberalism. The net result is oligopolistic competition in many manufacturing industries, with revived competition in activities where it does more harm than good, such as in health care, public broadcasting, or public transport.

In a very real sense – though not in the sense of a cabal – rapid technological progress amounts to a conspiracy of the developed countries against developing countries; a conspiracy of the rich against the poor. The faster technological progress becomes, the more difficult it is for developing countries to close the technological gap. They, too, have to run faster, and yet are condemned to fail in their attempt at catching up. The fast rate and high cost of technological progress puts it well out of the reach of developing countries and condemns them to a permanent technological dependence.

The Macro-Economic Role of Innovation

Current thinking on the subject of Technology and Economic Growth is summed up in a recent report by the OECD which states, inter alia:

> *Greater investment can increase total factor productivity (TFP) and therefore economic welfare in the long run in two principal ways. First, it may lead to the more rapid diffusion and adoption of new production methods and techniques. A key aspect of the 'quality' of the capital stock is its technical sophistication, and because new inventions and techniques are largely embodied in new machinery, newer capital should be more productive than older capital. By increasing the rate of substitution of new for old capital, higher rates of gross investment would raise the rate of growth of productivity* (OECD 1992: 167).

The emphasis is on improvements in total factor productivity caused by more efficient methods of production, and on improvements in the efficiency and quality of the economy at large caused by better education and training and, in effect, more and faster technological innovation. The so-called new growth theories claim even greater benefits from R&D and training because of alleged large multiplier effects (op cit: 173-4; Hanappi and Wagner: 209–30, in Matzner and Streeck 1991).

Because of these convictions, all advanced countries make strenuous efforts to increase their national potential for technological innovation and attempt to increase the effectiveness of what has been termed the national system of innovation (Nelson: 312, in Dosi et al 1988). The national system of innovation is a complex web of interrelated facts, activities, beliefs and relationships. The system has many ingredients, or sub-systems, such as the educational system, the system for basic research, the system of protection of intellectual property, the industrial R&D system, industrial management capabilities, the venture capital system, the market for investment capital, the market for technological goods and, last but not least, the labour market. The four main determinants of the capacity of a country to create technological innovation are:

1. human capital, ie the availability of well-trained skilled labour and of scientific, engineering, management and commercial skills;
2. investment capital, ie the existing industrial structure and its equipment, as well as the capacity to raise sufficient investment for R&D and for new production facilities;
3. R&D structure, ie the availability of properly equipped and staffed research, development and testing facilities;
4. infrastructure and markets, ie the availability of good communications and transport, availability of clean water and adequate power, functioning markets for all kinds of goods, a functioning legal system, etc.

The above list shows that the capacity for innovation of a country is not simply a matter of investing enough into R&D; it depends on the proper functioning of the whole economy and society. What is not shown in the list, but is regarded as important by many observers, is the ambience or, as it is now commonly called, the culture of a country (not to be confused with Culture). If industrial and engineering traditions are weak and are not held in high esteem, and if speculative investment in phoney office developments and dubious financial services are preferred to investments in industry, then the capacity of the system of innovation will be weakened. If easy speculative gains are preferred to the hard steady grind needed for industrial success, industrial success will prove elusive.

Much of the efficacy and efficiency of the national system of innovation is inaccessible to quantitative measurement and, at best, can be described in qualitative terms. Two quantitative measures – total national expenditure on R&D, particularly on civil R&D, and the total of scientific and technical personnel engaged in R&D and related activities – are the only measures available to describe the input into the innovation system. As a measure of output, the number of patents can be counted relatively easily, although the meaning and significance of such counts is controversial. An even more problematic measure, the high technology content and the degree of novelty of manufactured goods can be estimated, although problems of definition are such as to make these measures subject to considerable doubt.

The above measures substitute for a quantitative description of a national system of innovation, much as GDP substitutes for a description of real standards of living. By common consent, these measures are used as the only ones available, in full knowledge of their inadequacy. A simple measure is generally preferred to a complex set of descriptions. We happily substitute a poor measurement for a good description. The trouble with truth is that it is generally too complex to be credible. Simple statements, preferably supported by numbers and graphs, however misleading, command more credibility than complex and multiply qualified descriptions.

It is likely that good complementarity and harmonious interplay between the sub-systems of the national system of innovation are more important than spectacular achievement in any single part. It is no use to have brilliant engineers at the forefront of the most esoteric basic research and, at the same time, to suffer an acute relative and absolute shortage of skilled crafts people on the labour market. It is no use to have large industrial R&D departments if management is incapable of harmonizing their efforts with the needs of the manufacturing and marketing divisions. Mowery and Rosenberg argue that a good fit between the national R&D system and its environment is essential if the economy is to reap the full benefits from its R&D effort (Mowery and Rosenberg 1989: 217).

An efficient national system of innovation is now regarded as the *conditio sine qua non* for the success of a national economy. As Table 2.1 and Figure 2.1 show, however, there is no close positive correlation between total civil R&D expenditure as a percentage of GDP, and GDP per head of population. Similarly, no close relationship exists between scientific personnel as a percentage of the total workforce and GDP. Nevertheless, it is clear that in general the wealthier and more successful industrial nations spend more on R&D and employ a higher percentage of scientific personnel than the poorer and less successful nations. Disregarding special situations, such as the oil-sheikhdoms, it is clear, as far as this can be meaningfully asserted on the evidence of statistical measures which themselves have only limited meaning, that large effort at technological innovation can be correlated, albeit only roughly, with a high standard of living. The wealthy advanced countries spend anything between 0.5 and 3 per cent of their GDP on R&D, but it is not necessarily the wealthiest ones that spend most.

Table 2.1 *GDP per capita in thousands of 1985 US$; average growth rates of GDP 1980–90; R&D expenditure as % of GDP in 1989; and average annual percentage growth in R&D expenditure 1975–89.*

Country	1980	1985	1989	1990	1980/ 90	RD/ GDP	1975/ 89
United States	15.11	16.62	18.39	18.26	2.08	2.8	1.4
Japan	9.57	11.12	12.95	13.63	4.24	2.9	3.7
Germany	9.54	10.16	11.08	11.39	1.94	2.9	1.7
France	9.01	9.48	10.48	10.71	1.89	2.3	1.9
UK	7.35	8.04	9.24	9.29	2.64	2.3	0.4
Netherlands	8.48	8.69	9.31	9.61	1.33	2.3	1.0
Sweden	11.06	12.05	13.03	13.02	1.77	3.0	4.7
OECD Europe	6.95	7.32	8.10	8.24	1.86		
OECD	9.94	10.88	12.14	12.30	2.38	2.4	

Source: OECD 1992, *National Accounts 1960–90*, Paris; OECD (1992) *Science and Technology Policy Outlook 1992*, Paris

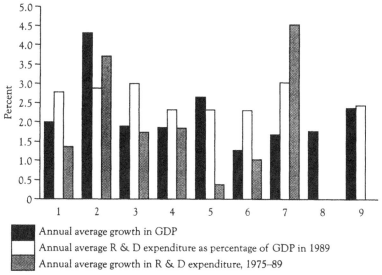

Annual average growth in GDP

Annual average R & D expenditure as percentage of GDP in 1989

Annual average growth in R & D expenditure, 1975–89

1. USA; 2. Japan; 3. FRG; 4. France; 5. UK; 6. The Netherlands; 7. Sweden; 8. OECD Europe; 9. OECD. (Values from Table 2.1)

Figure 2.1 *Annual average growth in GDP, annual average R & D expenditure and annual average growth in R & D expenditure, 1975–89*

Despite the fact that the relationship between total R&D expenditure and economic growth is, statistically speaking, a tenuous one, virtually all countries make strenuous efforts to increase the share of R&D in their national budgets. The fact that there is a vaguely positive relationship between R&D and technological innovation on the one hand, and between technological innovation and economic growth on the other, is sufficient reason for countries to attempt to spend more on R&D. In fairness, policies for economic growth consist of more than just increasing R&D expenditure, but R&D expenditure is the main measurable indicator of innovative effort and forms the very core of all public attempts to foster innovation.

Soete, Verspagen, Patel and Pavitt (OECD 1989) plotted R&D expenditure as a fraction of industrial output against industrial labour productivity for several countries over a number of years. The relationship is very erratic indeed. While in Japan and the FRG the function is almost monotonous, though quite irregular, for the US and the UK there is no discernible functional relationship between the two figures. The same authors also plotted R&D expenditure as a percentage of industrial output against per capita GDP for the years 1967–85. While for Japan there is a monotonous, though irregular relationship, for the US this plot is almost as erratic as the previous one.

Table 2.1 and Figure 2.1 show that there is no correlation between annual growth in R&D expenditure in the years 1975–89 and annual growth of GDP per capita in the years 1980–90, nor between average expenditure on R&D in 1989 and the other two variables. The UK seems a very special case, as a short spell of rapid growth in GDP was followed by a period of very slow growth, then substantial decline (followed by very slow recovery in about 1993–94).

Investment in R&D is based mainly on the expectation that high R&D expenditure will lead to a high rate of technological innovation, which will provide the competitive edge that is supposed to ensure economic success and economic growth. Of equal importance is the fact that R&D activity forms part of general technological competence, and it is this competence which is a necessary condition for successful industrial production. High R&D expenditure is based on the expectation of growth in GDP, and high GDP is a condition for high R&D expenditure. As usual, it is very difficult to separate cause and effect, but it is clear that high R&D expenditure alone is no guarantor of industrial success.

There is a general belief that more R&D expenditure will lead to more innovation, and more innovation will lead to more economic growth. In my view, the linkages are rather tenuous and conditional upon circumstances, and there is no compelling reason to believe that more R&D necessarily leads to a more successful economy. There is even less reason to believe that the maximum possible rate of innovation is the correct rate, or indeed that the highest rate of innovation gives the best return in terms of growth in GDP. It seems far more likely that a very low rate of innovation is as bad for economic growth as a very high rate, and that indeed there is an optimum rate for each industry, determined by the general state of this industry and of the economy at large. Although it is not possible to provide a proof or quantification of this theorem, there are many arguments in its favour and these are spread throughout this book.

Soete et al (OECD 1989) make the point that the measurement of R&D expenditure as the sole measure of innovative effort underestimates the total effort made to create new technology. First, small firms do not have separate R&D departments and their R&D effort is underestimated in statistics. Secondly, many innovations, particularly improvement innovations, do not involve R&D at all but are merely the result of normal engineering effort. Thirdly, expenditure on software development in the service sector, which has become quite substantial, does not enter industrial R&D statistics. Soete et al consider that total expenditure on the production of technology could amount to anything between two and three times the officially measured expenditure on R&D activities.

Because of the multiple links between industrial production, R&D and economic activity, developing countries face an extremely difficult task in moving from the vicious circle of poverty, with poverty breeding poverty, into a benign circle of wealth, with wealth breeding wealth. The only way to break into the vicious circle appears to be via education and simultaneous industrial investment. Only an educated workforce can achieve success in technology, but education leads to frustration if there is no industry ready to employ the educated. Only a two-pronged attack of improving education and simultaneously investing in industrialization can lead to development. The well-known obstacles are, however, so formidable that only very few developing countries have so far managed to break the deadly stranglehold of the vicious circle of poverty.

We return to the developed countries and to an apparent puzzle that has exercised the minds of economists in recent years. As Table 2.2 shows, the growth in productivity of the advanced economies has slowed down very considerably, despite no apparent slow-down in technological innovation or R&D expenditure. The productivity of an economy is a compound measure relating outputs to inputs and its measurement is bedevilled by many difficulties. It is particularly difficult to measure the productivity of some services, eg administrative services, as their outputs are indeterminate. Industrial efficiency, in theory, should be largely determined by the vintage of its capital equipment, on the assumption that each successive generation of capital equipment is more efficient than its predecessor. Hence, industrial productivity should grow with capital investment and with the replacement of old machinery by new equipment.

Table 2.2 *Average percentage change of productivity in selected countries.*

	Total factor productivity			Labour productivity		
	1960–73	1973–9	1979–88	1960–73	1973–9	1979–88
USA	1.6	−0.4	0.4	2.2	0.0	0.8
Japan	6.0	1.5	2.0	8.6	3.0	3.2
Germany	2.6	1.7	0.7	4.5	3.1	1.6
France	4.0	1.7	1.6	5.4	3.0	2.6
UK	2.3	0.6	1.8	3.6	1.5	2.4
NL	3.0	1.4	0.8	4.8	2.7	1.6
Sweden	2.9	0.5	1.2	4.1	1.5	1.8
OECD Europe	3.3	1.4	1.2	5.0	2.6	2.1
OECD	2.9	0.6	0.9	4.1	1.4	1.6

Source: OECD (1992) *Technology and the Economy*, OECD, Paris: 168

Numerous explanations have been offered for this slow-down in the growth of total factor productivity, consisting mainly of a decrease in capital productivity. Most commentators agree that the slow-down is real and not caused by errors in measurement (OECD 1989). The growth in productivity in the immediate post-war years in many countries was exceptionally large, as the European and Japanese economies were catching up with the traditionally higher US productivity (Abramovitz, in OECD 1989). Nonetheless, the slow-down is puzzling. The three main factors that might be responsible for this phenomenon are:

1. Reduced opportunities for catching up with the technological leader, the US;
2. A fall in the effectiveness of R&D expenditure, as measured by the fall in the number of patents per unit of R&D spending;
3. The prolonged and large under-utilization of resources in the 1970s and '80s, following the two oil shock crises (OECD 1992: 175).

It is the second of these factors that we have mainly addressed under the term 'law of diminishing returns'. Abramovitz has called it a decline in the 'potency' of technological effort (OECD 1989). Overall productivity is also held back, particularly in the USA, by some parts of the service sector where little technology and much unskilled low-paid labour is employed.

If indeed the law of diminishing returns is valid for R&D and if technological advance is one of the main causes of rising factor productivity, then a slow-down after a period of rapid growth is only to be expected. At any given time a number of technologies will be at a stage of development where progress is easy, and a number will progress only with great effort. If the majority of R&D effort goes into the latter category, real technological advance will be slow and total factor productivity will grow slowly, if at all. Circumstances have to be very exceptional for rapidly advancing technologies to predominate.

Capital productivity is affected by such factors as aggregate demand, but also by the rate of amortization of capital equipment. If the life-span of the equipment is very short, it will not have a chance to pay back its cost to the investor, even if new vintages of capital equipment are more productive than older vintages. The extra cost of early replacement must be repaid by higher profits, caused by the higher productivity of the new machinery, over the life-time of the equipment. Thus, whether the replacement of old equipment by new is worthwhile depends both on the life-span of the new equipment and on the increase in productivity achieved by it.

Of possibly even greater importance is the cost of introducing new equipment, over and above the cost of the equipment itself. Change is expensive, as it involves planning, disruption of production, re-training of staff, reorganization, ironing out initial problems, and a considerable amount of learning to use the new equipment to best effect. It will probably be necessary to remove new bottlenecks arising out of the higher productivity of the new machinery; disputes over pay and staffing may arise; problems with components and materials may occur. Generally, therefore, it will take a great deal of money, time and effort to make the best use of new equipment. If it becomes obsolete very rapidly, then the total cost, consisting of the cost of change added to the cost of the equipment, may not be repaid by its increased efficiency.

The slow-down in the rate of increase of total factor productivity in the face of rising expenditure on R&D may be an indication that innovative effort is not too slow but, on the contrary, too fast.

Many commentators speak of a new industrial paradigm as part of the information age, with Fordism and Taylorism being replaced by Toyotism. This includes just-in-time deliveries instead of buffer stocks, flexibility in terms of products and work methods, reduced hierarchies, faster response time to market demands, etc (see eg Bessant 1991 and Womack et al 1990). Some authors dispute that a change in paradigm has taken place.

> Indeed, no major change in the general trajectory of technology is apparent. Computer technology has facilitated a degree of convergence of mass and batch production principles and techniques in the form of flexible manufacturing systems (FMS) and computer integrated manufacturing (CIM) systems. It is now possible to automate even under conditions of market fluctuations and unpredictability (Scarbrough and Corbett 1992: 88).

Everybody is free to call the modern methods of mass-production a change in paradigm, but the changes appear to be refinements of the same basic industrial philosophy of obtaining as much output as possible with as little input as possible, and selling the largest possible amount of manufactured products. A change in paradigm to me would be a change from the goal of the highest possible production for the highest possible consumption to a goal of the greatest possible protection of the natural environment.

The existence of relatively stable socio-economic paradigms, with investment opportunities into technologies that develop along reasonably predictable trajectories, is postulated as the cause of relative stability in the economy by the school of economic thought that regards technology as the main driving force behind economic growth. A socio-economic paradigm includes institutions, such as markets and regulatory regimes, as much as dominant technologies and dominant ways of doing things. Within a given socio-economic regime continual change is regarded as normal and reasonably regulated, whereas a change of paradigm is a rare revolutionary occurrence. As change is normal, only organizations that are capable of adapting, ie learning, can succeed (Dosi and Orsenigo: 13–37, and Freeman and Perez, 38–66, in Dosi et al 1988). Unfortunately, once technology proceeds along a given trajectory, it is bound to run into the barrier of diminishing returns. Equally unfortunately, theories of economic growth, based on technological innovation, rarely discuss the question of whether or not there is an optimum speed of innovation and, if there is, how it might be determined. Is it not possible that the costs of change might become so high as to cause a slowing down, rather than a speeding up, of economic growth? Freeman and Perez argue that major changes in technology are a major cause of change in institutional arrangements. If this is the case, then certainly major technological change causes instability. Although Freeman and Perez only point to institutional change brought about by major technological changes, the argument can be extended to smaller changes, which bring in their wake more modest organizational change. Our argument is that even such change might proceed too fast and cause more than a desirable amount of instability. Too much instability is as harmful as too much stability, and too much technological innovation is as harmful as too little.

The rise of an entirely new family of technologies, such as information technology, is a rare event and, on the face of it, a highly desirable one. For what can be more desirable than the introduction of a whole new range of technological artefacts which satisfy a whole new range of previously undiscovered human wants? If, in addition, the new technology is so universal, so all-pervasive, that it permeates into virtually every existing industry and transforms its products and its manufacturing technology, we can expect a tremendous fillip to economic growth as a great deal of work needs to be done to accomplish all this transformation, and huge new markets arise for the new production machinery and transformed consumer products. If, to crown its achievements, the new technology transforms all administrative procedures in industry and in all services, and introduces, for the first time, a need for much investment capital into areas which previously managed with very little, then, one might think, we must look forward to an unprecedented period of economic growth, with new need chasing new need.

Reality, as is its wont, is rather different. The new is not simply added to the old; it often replaces it. The semiconductor industry rose out of the ashes of the older electronics industry and the many new products and services displaced older ones. That, in itself, need not be tragic. Although all change is difficult and causes transitional problems, the net result can nevertheless be positive. In the case of information technology, there is very serious doubt whether the net result is positive in terms of economic growth, total employment, enhancement of skills, and, for want of a better word, increase in human happiness.

There are many reasons for keeping the jury out for a very long time, if not for ever, when it comes to judging the net effects of IT. Even if we do not ask for a definitive answer on whether the sum total of human happiness has increased but restrict our questions to easier matters, we cannot know for sure, because technology is just one of many factors influencing the course of human destiny and even the direct influences of technology are usually ambivalent.

Take, for example, the question of employment. As information technology produces many new or considerably altered products, we would expect total demand for these new goods to give a considerable fillip to industrial production. Similarly, because information technology makes many new services possible, we would expect total demand for services to increase. These positive influences on demand and hence, other things being equal, on employment, are balanced to a greater or lesser extent by negative influences. The most important among these is the enhancement of productivity in both manufacture and services. Computers can be used to replace people and, unless the displacement effect is balanced by greater demand, unemployment must ensue. Although increased productivity is an economically desirable development because it means that more demands can be satisfied with the same amount of effort, in practice, demand is limited. Many thousands of words have been written, many complex computer programmes have been produced, and a large number of highly trained, highly skilled and highly intelligent people have spent untold hours in an attempt to find an answer to the simple question whether the sum total of employment effects of new information technologies has been positive, negative or zero. The answer you obtain still depends on who you ask, which means that no scientifically valid answer has been obtained, despite the vast effort. (For reviews see eg Freeman and Soete 1991; Matzner et al 1988; Freeman et al 1982).

The seemingly simple question of whether information technology has a positive or negative effect on employment is extremely complex and, most probably, unanswerable. Total employment in an economy depends on so many factors that it really is impossible to single out just one, even if the one is of such great significance as IT. We know that technology is the way we do things and doing things means employment. Yet we can determine the influence of a particular technology only in specific instances, if at all, and have no way of summing up over a whole economy, which uses thousands of different information technologies in thousands of different settings.

The crucial issue which limits the positive employment and growth effects of new products, services and technologies, is the limitation of demand. Why does demand not increase to absorb all gains in productivity; why, we must ask, does demand not absorb all products and services that an economy is able to offer? The answer contains several elements and we shall discuss some of these, albeit briefly, in arbitrary order.

One of the major inputs into an economy is labour, but the production of goods and services does not merely depend on the sum total of available labour. Those seeking work must be of the right quality and kind – ie the qualifications, knowledge, attitudes and abilities must match requirements. As an ideal match can never be achieved without adjustments at the micro-level, one of the fundamental conditions for achieving the best match between available and required skills is the willingness of both employers and workers to make adjustments. The match can be achieved, to a considerable degree, by workers being flexible in what they do and employers being flexible in providing training to those workers whose experience does not exactly match what is wanted.

The constant cry about shortages of qualified labour is true in a country such as Britain, where training and education have been neglected for decades and the overall level of skills is inadequate, but is likely to be less true in a country such as Germany, where general standards of training and education are high. With a sufficient level of education and training, which matches requirements in the most general and vaguest way, goodwill on the part of workers and employers can overcome many of the problems of mismatch between what is on offer and what is, ideally, required. Rapid technological change makes the process of adaptation both more difficult and more costly, yet more necessary (Matzner et al 1988). A skilled turner can be trained to operate a computer-controlled work-centre; a skilled physicist can operate effectively as an electronics engineer; a skilled typist can adapt to the use of a word-processor. The investment in retraining, however, must be given a chance to be repaid in the output of the newly trained worker. In the extreme, if the rate of obsolescence of skills were to become equal to the rate of retraining, no output whatsoever would be obtainable.

One of the many costs of rapid innovation is indeed an inevitable mismatch between the skills on offer and the skills required. The obsolescence of skills is a cost which needs to be balanced against the benefits of rapid innovation. Indeed, it is not merely formal skills, nor even only tacit technological knowledge, which become obsolete; as work organization and the interaction and interdependence between workers are all subject to change with changing technology, each worker has to adapt his/her customs and daily routines to constantly and rapidly changing circumstances. Some people, and not only the elderly, find this difficult. The cost is unease and sub-optimum efficiency, yet despite the magnitude of the problem, it is not possible to put a quantitative measure to it.

In an advanced economy, where more and more jobs are either fully automated or require highly skilled labour inputs, there is a large number of residual jobs to be done which are difficult to automate, yet require very little skill. There is all the minding, watching, guarding, loading and unloading, cleaning and tidying, fetching and carrying, that need to be done by humans. Although the activities are essential for the maintenance of civilization, their value is generally difficult to assess in monetary terms and those who do these jobs have become marginal. They require no special skills and are thus interchangeable; the value of their work is indirect and thus subject to cuts and savings. Wages are often so low that it is hard to fill available positions, except by citizens who are themselves marginal, whether because of their immigrant status, or the colour of their skin, or because of some form of social or physical handicap. The machinery that churns out technological innovation produces, among its many by-products, considerable numbers of marginal citizens.

The potential for enhanced productivity of new computer-controlled machinery is not fully realized because the full utilization of such machinery requires major organizational changes, and the cost of such change, added to the cost of rapid obsolescence of the machinery, is very high indeed. The gain in productivity may be cancelled out by the cost of rapid change. Perhaps the full gains will be realized if and when information technologies settle down to a steadier state. In addition, for one reason or another, industrial capacity is not currently fully employed – most industries work below capacity – and this in itself reduces capital productivity. Some people hope that this lack of demand will cure itself for cyclical reasons and, if that is not sufficient, that product innovation will help to cure it by overcoming the problems of the saturation of markets. Time will tell, but surely only a relatively sedate pace of innovation can cure problems of saturation without imposing intolerable costs.

One of the macro-economic theories on the role of technological innovation goes back to Schumpeter and has been developed by several recent authors, such as C Freeman and his school. Essentially, the theory attempts to explain long-term upswings and downturns in economic activity (the so-called Kondratiev waves) by the introduction of major new techno-economic systems. The new technology – eg the railways in the 19th century – offers many new profitable opportunities for investment and stimulates much new activity and demand. Once this stimulus has run its course, the economy begins to slow down until the next stimulus begins to raise activity (for a detailed discussion see eg Freeman et al 1982). The theory is not without its critics, or sceptics, who find it hard to accept the historical evidence for such cycles and even harder to accept the assignment of technologies to the role of more or less regularly recurring stimulants of such waves (see eg Rosenberg and Frischtak: 62–84, in Rosenberg 1994).

Optimists still believe that computer technology, perhaps combined with biotechnology, will eventually cause the economic upswing which the theory of long waves confidently predicts. Pessimists believe that not all technologies, however revolutionary, can cause upswings and that the currently dominant technologies, because of their strong labour-saving characteristic and their limited capacity to add to total demand, are unlikely to cause a new long-term economic upswing.

The need for industrial investment increases with rapid technological change. As equipment becomes obsolete for technical reasons, rather than because it is worn out, new modern equipment has to be purchased to replace the old-fashioned machinery. With the availability of ever new production and office equipment, companies dare not refrain from purchasing the latest machines for fear of becoming noncompetitive, yet they often cannot afford to buy it because of shortages, or the excessive cost, of capital. New equipment has an unproven record, and investment in unproven equipment is largely an act of faith. To this day it is very hard to justify purchases of many items of information technology in cash terms. For example, the computerization and networking of office work is carried out in the belief of achieving greater efficiency. However, efficiency in the office is a virtually immeasurable quantity because the outputs are ill-defined, and it is impossible to put a figure to the improvement of a quantity which cannot be measured in the first place (Peissl 1989).

As with shortages of skills caused by their rapid obsolescence, so shortages of capital can arise because of the rapid obsolescence of capital goods. If we take this case to its extreme limit, then capital goods have to be written off at a rate which never allows them to earn their keep. In other words, if production equipment becomes obsolete before it has produced enough profit to pay for its replacement, then there is no incentive to invest capital into such equipment, as no dividend can be achieved on such investment.

A vicious circle can arise. Competitive pressures can create a need for rapid technological change, and this can reduce profits because of the costs associated with R&D and with rapid obsolescence. Whereas rapid technological change requires increased investment, the costs associated with it may reduce the expectations and the prospects for profits, and thus reduce actual investment. If competitive pressures persist, then such shortfalls of investment lead to inevitable decline. If this is the case, there are two possible remedies: increased investment, whether private or public, or an attempt to decrease international competitive pressures on the speed of innovation. In the long run, only the second option can succeed.

The fact that high rates of innovation cause the demise of many small firms and change the competitive regime to an oligopolistic one, undesirable as this is on many grounds, offers the hope of reducing the rate of innovation. In an oligopolistic competitive regime the chances of some sort of agreement, tacit or otherwise, to reduce the rate of innovation are high. Because the cost of innovation is increasing, firms will tend to limit its rate unless they are forced to increase it by pressure of competition. If competition is oligopolistic, the chances are that the limitation of the rate of innovation, deemed desirable by all the remaining competitors, will actually take place. Thus industry is likely to reduce the current rates of innovation. The last thing governments should do is to attempt to force, or support, a higher rate of innovation.

If the cost of capital is too high, then some sectors of the economy may be less able than others to achieve the profits necessary to provide the rate of return demanded. These sectors will be particularly affected and their rate of investment will fall, with a consequent decline in their competitiveness and general activity. Rapid technological innovation increases the need for investment in industry, and this can cause two problems: one is the starvation of investment in other sectors, with possibly negative consequences on the whole economy and on the quality of life; the other is the starvation of industry, with the consequent loss of international competitiveness. Because the cost of capital is largely determined by international movements of capital, by the need to protect the exchange rate of the local currency, and by the need of governments to borrow money, the large needs of industry often are not properly met. The need for capital increases with the pace of technological innovation and this need for industrial investment may cause serious shortfalls either in industry or elsewhere. A lower rate of innovation might provide all the goods needed with a reduced requirement for capital investment.

Although obtaining sufficient investment for industry has been a British problem for a long time, it is not generally the main problem that industrial societies face. The main problem is the financing of public goods. Whereas there is sufficient cash to purchase, say, cars and their use far in excess of what the social fabric can bear, there is insufficient cash to provide care for the sick, care for the disabled, care for the elderly, housing for the poor, public transport for everybody, and so on. Nor is there sufficient cash in Britain or the US to support the unemployed; we prefer to pretend that they do not exist by giving them very low-paid, part-time or occasional jobs. There is also inadequate cash to protect the environment, to clean up the mess left by early industrialization, to provide decent educational and training facilities. As has often been remarked, it is still private affluence and public squalor, not to mention the private squalor of the millions of poor.

Britain may have problems of financing even commercially viable technological innovations, but this is not the general world problem. Innovation constantly seeks to find new products and processes that might find buyers. It does, of course, fail occasionally, but on the whole technology does increase its performance and does expand demand into areas of previously unknown wants. What purely market-oriented technological innovation cannot do is to be guided by social needs. Those needs that cannot be satisfied by private finance cannot be met by privately financed technological innovation either. And even where public support is given for technological innovation, it is given on the same criteria as private support, rather than on the criteria of social need. Social criteria would mean the environmental compatibility of normally traded goods, including their durability, safety, low energy consumption, etc. However, social criteria go considerably beyond this to finding socially desirable goods that normal markets cannot support, such as environmentally benign technologies that are insufficiently developed and therefore too expensive to be bought privately, for example heat-pumps; and to develop public transport systems that private demand cannot create because of the ubiquity of cars. Things might improve if industrial products were to compete on their true quality, which would include environmental criteria.

The issue is aggravated by the fact that industry now accounts for relatively little employment, so a high proportion of investment fails to secure a high proportion of employment. It is very hard to imagine rates of industrial growth that would suffice to provide full employment, unless other sectors of the economy were flourishing and employing people. However, those countries whose share of industrial employment has fallen least are doing economically best. So much for the post-industrial age!

The reasons for such economic success are not difficult to find. First, the much-praised services, including those services related to the manipulation of information, often do not provide products for final consumption, but serve merely as inputs to industry. Thus any decline in industrial activity causes a decline in industry-related services. Secondly, a country whose industry is not able to supply a high proportion of domestic demand for industrial products and to capture sufficient international markets to help pay for necessary imports, will inevitably suffer balance of trade problems.

Although services can earn foreign currency – eg in the tourist industry, in shipping, in insurance and in financial services, or even in professional services such as industrial or fashion design – it is only in very exceptional circumstances that an economy can flourish without a large and well-developed industrial sector. Generally, only services built upon a local industrial base are strong enough to be able to take the difficult leap into exporting their service. It should not be forgotten that services themselves need large inputs of capital equipment. Many services can hardly be traded internationally – eg, local transport, legal services, personal services, administration, health services, education. Total international trade in services is far less than trade in raw materials, fuels, agricultural produce and manufactured goods, and the chances of achieving a healthy international trading surplus in services alone are slim. A healthy economy requires a healthy industry.

A healthy industry must be internationally competitive, unless it is protected by much frowned-upon barriers to trade. Competitiveness means the ability to provide goods with competitive price/performance ratios. This means achieving some competitive combination of productivity, wages, profits, quality and technological novelty. The most desirable of these combinations is, obviously, high productivity, high quality and high novelty, as this can be combined with high wages and high profits without detriment to competitiveness. The least desirable combination is low wages and low profits, as international competitiveness is then achieved without great benefit to the local economy. The advantage of this combination is that it is technically easier to achieve, because no great demands are made on quality or technological novelty. The success or failure of modern industrial nations depends, *ceteris paribus*, on the ability of their industry to be internationally competitive with goods that sell at prices which allow domestic high wages and high profits. These in turn assure high purchasing power and thus further demand for goods and services, and enable industry to retain sufficient profits to finance its investment needs without excessive recourse to capital markets.

The faster the rate of technological innovation, the harder it becomes to remain competitive and the less likely it becomes that industry, on average, will be able to generate sufficient profits to underpin its investment requirements.

Technological Innovation and Defence

One of the greatest pressures for technological innovation comes from defence requirements. Weapons have always been among the favourite implements produced by humankind, and the application of modern science and engineering to the production of ever more sophisticated and devastating weapons has always had high priority. Indeed, in many countries the share of military R&D in total R&D has been very high, as shown in Table 2.3.

Table 2.3 *Military R&D as % of total government R&D, 1987*

United States	68.6
United Kingdom	48.4
France	43.2
Germany	11.6
Japan	4.4

Source: OECD (1992) *Technology and the Economy*, OECD, Paris: 246

Military technology is a prime example of a technology that cannot stand still, where the impetus for rapid innovation stems from the need to keep abreast and ahead of all potential enemies. In peacetime, or at times of limited warfare, the rapid obsolescence of weapons systems is also the only means of keeping orders flowing. If arsenals are not depleted by enemy action, how can the armaments industry keep going without the obsolescence of weapons? As in the civilian industry, obsolescence becomes the main tool to fight market saturation.

Because many citizens doubt whether, indeed, all weapons research can be justified on the grounds of pure defence, much has been made of the benefits of defence R&D for civilian technological innovation. First, it was claimed that defence R&D and its not so distant relation, space research, produce incidental unplanned spin-off benefits for civilian use. Often quoted examples are the military orders for early integrated circuits which greatly accelerated the development of this technology; the famous ceramics developed for space applications and later found useful for kitchen utensils; and satellite communications which might have been delayed by many years if rockets had not been developed for military purposes.

As the spin-off theory has met a more and more sceptical reception of late, it changed to a theory of co-development. Electronic circuits, computer systems and advanced materials are now said to be developed simultaneously for civil and military uses, thus increasing the efficiency and reducing the cost of R&D for both purposes. On the premise that military R&D remains necessary, this argument is reasonably convincing. Whether the premise remains convincing, is quite another matter.

> *Today, the direction of decisive technological flows has reversed. The defence sector depends strongly on the results of competitive industrial R&D ...Military technology has developed over the years a number of distinctive features. ...All these features accentuate the non-generic, highly customised features of military technologies and their very low degree of transferability to civilian uses* (OECD 1992: 246).

As the threat of a major war receded in the 1980s, very high hopes were pinned upon arms conversion. The old slogan of swords into ploughshares was revived as many people of goodwill attempted to find civilian work for military R&D and production establishments. Many sophisticated and useful products were proposed: kidney machines, heat-pumps, high-speed trains (see eg Elliott 1985). Unhappily, not much of this conversion actually happened and the net result of the reduction in defence budgets is unemployment among former defence workers.

On the face of it, this is not only disappointing but also counter-intuitive. The reasons can only be conjectured. For one, there is an institutional mismatch. Defence firms simply do not know their way round civilian markets and civilian ways of doing things. For another, there is no shortage of industrial capacity for the production of sophisticated goods; the shortage is in demand. Perhaps we do need more kidney machines, but the health service (at least in Britain) cannot afford to buy more. Perhaps we do need high-speed trains, but the impoverished railways certainly cannot afford to invest in them (at least in Britain). Heat-pumps may be the ideal way for heating and air-conditioning buildings, but, given the low price of fuel, they are not able to compete on price with conventional methods without public subsidies. The unpalatable fact is that there are worldwide over-capacities in shipbuilding, steel, armaments, motor vehicles, computers, electronics and most other manufactured products. Although there is a need for more of some of these products, need without the backing of cash does not count.

Perhaps we are simply too impatient, and the achievement of such a major shift to different products and different markets takes a long time. It probably also needs considerable assistance from government. Although in the UK some firms, such as Racal, have been successful in switching from military to civil production, most firms have not. In Germany, for example, a much more concerted effort is being made, aided and abetted by public policy (POST 1991).

It used to be said that defence expenditure in the US and Britain, to name but two examples, is vital to keep the technological innovation system and, thus, the economy as a whole at a high level. The argument is obviously spurious; for did not the German and Japanese economies, with far less significant defence commitments, thrive rather better? And did not the Soviet Union, for all its vast defence budgets, turn out an utter economic failure?

Our problem is not to produce ever more sophisticated goods, but to create the worldwide purchasing power to buy the goods we can produce. If we did this, however, we would soon run into the buffers of environmental catastrophe; thus it becomes clear that we must not only change our ways of financing purchases, but our whole way of technological thinking to make it compatible with environmental survival.

Chapter Three

TECHNOLOGY POLICY

◆

Technology and Politics

Technology is now deemed too important to the lives of nations to be left to the technologists. What is more, it is even deemed too important to be left to industry. As a consequence, virtually all governments and political parties lay claim to policies for technology. Technology has moved close to the centre of the political stage. Because politics deals, among other things, with the distribution of wealth, it has unavoidably become involved in the creation of what is to be distributed. As technology is now seen as one of the dominant factors in the creation of wealth, politics has become involved in technology. From this point of view, politics endeavours to support technology in order to facilitate the maximum possible creation of wealth for the nation. The support of technology, in one form or another, has become a firmly established part of the political agenda.

There is more to technology than the creation of wealth. The use of technology is a prime social activity. It is a dominant influence on the way we work, on the way we live, and on the way we interact with each other. Politics deals with all these matters and hence cannot avoid dealing with technology. In view of the very large potential for a conflict of views and interests, it is surprising that there is so much consensus among political parties on matters of technology. Until the relatively recent advent of the green parties, consensus in principle was almost complete and all parties simply claimed that they were better able to support technology to the hilt and thus extract maximum possible benefit from it.

Disregarding early opposition to technology from the time of the Industrial Revolution, doubts about technology as purely benign and wholly beneficial began to be voiced by critical writers from the early Sixties. Their main concerns were environmental pollution and the exhaustion of natural resources. Books such as *Silent Spring* (Carson 1965), *Only One Earth* (Ward and Dubos 1972), *Murderous Providence* (Rothman 1972), and *Limits to Growth* (Meadows et al 1974) were highly influential and inspired a small but vociferous political movement which eventually led to the formation of effective pressure groups and green parties in many countries. The green parties have remained small and far removed from political power, but the combined influence of environmental pressure groups and the green parties on the major parties and on the general political ambience, has been substantial. The public at large has become convinced, to a stronger or lesser degree, that the natural environment matters and that something ought to be done to safeguard it from the ravages of technology. Most major parties have added a green hue to whatever colour they traditionally adhered to. The green parties are, of course, much more radical in their critique of technology, but some of their thinking has penetrated the major parties and has even gone on the statute books and become part and parcel of official policies. The United States came first with its Environmental Protection Act and the Environmental Protection Agency, and most political entities, including the European Union, now have environmental policies and environmental legislation and enforcement agencies.

A number of spectacular and well-publicized accidents, such as tanker disasters, major explosions, leaks of poisonous fumes such as at Bhopal, the near nuclear disaster in Three Mile Island and the actual disaster in Chernobyl, have all contributed to the general public's unease about technology and to an undermining of its faith in the infallibility of technologists.

Not that these acts and activities are without precedent. To the contrary, governments have found it necessary to curb some dangers caused by technology for a very long time. In the US, the example of the control of the construction of steam boilers, in response to numerous explosions on Mississippi steamers, is quoted as an early instance of regulatory technology policies; while in Britain the famous Alkali Act aimed to control noxious emissions from early factories. At that time, and until quite recently, such technological hazards were simply viewed as threats to be dealt with as and when they arose. It was part of the duties of government to guard the population against excessive hazards in general, and the control of technological hazards was viewed much in the same vein as issues of public order or crime control. The view of technology as a single complex, to be made subject to policy and an important part of the political agenda, is of quite recent origin.

Although it is generally acknowledged that a policy for technology is important, in practice governments find it difficult to take a unified approach and designate a single ministry in charge of technology policy. The very fact that technology permeates all spheres of society and economic activity makes it almost impossible to separate technology from other political activity and to put a single ministry in charge. Most countries grapple not so much with the problem of formulating a single technology policy by a single ministry, as with the problem of coordinating the various technology policies pursued by several departments of state. Industrial policies, for example, are inextricably intertwined with technology policies, and, similarly, it is hard to separate R&D policy and aspects of education and training policy, or state procurement policies, from technology policy.

Germany and Japan have, perhaps, gone furthest in an attempt to assign the task of technology policy formation to a single ministry. In Germany it is the Bundesministerium für Forschung und Technologie (Federal Ministry for Research and Technology), while in Japan it is the Ministry for International Trade and Industry (MITI). In both cases these ministries play an important and successful role in formulating and carrying out technology policy, although in neither case do they have a monopoly in this area. Rivalries between ministries and their policies occur frequently. In Japan, for example, the Ministry of Communications plays a dominant role in telecommunications and wishes to determine technology policy in this area, while MITI also wants to be a player in this internationally important field. It is interesting that technology policy in Japan originated from a ministry whose task it is to foster an industry that is successful in international trade – ie the impetus for technology policy came from the desire to enhance the ability to compete internationally and to promote 'Japan Inc'. In Germany, on the other hand, with its strong scientific tradition, the impetus came from the desire to harness research and technology into a powerful team for economic advance. The approaches to technology policy in the two countries differ considerably, yet the results, in terms of success in world trade in advanced industrial products, is much the same in both countries and is very likely to be related, to some degree, to their technology policies. It cannot be doubted, however, that it takes more than a good technology policy to achieve success in world markets.

Technology policy consists of two fundamentally different, though complementary, aspects. On the one hand, it tries to foster and support technology, technological innovation and the application of technology, in order to support economic growth and international industrial competitiveness. On the other hand, technology policy attempts to regulate the use of technology in such ways as to minimize dangers to health, damage to the natural environment, risks to life and limb, and social conflicts arising out of the use of technology. The support of technology and the control of technology are the two faces, the yin and yang, of technology policy.

Support Policies for Technology

State support for technology can take a variety of forms. We shall try to pick the main principles out of the vast number of different examples; rather like picking the basic tune out of a complex set of variations. The basic measures available for the support of technology are rarely used in a pure form; in reality different aspects of support are woven into a fugue-like pattern which is supposed to yield optimum results at the least cost. Any policy has one or more aims and consists of a number of measures, addressing different target areas.

The aims of support policies may be classified according to their generality. We may wish to support technological innovation in general, or a specified generic technology, or a specific innovation. We may wish to strengthen the innovation system of a state (or a federation such as the European Union) in general, in the hope that, as a result of the measures taken, it will produce more successful innovations than hitherto. On the other hand, we may decide that biotechnology is extremely important for the future well-being of the state and that private industry is not doing enough for the development of this generic technology. We may then decide to take supportive measures to strengthen all aspects of biotechnology in the hope that these measures will strengthen this generic technology and thus lead to economic success which might have eluded the state in the absence of such supportive measures. Finally, we may decide to lend support to a very specific innovation project – say, the development of carbon fibres or, to use a contemporary example, the development of a broadband telecommunications system, recently renamed communications super-highway and probably destined to become a hyper-highway in the near future. Such support will be given in the belief that it is a worthy project which, in the absence of public support, might not be undertaken at all, or might falter, or might advance too slowly to beat the international competition, and thus opportunities for the industry and the economy might be lost.

The target area for support measures may be classified along two dimensions. The first is the stage of the innovation process. Although the linear view of the process of technological innovation is now discredited, we can still distinguish different innovative activities which form a temporal sequence. We do not wish to suggest that pure research reaches a conclusion and is then followed by applied research, which in turn reaches a conclusion and is followed by development, and so forth. Obviously all these activities are carried out simultaneously and weave into a complex pattern of interactions and feedbacks. Nevertheless, whether we consider any specific innovation or the innovation process in general, there is a functional and temporal dependence between the various stages of the activity. Pure research may not always play a role in an innovation, but if it does, then at least some parts of the pure research will have preceded the stage of development.

Development, or at least a substantial part of the development effort, precedes marketing and production. This is not to say that development will not continue even when production has started, but it means that the function of development takes temporal precedence over the function of production in any specific chain of innovative events, even if several such interdependent events are running in parallel. Discredited as the so-called linear model of innovation may be, some aspects of this view have to be taken over into our new view of the process of technological innovation. And, hence, target areas for support measures may be classified according to the dimension 'stage of the innovation'. This means that a distinction may be made between measures supporting pure goal-oriented research, measures supporting applied research and development, measures supporting engineering development and design, and measures supporting preparations for production, preproduction, early production and product launch. Within the same dimension we may also identify measures to support early diffusion, such as government aid for the purchase of new production machinery, or for the training of operatives or maintenance engineers for a new process technology.

The second dimension for classification of the target area for policy measures is the socio-economic sphere which they address. Braun (1984a: 134) distinguishes five target areas at which support can be aimed: political ambience, industry, commerce, foreign trade and consumers. It is useful to add services and infrastructure as two further likely target areas.

Having defined the two dimensions of targeting for support measures, it remains to describe individual measures as examples of the possible ingredients of a package from which a policy is constructed. The types of measures listed in Braun (op cit: 126) are: financial, taxation, legal and regulatory, educational, procurement, information, public enterprise, public services, political, scientific and technical, and commercial.

Aims of support policies for technological innovation		
Innovation in general	Generic technology	Specific innovation

Target areas for policy measures		
Stages of innovation	Socio-economic sphere	

Policy measures		
Financial and fiscal	Legal and regulatory	Educational
Information and cooperation	Public enterprise	Government R & D
Political	Infrastructure	Public procurement

Figure 3.1 *Classification of support policies for technological innovation*

A two-dimensional 'target space' at which support measures can be aimed is obtained. The dimensions are 'stage of innovation', and 'socio-economic sphere'. The individual policy measures, which can range from direct financial support to the provision of information and include purely symbolic measures, such as the award of honours to innovators, can be aimed at one or more target areas, located somewhere in target space. Figure 3.1 summarizes the above points.

Examples of Support Policies

In England the responsibility for technology policy is now divided, in the main, between the Department of Trade and Industry and the Office of Science and Technology, the latter located in the Cabinet Office under the Minister for Public Service and Science, also known under the quaint title of Chancellor of the Duchy of Lancaster.

In the spring of 1993 the Minister for Public Service and Science presented a White Paper to Parliament, setting out a strategy for science, engineering and technology (Cabinet Office 1993a). The document sets out, elegantly and succinctly, everything we have termed conventional wisdom about the role of technological innovation in the economy. Practically nothing is said about problems of the environment, nor is any critical thought about technology allowed to rear its ugly head. Technological innovation receives unadulterated praise for its role in supporting economic growth and international competitiveness.

> *The nation's first priority must be to improve the*
> *performance of the economy to meet the competitive*
> *challenge of making the goods and providing the services*
> *which others, at home and abroad, choose to buy.*
> *...Innovation is essential across the whole range of goods and*
> *services* (loc cit: 11).

In terms of our classification of aims, the policy set out in the White Paper clearly aims to support innovation in general, as is to be expected from a strategic document of this kind. Within the general aim, some specific policy measures receive special attention: for example, awareness and cooperation are singled out for repeated mention in the belief that managers are insufficiently aware of the need to innovate, and that resources can be better utilized by cooperation between firms and between firms and research institutions. Among the target areas for support, it does not come as a surprise to learn that pre-competitive strategic research is singled out for special mention.

> *Strategic research – where the work, although directed*
> *towards practical aims, has not yet advanced to the stage*

99

> *where eventual applications can be clearly specified –*
> *represents an important area of shared interest between*
> *industry, Government, research charities and other*
> *organisations* (loc cit: 15).

The paper stresses information and cooperation measures above all others. This indicates a belief that Japanese success is largely based on cooperation between all parts of the innovation system, facilitated and coordinated by government. The fact that these measures are cheaper and easier to implement than most others may also play a role. The Japanese, meanwhile, are beginning to worry that their system does not carry out sufficient basic research to provide the foundations for future technologies (Science and Technology Agency 1989).

The White Paper reiterates what has been said many times before: although the government is willing to support some basic research as a cultural activity, it is far more interested

> *...to harness the intellectual resources of the science and*
> *engineering base to improve economic performance and the*
> *quality of life. ...support should be much more clearly related*
> *to meeting the country's needs and enhancing the wealth-*
> *creating capacity of the country* (Cabinet Office 1993a: 26).

The concept 'quality of life' is not defined. The science and engineering base is essentially the basic research and training capacity, residing in universities and other institutions, and supported through the Higher Education Funding Councils, the Research Councils, charities and donations.

The Research Councils are not only reorganized, they will also each be 'provided with a mission statement which recognises the importance of research undertaken to meet the needs of users and to support wealth creation' (loc cit: 27).

One of the programmes of the Department of Trade and Industry (DTI), which is specifically mentioned in the White Paper, is the LINK programme. This aims to promote cooperation between R&D institutions and commercial firms within the UK by contributing 50 per cent of project costs. Total government funding for the LINK programme is about £80 million per annum. LINK involves not only the DTI, but also the Research Councils.

> *LINK aims to accelerate the commercial exploitation of*
> *government-funded research. The initiative will focus on*
> *advances in science and engineering with particular*
> *commercial promise. It will stimulate collaboration between*
> *industrial and science-based partners on projects in key areas*
> *of science and technology.* (From a leaflet prepared by the
> DTI for the LINK secretariat in May 1991).

The prescription is similar to other DTI programmes: a mix of direct financial support and information. In this case, the aim is the support of specific technologies and the policy measures include the utilization of government-funded research.

In a statement of its objectives, issued in October 1992, the DTI proclaims as its aim 'to help UK business compete successfully at home, in the rest of Europe, and throughout the world'. Thus the overall aim of the DTI's technology policy, which is intimately linked with trade and industrial policy, is support for increased international competitiveness, and thus for innovation in general. Individual policies cover a wide range within this very broad aim.

In the DTI leaflet 'Technology and Change' (May 1991), innovation is defined as 'the commercial application of knowledge or techniques in new ways or for new purposes', thus addressing all businesses, not only those able and willing to carry out their own R&D. The DTI classifies its help into three categories: consultancy help; technology transfer services; grants for research and development.

The technology transfer programmes concentrate mainly on information services and on fostering cooperation between firms, and between firms and R&D laboratories, but include some educational measures – eg the placement of postgraduate students in so-called teaching companies. The aims of the policies are either specific generic technologies – eg biotechnology or knowledge-based systems; or else they aim at innovation in general by measures that promote advanced methods of management.

The DTI leaflet describes a range of policy measures:

- SPUR: 'a scheme to help firms with up to 500 employees develop new products and processes';
- SMART: an annual competition for firms with fewer than 50 employees;
- Club Research and Development: a scheme to enable small firms to benefit from R&D in major organizations at subsidized rates;
- Regional Innovation Grants: given to firms with fewer than 25 employees in specified geographic areas;
- finally, there is an offer of subsidized consultancy advice.

SPUR offers a grant of up to 30 per cent of eligible costs to 'develop new products which involve a significant technological advance for the industry concerned'. It is thus a financial measure aimed at innovation in general, but one that is confined to small firms. A programme for research collaboration aims to support specified technologies – eg the aims are specific and the measures include financial support and promotion of cooperation at a pre-competitive stage of an innovation project.

The DTI is also responsible for UK participation in the well-known EUREKA programme, a pan-European scheme which concentrates on financial and information support of innovation projects involving several European firms. The projects must be nearly ripe for international marketing and the overall goal of EUREKA is to increase the competitiveness of Europe as a whole. All these policies aim at specific technologies, but vary as to the stage of innovation. They all include financial support and support by the supply of information and the fostering of cooperation.

A set of support measures in a similar vein, the Advanced Technology Programmes (ATP) are described in a leaflet published by the DTI in June 1992. The programmes are concerned with the development of specified generic advanced technologies at a pre-competitive stage of R&D. They are jointly funded by the DTI and industry and must involve collaboration between several firms. Often included among the partners are government and other research laboratories. ATP clearly consists of direct financial support and includes encouragement of collaboration. It is aimed at generic technologies and targeted at early stages of the innovation process.

Among the roughly 220 programmes run by the DTI only one more shall be mentioned. It is targeted at the last stages of innovation and aims to foster a particular technology: Gallium Arsenide integrated circuits. The research is carried out in industry and receives funding of £30 million from the DTI and £10 million from the Science and Engineering Research Council.

The great stress on cooperation is a response to three factors:

1. the escalating cost of R&D, which it is hoped to reduce, or make bearable, by cooperation;
2. the fear that small and medium-sized enterprises cannot keep up with technological developments except by cooperation among themselves and/or with larger firms and research establishments; and
3. the wish to make publicly financed R&D more readily available to industry.

But cooperation in R&D between disparate firms, whose heads have been knocked together by some government programme, can be problematic. One experienced industrial researcher who participated in the so-called Alvey programme (a large DTI programme in support of IT in Britain) suggested that such partnerships did not work because each firm still pursued its own interests, and because it was difficult to get them all not only to pull in the same direction, but also to pull their full weight individually. The Alvey programme has now been succeeded by another IT programme, run jointly by the DTI and the Science and Engineering Research Council, but despite all these programmes, the British IT industry is not doing well.

The concept of pre-competitive research has recently come into vogue. Industrial firms and research organizations are supposed to form collaborative networks, jointly performing R&D into advanced technology at a stage before individual firms adopt their individual competitive solutions and designs. Although the concept is controversial, and the boundaries between competitive and pre-competitive research are blurred, a great deal of such research is being carried out, much of it under the auspices of international programmes. One example is the RACE programme (Research into Advanced Communications for Europe) of the European Community. Virtually the whole European telecommunications industry got together with almost all the public telephone operators and a host of large and small research organizations to investigate, research, develop and foster the introduction of broadband telecommunication networks in Europe. This is a large and ambitious programme with a very clear aim: to foster one specific innovation in order to first increase the competitiveness of the European telecommunications industry and secondly increase European competitiveness in general by providing a better telecommunications infrastructure. The target of policy measures is somewhat confused: on the one hand, the research is supposed to be pre-competitive; on the other hand, it is intended to achieve the actual introduction of a universal broadband network. In fact, RACE combines the role of a research programme with that of a pressure group. The measures taken are the same mix we have encountered before: direct financial support and a great deal of effort to foster and coordinate cooperation.

An example of a programme supporting European cooperative R&D in a generic technology is the ESPRIT programme on information technology. In the first phase of this programme, completed in 1988, 1,500 million ECU was spent, half of which came from the European Community. The emphasis was on obtaining actual products, but this emphasis shifted somewhat for the second phase.

> *The acceleration in the application rate of knowledge of*
> *fundamental microelectronics, computer science and artificial*
> *intelligence should not be to the detriment of the necessary*
> *reservoir of fundamental knowledge. For this reason, basic*
> *research has been included in the ESPRIT programme* (Cadiou,
> ESPRIT in 1988: an overview, CECDG XIII, Brussels).

As a further illustration of government programmes for the support of technologies, this time in the field of microelectronics in the widest sense, we shall briefly describe three programmes of the German Federal government.

1. The programme 'Application of Microelectronics' ran from 1982 to 1984 and aimed to support the generic technology. The

specific goals of the programme were: to increase the range of microelectronic applications and microelectronic-based product innovations; to secure the position of domestic component manufacturers; and to promote applications in the capital equipment sector. Up to a maximum of DM800,000 was granted to individual firms to cover up to 40 per cent of development costs and up to 20 per cent of associated investments. An extensive evaluation at the end of the programme came to the conclusion that the programme had helped to increase the range and to modernize many of the products of the 1,740 participating firms. The improvements were mainly in the areas of material handling, process and production technology, and in communication and media technologies.

2. The 'Microperipherics Programme' ran from 1985 to 1989 and aimed at: securing the availability of microsensors; enhancing the diffusion of miniaturizing technologies in sensor elements; and strengthening the technological base of sensor manufacturers. This programme, aimed at enhancing a specific technology deemed to be a weak link in automation and to offer many commercial opportunities, was targeted at the fairly early stages of the innovation process, up to the development of prototype sensors. The policy measures were similar to those of the previous programme and consisted mainly of financial support, although the provision of information was included.

3. In the summer of 1989, a new comprehensive programme 'Information Technology – a Concept for the Future' was jointly introduced by the Federal Ministries for Research and Technology and for Economic Affairs (Bundesminister für Forschung und Technologie & Bundesminister für Wirtschaft, 1989). This is a policy framework with the overall aim of helping the German economy to participate as much as possible in the rapidly advancing and growing generic technology. The programme is a good illustration of the very wide scope of technology policy measures.

The goals of the programme, in loose translation, are the following:

- Economic and technological conditions are to be developed to allow an even wider and more efficient use of information technology (IT), thus creating new markets, strengthening competitiveness of the German economy, and securing and expanding employment.
- Opportunities are to be maintained and enhanced for German firms to participate in the development, production and sale of components, equipment, software and services in the field of IT, to ensure that they benefit from the above average growth of this branch in internationally open markets within the international division of labour.

- Basic research in the field of IT is to be strengthened, cooperation between industry, research organizations and universities should be improved, and the development and application of IT in small and medium-sized enterprises (SMEs) should be supported. SMEs should increasingly participate in early stages of R&D.
- All possibilities of using IT for the solution of environmental problems, for the improvement of working conditions, for the rational use of energy, and for carrying out government tasks should be systematically explored and utilized.
- In the long-term planning of the development of the telecommunications and transport infrastructure consideration shall be given to the full utilization, within economic constraints, of the technical possibilities of IT.
- All sectors of the education system (schools, universities, professional, continuing and further education) must come to grips with IT and must make their contribution to enable people of all ages and all levels of education to participate in these developments and to contribute to the humane use of IT.

The programme enlists virtually all the policy measures mentioned in our categorization for the achievement of its far-flung aims. This is possible because of the participation of the powerful Ministry of Economic Affairs, in addition to the ministry directly responsible for technology. Almost equally important is the fact that the federal states (Bundesländer) also participate in the programme, thus giving it support at all levels of government. The regulation of telecommunications, the law on cartels, company taxation, public procurement, and intellectual property rights are specifically mentioned among economic conditions influencing the use of IT.

The framework concept does not describe detailed measures, but we may glean the scope of the measures by listing the topics dealt with in some detail in the document describing the concept (Bundesminister für Forschung und Technologie & Bundesminister für Wirtschaft, 1989):

1. further development of economic conditions;
2. creation of the single European market;
3. intensification of international cooperation;
4. development and introduction of technical standards;
5. support for small and medium-sized enterprises;
6. support for research;
7. securing the technological foundations;
8. development of the telecommunications infrastructure;
9. education;
10. application of IT in the implementation of governmental tasks;
11. assessment of the impact of IT.

Even from these chapter headings it is clear that the concept is not only far-reaching, but that it asks the right questions about using IT for human and environmental purposes. IT is not to be supported merely for short-term thoughtless gain and for the sake of keeping up with the Joneses, but its role in society is to be properly considered lest the disadvantages outweigh the benefits.

All governments have large R&D programmes, and all of them struggle with two policy problems: how to set priorities for the allocation of resources and how to balance pure and applied research. Recent thinking on the latter question may be summed up by saying that basic research is good, but if it leads to applications it is even better. The German Federal government is increasing the proportion of support for basic research within its research budget because of two beliefs: first, that the distinction between basic and applied research is largely artificial and becoming increasingly difficult to maintain; and secondly, because it believes that directly applicable research should be done by those who wish to apply it, ie by commercial firms. The Federal Ministry for Research and Technology spent 38.9 per cent of its R&D budget in 1988 on basic research, as against only 26.5 per cent in 1982.

The setting of priorities in R&D is fraught with difficulties. It is notoriously difficult to pick winners, and almost equally difficult to avoid band-wagon effects. Both by missing winners and by joining – possibly belatedly – a band-wagon, and thus duplicating effort, scarce resources are likely to be wasted. On the other hand, broadcasting support may mean sub-critical size for some important projects and over-generous support for others. Peer review may be sufficient to provide quality assurance, but cannot readily help in the setting of priorities. This task can only be performed by high level advisory bodies, providing an institutionalized combination of political and scientific wisdom.

One of the new policy initiatives, announced in the recent British White Paper *Realising our Potential* (Cabinet Office 1993a), is technology foresight.

> *The central thesis of this White Paper is that we could and should improve our performance by making the science and engineering base even more aware of and responsive to the needs of industry and other research users, and by encouraging more firms and other organisations to be more aware of and receptive to the work being done in other laboratories, especially those of the science and engineering base. ... the Government has concluded that this country could and should benefit from the application of technology foresight, not only as a means of gaining early notice of emerging key technologies but also as a process which will forge a new working partnership* (loc cit: 16–17).

The conviction that if only industry and the science and engineering base knew more about each other's needs, all this tremendous research potential could be harnessed to the creation of wealth is, alas, not a new one. It is only reiterated and recast, and now given the new mantle of technology foresight.

The technology foresight initiative is underpinned in a commissioned research report, published a couple of months before the White Paper (Cabinet Office 1993b). What technology foresight actually means is open to a wide range of interpretations. As far as I understand the above document and the relevant sections in the White Paper, it means spotting band-wagons early, preferably before they start rolling, in order to secure a good seat on them. Much is made of responding to technology-push and to demand-pull. Technology-push means spotting opportunities offered by new scientific/technical developments in their early stages. Demand-pull is interpreted with some modesty; it appears to mean R&D requirements of industry for the development of technologies already in or near production. Virtually nothing is made of demand-pull in the sense of seeking solutions for social and environmental problems; a very brief mention is all this vital issue is deemed worthy of.

The government is setting up a Technology Foresight Steering Group which will draw up lists of technologies to be the subject of foresight assessments by panels of experts. The foresight exercise is driven by the belief that if a strong network of formal and informal contacts between knowledgeable people can be organized, then barriers to cooperation can be broken down and potential winners can be spotted early. Although it is undoubtedly true that ignorance and lack of communication is a frequent barrier to cooperation, there are many other barriers that cannot be overcome by contacts. Perhaps the most important barrier is commercial secrecy; if any firm thinks it has a potential winner in its laboratory, the last thing it will want to do is to broadcast this information. The second fundamental difficulty is to spot potential band-wagons and to judge their importance in advance, even if the search for them were genuinely collective and open. Horse-racing or soccer spring to mind as painful analogies. Even punters equipped with excellent knowledge of form cannot be sure of spotting the winners.

This is not to condemn efforts at foresight; it is certainly better to attempt to look into the future than to rush blindly into it. But these foresight exercises are not attempting to harness technology to real problems and furthermore are not endeavouring to link the foresight of the consequences of technologies with the foresight of their likely take-off. In my view, technology foresight should be closely linked to technology assessment. Funding for R&D should not depend on the likelihood of commercial success alone, but also on the likelihood of generally beneficial consequences of the technology. This sort of advice is likely to fall upon the deaf ears of a purely market-oriented government: for them, commercial success is the only criterion of benefit.

In general, R&D priorities are set by a combination of four factors, each given a political weighting:

1. national aims – eg military strength, economic competitiveness, use of specific resources;
2. the need to solve acute problems, such as environmental pollution or rising levels of crime;
3. the realization of scientific/technical opportunities, such as the current rapid development of molecular biology and genetic engineering;
4. local presence of strong research schools or a strong industrial base.

The quest for R&D priorities is driven by opportunities as much as by problems.

The lists of priorities in different countries make interesting reading. A number of topics are listed among the research priorities in virtually all OECD countries, and most of them have been on the lists, in one form or another, for many years. Major research areas do not go out of fashion very quickly and new significant topics are added only very occasionally. International collaboration within the scientific community is very strong and the fashion for certain research topics spreads internationally, almost as fashions in clothes or pop-music. On the other hand, many countries have, in addition to the universal topics, specific research priorities related to cultural heritage, political interests, industrial and scientific strength, or to natural conditions.

Recurring topics for research are: materials technology; energy; health; information technology, including telecommunications and electronics; the environment; and, the most recent universal addition, biotechnology. In many countries agriculture, fisheries, forestry and food technology play an important role. Space research is significant in many countries, whether for telecommunications, military purposes or astronomy and astrophysics.

With the end of the Cold War in the Eighties, a slight reduction in priority and expenditure on military R&D has occurred. A trend is discernible toward less emphasis on supporting R&D in purely military technology and coupling this with the hope of civilian by-products. Instead, dual technologies, with both civilian and military applications, or civilian technologies with possible military applications, are often spoken of. 'In years past, military research produced important spinoffs for the commercial civilian economy. Today, improvements in military technology frequently depend on innovation in the civilian sector' (Erich Bloch, Director, National Science Foundation, in his testimony before the US Congressional subcommittee on Science, Technology and Space, US Government Printing Office, Washington DC, 1989).

A degree of disillusionment with the efficacy of military R&D for civilian economic success has obviously set in. The old argument that the immediate purpose of R&D is less important than the fact that it is carried out at a sufficient level, seems to have lost much of its power of conviction. The great success of Japan, with very small military R&D and highly purposefully directed civilian R&D programmes, has dented the faith in military R&D as a vehicle for civilian technological innovation and economic success. Even the development of microelectronics owes less to direct military involvement than to civilian aims, though aided and abetted by military purchases and requirements.

The following two tables give some quantitative information on R&D expenditure in recent years. Table 3.1 shows government R&D expenditure by socio-economic objective in various countries for the two years 1985 and 1989. Table 3.2 shows total R&D expenditure, both public and commercial, as a percentage of GDP in various countries.

While the prime interest of governments is directed towards economic strength, economic growth and competitiveness, problems of the natural environment are seen by many as a brake on all these aspirations. Hence a considerable amount of effort is being put into finding ways around the apparent natural limits to economic growth, and matters such as environmentally benign technology and sustainable growth appear high on the list of priorities of some countries. Motivation for supporting environmental research and environmental technologies is mixed: genuine concern about a possibly intolerable deterioration of the natural environment, coupled with the desire not to let this concern interfere with economic growth, and the hope of developing new markets in equipment and services for environmental protection. As an example of growing government expenditure, the German Federal government spent DM 632 million on environmental and climate research in 1987, while in 1990 it spent about DM 930 million (BMFT Faktenbericht, Bonn, 1990: 116).

European thinking on problems of economic development to combat unemployment has recently been summarized in a White Paper issued by the European Commission (European Commission 1994). The White Paper is based on inputs provided by governments of the member states, and these inputs were published separately as part C of the White Paper (Commission of the European Communities 1993).

Most of the inputs are concerned with macro-economic policies and do not say very much about technology. The British contribution, for example, provided by the Department of Employment, essentially amounts to a treatise on liberal political economy and the German contribution is not very different, although it mentions briefly the environment, telecommunications and transport. The Danish contribution makes, from our point of view, more interesting reading. The Danish government suggests that taxation should be shifted from labour to, among other things, 'green' taxes. It also sug-

Table 3.1 Government R&D expenditure on selected socio-economic objectives by selected countries in million 1985 US$

	Socio-Economic Objective							
	Industrial Development		Infrastructure		Environmental Protection		Health	
	1985	1989	1985	1989	1985	1989	1985	1989
US	114.0	112.9	1080.0	1002.2	258.0	291.2	5611.0	7032.3
UK	766.9	709.8	95.3	104.1	94.1	92.2	287.2	368.3
Norway	58.8	83.7	25.2	37.8	10.7	15.4	28.7	31.7
Greece	11.6	23.7	0.7	1.4	5.2	5.5	11.3	14.5
FRG	1200.2	1097.7	162.9	171.9	267.0	288.8	257.1	267.0
France	1126.7	1324.6	288.9	84.1	44.0	71.1	368.7	330.4
Finland	104.7	137.6	8.5	12.1	5.6	8.3	7.6	9.9
Austria	34.7	40.6	5.4	7.5	3.9	7.1	6.4	8.2

	Earth and Atmosphere		Defence		Knowledge		Total R&D	
	1985	1989	1985	1989	1985	1989	1985	1989
US	568.0	555.5	33698.0	35792.2	1862.0	2089.8	49887.0	54702.7
UK	136.5	192.5	4113.8	3445.8	1502.5	1433.0	8061.3	7290.4
Norway	9.3	11.5	44.7	38.8	171.5	224.6	442.3	569.5
Greece	8.2	10.7	4.4	3.4	51.6	61.7	150.0	182.4
FRG	179.5	188.3	1012.5	1131.7	3634.3	3890.1	8487.0	8488.1
France	136.2	163.0	3077.5	3698.7	2442.6	2705.2	9455.2	9990.1
Finland	23.1	25.9	6.7	7.8	137.5	178.5	380.7	487.5
Austria	5.0	4.8	0.1	0.3	363.2	393.7	454.2	499.0

Source: OECD statistics

Table 3.2 *Expenditure on R&D performed in the business enterprise sector (GERD=Gross Domestic Expenditure on R&D); Funding of GERD by industry and by government*

	% of GDP		% of GERD		Ind	Govt
	1981	1989	1981	1989	1989	1989
USA	1.72	1.98	70.3	70.2	49.6	48.3
Japan	1.41	2.12	66.0	74.3	72.3	18.6
Germany	1.70	2.10	70.2	73.0	65.1	32.8
France	1.16	1.40	58.9	60.3	43.9	48.1
UK	1.49	1.37	61.8	66.6	50.4	36.5
Netherlands	1.00	1.32	53.3	60.0	53.4	42.7
Sweden	1.46	1.83	63.7	66.2	n/a	n/a

Source: OECD 1992, *Technology and the Economy*, OECD, Paris: 31

gests old Keynesian remedies for stagnation – ie, public investment into infrastructural projects. It further advocates that all member governments ought to meet the UN target of using 1 per cent of GNP for development aid. An important part of the Danish contribution deals with the environment:

> *Increased integration of environmental considerations in all Community policies is of decisive importance to a sustainable development of the Community (loc cit: 90). Furthermore, the Community should strengthen its programmes developing new capital equipment which is able to produce environmentally benign products. These products could solve environmental problems in the Community and at the same time become an export commodity for the Community (loc cit: 91).*

The Danish paper lauds the fact that the new Structural Funds Regulations, covering the period 1994–99, include stipulations for environmental impact assessment on proposed projects and urges that the environmental goals of these funds should be respected.

The White Paper itself (European Commission 1994), pays considerable attention to several technologies. Pride of place is given to information technology and the information society.

> *The dawning of a multimedia world (sound – text – image) represents a radical change comparable with the first industrial revolution;...It can provide an answer to the new needs of European societies: communication networks within companies; widespread teleworking; widespread access to scientific and leisure databases; development of preventive health care and home medicine for the elderly (loc cit: 13).*

The first of these statements is a matter of opinion. The second expresses hopes that IT will provide solutions to several problems, such as increasing opportunities for action by reducing information bottlenecks; easing of traffic congestion in urban areas and providing employment opportunities in rural areas by teleworking; reducing the cost of medical care, especially for the elderly, by providing medical advice over telecommunications networks. Teletraining and telemedicine are two examples of the principle that advanced telecommunications can put into practice: do not bring the experts to the problem, bring the problem to the experts.

The White Paper also foresees an enormous upswing in entertainment: 'by the end of the century there will be 10 times as many TV channels...' (loc cit: 13)

The total investment required between 1994 and 1995 to achieve the desired information highways and their applications is estimated at 67 billion ECU. Of this, 20 billion will be needed to establish high-speed communication networks, 15 billion to consolidate the integrated services digital network, 1 billion to develop electronic access to information, 1 billion to develop electronic mail, 10 billion to develop electronic images and interactive video services, 3 billion for teleworking, 7 billion for links between administrations, 3 billion for teletraining and 7 billion for telemedicine (loc cit: 27). The investment required to the year 2000 is estimated at 150 billion ECU, but most of the capital should come from private sources. The Community is planning to spend only about 5 billion, and individual governments are not expected to provide more than some pump-priming and R&D support.

The development of transport and energy networks will swallow even larger amounts of capital; the estimate is 250 billion ECU by the year 2000. The Commission has agreed on 25 transport projects and 10 energy projects as priority developments for the next five years. The Commission itself plays mainly a coordinating role, although it also contributes 5.3 billion ECU annually from its own budget. The Community offers loan guarantees, interest rate subsidies and supports feasibility studies. Further loan finance will be provided by the European Investment Fund, and some special bonds will be issued to raise further capital. It is generally accepted that such major capital projects are 'a key factor in the economic recovery of Europe', but their main aim is to improve the European infrastructure. Fortunately, the transport development will include a good deal of high-speed railway links, although it will also include further road development. Examples of projects are a rail link over the Brenner pass between Austria and Italy, which will serve traffic from north-western to southern Europe. An interesting example is a planned motorway link from Berlin to Warsaw and Moscow. This is an attempt to improve access and trade between the Community and the former Eastern bloc. Energy projects are mainly concerned with interconnecting existing networks in an attempt to utilize better existing generating capacities, and with building further gas pipelines, anticipating that the whole of Europe will be supplied from the North Sea, Algeria and Russia.

What the White Paper refers to as environmental projects is mainly concerned with waste water treatment plants and the renovation of water-supply distribution systems. The estimated cost of these projects to the year 2000 is 174 billion ECU.

The White Paper has to much say on the support required by industry to increase its competitiveness.

> 'Four overriding objectives must be pursued jointly by industry and the authorities:...
> ■ Helping European firms to adapt to the new globalized and interdependent competitive situation.
> ■ Exploiting the competitive advantages associated with the gradual shift to a knowledge-based economy.
> ■ Promoting a sustainable development of industry.
> ■ Reducing the time-lag between the pace of change in supply and the corresponding adjustments in demand.'

It is not easy to know what these sentences mean, but my interpretation is that:

1. Global competition is now so severe that industry needs all the help it can get to survive;
2. Those who use IT more quickly and more extensively will gain competitive advantage over laggards;
3. This might mean that industry ought to think about the long term, including considerations of environmental impacts and the use of natural resources;
4. Demand had better hurry up to decide that it needs what industry wishes to supply!

The Community identifies, and wishes to redress, the following weaknesses of European industry:

1. The trade performance. European exports now exceed imports only by a few per cent, whereas in the early Eighties there was a surplus of 30–40 per cent.
2. European 'performance deteriorated on markets with high value-added, such as office automation, information technology, electronics, and medical and surgical equipment' (loc cit: 73).
3. Investment in R&D has grown more slowly than in Japan, and that from a lower level. In 1991 total spending on RTD (Research and Technological Development, a new synonym for R&D) averaged 2 per cent of GDP in the Community, 2.8 per cent in the USA, and 3 per cent in Japan. This is 302 ECU per inhabitant in Europe, 493 ECU in the US, and 627 ECU in Japan!

The share of investment, as a percentage of GDP, is also much lower in Europe than it is in Japan, as is the share of researchers and engineers in the workforce.

The White Paper briefly discusses the relationship between growth and employment. At one point it echoes arguments put forward in this book:

> *It is nevertheless the case that we are once again passing*
> *through a period in which a gap is opening up between the*
> *speed of technical progress, which is concerned primarily*
> *with how to produce... and which therefore often destroys*
> *jobs, and our capacity to think up new individual or*
> *collective needs which would provide new job opportunities*
> (loc cit: 11).

And we all thought that innovation occurs only in response to needs!

Apparently, the labour intensity of growth is much higher in the USA than in Europe. The White Paper argues that a higher labour intensity of growth can be achieved only by lowering the cost of unskilled labour, on the US model. It seems to me that the same effect can be achieved by finding new forms of financing for socially desirable and needed work, which at present is left undone because of lack of finance. And perhaps a higher employment density of growth might be achieved by lowering the cost of professional labour?

The White Paper bemoans the fact that R&D projects are not sufficiently coordinated. This is a recurring worry: if only we could coordinate, cooperate and disseminate information better, then the existing effort could be so much more productive. Another recurring theme in a similar vein is the lack of coordination between industry and academic research institutions. It is thought that this is to blame for a 'comparatively limited capacity to convert scientific breakthroughs and technological achievements into industrial and commercial success' (loc cit: 102).

A factor which seems to be much more to the point than the allegedly weak link between academe and industry is 'the lack of risk capital to help firms through the development phase and the reluctance of private-sector financiers to invest in activities if they consider the risks too great or the return too uncertain' (loc cit: 102).

The remedies sought, apart from the usual wish for better coordination, for more support for small and medium enterprises, and for higher R&D expenditure, are: the desire for an expansion into new trading areas, including the countries of Eastern and Central Europe; and the desire to fulfil 'the emerging needs of society'. The new needs are to be found in the environment, health and the media. I can but applaud the first two, while expressing doubts about the last.

Environmental products and services, such as detection and monitoring equipment, improvements in conventional technologies to make them cleaner or more energy efficient, entirely new environ-mentally benign technologies, or environmental services such as water treatment, are estimated to reach an annual worldwide market value of 270 billion ECU by the year 2000.

Health care includes not only new pharmaceutical products, but also preventive and diagnostic technologies and methods 'allowing treatment in the home'. Biotechnology also receives a positive men-tion as 'offering the greatest potential for innovation and a particularly rich source of growth' (loc cit: 104).

In the media field, it is the multi-media products and related hard-ware that raise the hopes of policy-makers.

Finally, in the last chapter (loc cit: 161–67), the White Paper pre-sents some thoughts on a new development model for the Community. This model concedes that labour resources are under-used, while envi-ronmental resources are over-used. The model is remarkably close to my opinions expressed in this book. I can but hope that eventually it will become a model for action, not just for thought.

> *The new integrated technology... should result in a reduced need for new environmental resources through:*
> 1. *Improved 'nature productivity' of products: eg increased energy efficiency, less raw material-intensive products (lighter cars, etc);*
> 2. *A longer product lifetime: making repair and control services more attractive, which are labour intensive activities par excellence;*
> 3. *More reuse and recycling: use the same raw materials or spare parts far more frequently;*
> 4. *Improved process technology: the production processes (and not the final consumers) generate the largest quantities of waste water, solid waste, etc.*

It is argued, undoubtedly correctly, that implementing such technolo-gies will bring many primary and secondary benefits. Not only will it save resources in the Community itself, but these technologies will create large export markets. Indeed, if developing countries are to develop, they will have to use this kind of technology. Environmentally sound technologies would reduce the strategic dependence of the Community on the import of energy and raw mate-rials. In the longer run, such pioneering effort at environmentally sustainable development would reduce world imbalances and lead to greater real prosperity for all.

The R&D support policies of the European Community are for-mulated in a framework programme. The Fourth European Community Framework Programme for Research, Technological Development and Demonstration Activities, for the period 1994–8, was produced by the Commission for Council Decisions in March

1994 (CEC, 1994). There are four areas of activity. The first, which is of most concern to us, is support for a variety of technologies:

1. Information and communication technologies – ie telematics, communications technologies and information technologies; industrial technologies – ie industrial technologies and materials technologies, and standardization, measurement and testing; environment – ie environment and climate, and marine sciences and technologies; life sciences and technologies – ie biotechnology, biomedicine and health, and agriculture and fisheries; non-nuclear energy (nuclear energy is an entirely separate programme); transport; targeted socio-economic research.
   The other three areas of activity are:
2. Cooperation with third countries and international organizations.
3. Dissemination and exploitation of results.
4. Stimulation of the training and mobility of researchers.

It would be unhelpful to try to summarize a lengthy document, instead we shall try to indicate the main lines of thought in just two parts of the programme: industrial and materials technologies, and the environment and climate.

The objectives of the industrial and materials programme are to boost industrial competitiveness by means of R&D as a major factor

> in stimulating innovation in respect of products, processes
> and business organization, and underpinning and prompting
> new industrial activities which will ease the transition from
> traditional sectors to new, emerging sectors... (loc cit: 129).

The programme aims to improve production systems to enhance competitiveness, but it does address concerns such as working conditions, clean technologies and rational use of resources. Further aims are research into new techniques for the design and preparation for new products; and research into transport technologies, especially aeronautical engineering.

In the area of materials, the programme restates their importance for all technological development and aims to improve their performance in traditional and advanced applications. In addition, however, it aims to undertake

> multidisciplinary research into materials aimed at enabling
> natural materials to be used cost-effectively in industrial
> products, at eliminating harmful substances, at increasing
> their suitability for recycling and at predicting the effects of
> repeated recycling on the structural and functional
> characteristics of materials (loc cit: 137).

The programme does offer financial support, normally on a 50 per cent share basis, for R&D projects within its objectives, but it will also attempt to target help for SMEs and to bring together interested parties. Overall, the programme mainly uses direct financial support for R&D, but information and coordination activities form no small part of the effort. The total cost is estimated at 1,623 million ECU.

The research programme on the natural environment will cost 532 million ECU. It will cover the following areas of enquiry:

1. Climate change and impact on natural resources; atmosphere physics and chemistry and biosphere processes and consequences; human dimension of environmental change.
2. Sustainable development and technological change; instruments, techniques and methods for monitoring the environment; technologies and methods to protect the environment; technologies to forecast, prevent and reduce natural risks.
3. Space techniques applied to environmental monitoring and research. (This is a highly laudable and comprehensive R&D programme in a vital area, but the sums of money allocated to it do not appear to reflect its importance.)

Should Government Support Technological Innovation?

Three questions arise:

1. Should governments support technological innovation at taxpayers' expense?
2. If the answer is yes, what targets and what measures are legitimate and desirable?
3. Are government support measures effective, irrespective of whether they are desirable or otherwise?

In simpler words: what, if anything, should and can governments effectively do in support of technological innovation?

We shall take the three questions in turn and attempt to answer them as well as their complexity allows. As this book argues that technological innovation generally proceeds too fast for the common good, it could be argued that governments should keep out of this matter, except to safeguard those public interests that the market cannot safeguard.

Public intervention in the economic affairs of a capitalist society can be justified on several counts:

1. to correct malfunctions of the market;
2. to safeguard the interests of the economically and/or socially weak and redress injustice;
3. to safeguard public and private interests which the market fails to

address – eg to protect the natural environment;
4. to provide, or assure and control the provision of, infrastructure – eg transport, communications, public health, sewers, garbage collection, water, electricity;
5. to safeguard the public against malpractices in business and in the provision of goods and services;
6. to set the general framework and conditions under which the economy can best operate to the benefit of the community.

The above list may not be exhaustive and may betray a personal bias in favour of the natural environment and of social justice and against 'sharks' of every description, but is nevertheless close to a fairly widespread consensus. The list omits other roles of the state and concentrates merely on economic activity. Each heading covers a multitude of sins and is open to a range of interpretations. I shall concentrate on technological innovation and interpret the above list solely from this point of view.

The prize question is whether the market can cope adequately with issues of technological innovation. My answer to this question is yes, provided we are dealing with innovation in commercial goods and processes. The market, however, is unable to cope adequately with many aspects of innovation in the public interest.

No government support is required if and when the results of technological innovations can be appropriated – ie the innovator can reap economic benefit from his/her investment in the innovation. It is the task of government to ensure that this is the case – ie it must provide adequate protection for intellectual property and take effective measures against industrial espionage and other criminal activities which might deprive innovators of the fruits of their labour. Leaving aside the possible need for the control of a new technology, government intervention is justified only if, in principle, innovators cannot reap profits from their investment, or are insufficiently motivated by potential profit to provide socially desirable innovations. It may be argued that governments must support basic research that benefits the community at large, whereas specific R&D aimed at a specific commercial innovation is the responsibility of the innovator. On the other hand, governments must support innovations that are in the public interest, yet have little or no chance of being pursued for commercial gain. The main examples for this situation are to be found in environmental protection. If there is no market failure, then there is no call for public intervention in favour of innovation. When the market does not operate, government must step in to safeguard the public interest.

At a deeper level, both the list of government duties and the arguments against intervention are about the purpose of the state and the welfare of society. If I were convinced that the welfare of society demands a rate of innovation that is unobtainable from the activities of market-driven enterprises, I would have invented a category of government duties 'to safeguard a rate of technological innovation commensurate with maximum benefit to society'. The fact that my 'book of government duties' includes no such category shows that I believe that commercial enterprise (irrespective of whether government does or does not hold shares in it) can produce technological innovations at a rate which is fast enough, or even too fast, for the public good, and any attempt by government to accelerate this rate would be detrimental to the public interest.

So far, we have dodged the question of whether or not governments should be involved in the support of 'generic technology' in our classification of target areas of support. The answer is a qualified 'yes'. Generally, governments should become involved in the support of technology if one or more of the following reasons prevail:

1. The technology is required as a general technical infrastructure – eg such things as transport and communication systems, sewage and waste disposal, the provision of water of suitable quality, and the supply of electricity or other energy. It is the responsibility of government either to provide the infrastructure or to see to it that it is provided by private enterprise under equitable and appropriate terms and conditions. If the utilities are run as private monopolies, then there is no reason whatsoever for government to invest in their innovations. It may, however, be necessary to control their technologies in the interest of safeguarding both the environment and the consumer.

2. Government requires the technology for one or another of the services it provides, directly or through some agency – eg for the armed forces, the police, emergency services, education, public health and other health services. Last, but not least, the essential functions of administration may, and do, require a great deal of technology which government at various levels needs to procure. Procurement at this level often requires more than simple purchase; indeed, it may require R&D to be undertaken and, on occasion, production of the necessary items in order to remain in the forefront of developments and to get reasonable deals from private enterprise.

3. The technology is of a universal character; its general spread throughout the economy is regarded as essential, yet private effort is unable to provide the necessary general facilities because the fruits of such efforts give public, but not direct private benefit. In other words, if some effort is required which does not yield benefits that can be privately appropriated, yet is of advantage to the community at large, then governments need to provide the required support. This statement may be too general to provide much guidance, but it is necessary to go back to fundamental principles on the role of government before deciding on each individual case.

A typical case in point is information technology in its various forms, and particularly in its early days. It was then thought, as indeed it is thought today, that information technology is a key technology which needs to spread as fast as possible throughout the economy in order to guarantee the economy's ability to compete in international markets. It was also thought that information technology has a large contribution to make to the enhancement of productivity, and hence could become a major contributor to the creation of additional wealth. Although even in the early days doubts were raised about the effects of information technology upon employment and upon some aspects of social well-being, the prevailing opinion was that information technology must be embraced, as the disadvantages of not doing so far outweighed the disadvantages the technology might bring in its wake.

Several obstacles to the rapid spread of information technology (at that time it was still called microelectronics) were seen in the Seventies. First and foremost, very few people knew anything about the technology and many did not even realize that it existed, let alone that it might be of any concern to them. Rightly or wrongly, it was thought that the awareness of this technology needed to be enhanced and the British government, in common with many other governments, started an awareness programme. The British programme attempted not so much to inform the general public as to inform industrial managers, to get them to consider the possibility of using the new technology in their firms and of developing products incorporating this technology.

Information technology is deemed a key technology because it can be used to enhance performance in a wide range of products, processes and services. The awareness programme went beyond providing information and offered financial and other help in obtaining consultancy services for individual firms in order to establish the feasibility of using the new microelectronics. If my view on the role of government in the support of technology is correct, then the provision of information and the attempt to get this information to those who need it is undoubtedly a task appropriate to government. Whether support for consultancy services provided to individual firms for their private benefit is a legitimate role for government, must be doubted.

Another legitimate task for government, which was also catered for to some extent in the British awareness programme, is the provision of training courses at all educational levels. A new technology that is deemed important needs new training facilities that cannot be provided by private firms but fall under the general educational responsibility of government. The reason is simple: a pool of new skills needs to be created which will benefit all firms and the country at large, rather than a particular firm.

A new technology also needs new research facilities, although only some aspects of research should be the government's responsibility. If a firm wishes to produce new products or processes from which it hopes to reap commercial benefits, such research must be its own responsibility. On the other hand, much research is not oriented directly towards the production of new commercially exploitable products or processes, but is inspired by curiosity and underpins technology only in the sense of replenishing a general pool of knowledge. The difficulties of deciding what is or is not a research responsibility for government should neither serve as an excuse for the wholesale support of private industrial R&D, nor as an excuse for curtailing government-sponsored R&D activities.

4. Innovation is required in the public interest, but cannot be secured by commercial activities because of market failures. A typical case in point is innovation for the protection of the natural environment, or innovation in the interests of health or safety. There is no commercial incentive to produce, say, a better filter for sulphur dioxide unless the government either supports the development, or imposes strict regulations that must be met by commercial firms. In practice, a subtle blend of regulation and support for socially desirable innovation will lead to the best results.

5. The setting of standards in technology may not fall exactly into the category of supportive measures for innovation, but governments must certainly oversee the setting of standards and arbitrate in national and international disputes over standards. Standards play an extremely important role in the development of technology, because standards ensure both the safe operation and the compatibility of technologies. To standardize too early in the life of a technology may freeze in undesirable properties, yet to standardize too late may cause unnecessary duplication of development effort and unwise purchases by many early users of the technology. The setting of standards is subject to fierce national and international battles, as the firm that develops a technology which eventually becomes the industrial standard has great advantages over firms that have to abandon their early designs and follow the leader.

Government Support for Research

The classification of types of research has a long academic history and has never been fully successful in separating different R&D activities into watertight compartments. Without wishing to enter into an exhaustive discussion of this topic, we shall attempt to classify sufficiently for our needs.

The first category is fundamental research, although terms such as 'basic' or 'curiosity-oriented' are sometimes used to denote the same activity. What we mean is research into natural phenomena which is driven essentially by the wish to know, although quite often researchers, and their sponsors, have the possibility of a practical pay-off in mind. A typical current example is high-energy particle physics. In this branch of physics scientists are attempting to find the inner-most and most basic structure of matter, with no real hope of ever producing anything that will be of practical utility, rather than merely satisfying the human wish to know and comprehend all aspects of the world we live in. Basic research is the responsibility of government, as there is no direct commercial beneficiary and this type of research merely satisfies a human need that may be classified under the heading of Culture. If we define Culture as meaning the soaring of the human spirit, the striving after an understanding of ourselves and the world we live in, the expression of our essential humanity, then science surely is a prime cultural activity. Basic research is a cultural activity which attempts to broaden our understanding and knowledge of the world, without any commercial objective and, generally, without results that can be commercially exploited. That the support of such research is a public responsibility is not questioned, although many painful questions must be asked about the total level of support and about the selection of individual projects or disciplines.

In addition to support by governments, there is some philanthropic support for pure science. Some philanthropists believe that scientific research is an activity of high intrinsic value, whether for the sake of knowledge, or for the sake of upholding the values of rational thought and objective evidence, or for the sake of ultimate benefit in medicine or technology.

Our desperate striving for ever-faster technological change is stripping science of some of its cultural meaning. Basic science has often proved to be of some utility to technology, and if the edifice of science is regarded as a whole, this whole is seen as an indispensable ingredient of technological innovation. Hence, basic science is being stripped of its cultural values, and terms such as 'goal-oriented basic science' are being invented to replace the cultural value by a utilitarian value. It is no longer regarded as valuable to indulge in curiosity or in knowledge for its own sake; we may only indulge in basic science if and when it serves utilitarian goals. There are still a few sacred cows being tolerated and fed, such as high-energy physics, although it is claimed frequently that the sophisticated machines produced for such research may improve our technological prowess in general and lead to commercial success. Most research fields, however, and almost all individual research projects, must now show that somehow they help to create technological innovations. To say that a project is interesting, that it tries to fill a gap in our knowledge, cuts no ice with hard-pressed funding bodies. What they want to hear is that the project is of direct interest to industry and that it will help to create successful new technologies. The modern view regards basic research as good, but basic research that eventually proves useful as better.

Goal-oriented basic research is a relatively new concept which arises out of the recognition that too narrow a definition of research goals leads to ultimate sterility. It is necessary to search fairly widely and deeply in order to come up with truly new ideas or original solutions to problems. Goal-oriented basic research is research aimed at producing technological innovation, but recognizes that too narrow a definition of goals stifles creativity, forecloses avenues of enquiry, and deprives research of many potentially fruitful results.

Should governments support this type of research? The answer must depend upon the goal. If the goal is one regarded as desirable for society as a whole, then basic research that aims to achieve this goal in the long term must be supported by society. If the goal is merely the achievement of a new product by a firm – the invention of a better mousetrap – then clearly the goal is the firm's goal and research aimed at achieving it must be financed by the firm. This is as far as one can go in general terms, except to add that to answer the question whether or not a goal is of general desirability for society is a political question that can only be answered by political processes. The desirability of goals depends upon systems of values and, hence, consensus or broad agreement can only be reached by debate, compromise and other political methods for the finding of acceptable solutions to questions on which differences of opinion prevail.

Goals associated with improvements in the natural environment, in health, safety, security, public order and so on, can easily be recognized as desirable for society as a whole, although some dissent on detailed aims and on the acceptability of some solutions or preferences for different approaches do occur. We are all against sin, although what is sinful is not quite so readily agreed upon now that the Church no longer holds the monopoly of jurisdiction on such issues.

When the goal of goal-oriented basic research is an improvement in the infrastructure of the state, yet the infrastructure is owned and operated by private companies, does the state have the duty, or the right, to invest in such research? The immediate benefits will accrue to the private company, yet, because the quality of the infrastructure is at stake, the general public is also a potential beneficiary. There is no clear general answer to this question, as all depends on details of circumstance. All that can be said at the general level, without becoming too abstract and convoluted, is that private companies must weigh up the risks and costs of research against potential benefits to them. Governments, on the other hand, must weigh the risks and costs of research against the benefits likely to accrue to society at large. In any individual instance, a solution to who bears the cost of R&D must be sought on the basis of such considerations. Unfortunately, neither the likely gains nor the probable costs or risks can be assessed with any accuracy and decisions must be taken on the best evidence, advice and analysis available and must be subject to continuous review as circumstances change and the action unfolds.

The next category of R&D is applied research. It is distinguished from goal-oriented basic research by its proximity to a technical realization. If the goal of the research is very close at hand, a technical device aimed at near achievement, then we call the research applied. If the technical device is merely a possibility, a distant aim, somewhat vague in shape, and the research seeks to establish new principles or fundamental properties that need to be known or understood for the realization of the technical ambition, then we speak of goal-oriented basic research. Clearly, these definitions are somewhat vague and many R&D projects could fall into either category. Indeed, how projects are classified is, to some degree, arbitrary and depends on tactical considerations. If it is thought that the funding body might prefer one category to another, a project can be slanted that way without changing its substance. The vagaries of research are such that no project runs exactly as described in the application for funds; thus, slanting it in accordance with the wishes of the potential financial supporters need not change the actual work significantly.

We need to ask again whether governments should fund applied research. The answer here must be as that given in the discussion of support for innovation in general. Applied research is close enough to actual technological innovation to be subject to the same criteria for government support: if the innovation is commercially driven, let commerce bear the costs and the risks, and reap the benefits. If the innovation is in the public interest but cannot be supported by market forces, let government bear the costs and the risks, and the public reap the benefits.

Finally, the last stages of the R&D process will be described. This consists of development and preparation for manufacture. At this stage, new knowledge is not gathered; the task is to obtain a workable product with the right properties at the right price. Price will depend, among other things, upon the manufacturing process, and this often has to be developed alongside the product.

Despite the neat enumeration and classification of R&D into different stages which form, to some extent, a temporal sequence, there are many overlaps of activities. Even when a project is at the stage of development it may be necessary to delve into basic unresolved scientific questions; and while goal-oriented basic research is still in full swing, actual prototypes and designs of products, based on present knowledge, may be produced and, possibly, even marketed. The activity of technological innovation is not neatly sequential; it is a rather messy conglomerate of parallel activities, always on the look-out for new opportunities.

In my view, governments should not support the final stages in the development and marketing of new products, unless these products form part of their own procurement activities and are being developed to fulfil government or public needs that market forces do not support.

Measures for the Control of Technology

Advocates of free markets claim that any control of technology imposes additional costs and retards technological innovation to the detriment of the countries with the strictest controls. Protagonists of controls claim not only that they are unavoidable, but also that suitably formulated controls create new markets – eg for anti-pollution equipment. Despite fierce controversies about the regulation of technology, all governments see themselves forced to adopt some regulatory measures. (For a fuller discussion of the dilemma faced by governments, torn between their wish to support technology and the need to regulate it, see Braun: 95–124, in Aichholzer and Schienstock 1994; and Braun and Wield 1994).

The old rule of 'buyer beware' is no adequate safeguard for consumers of sophisticated and complex products of modern technology. A rule of conduct that is adequate for the consumer of simple goods and possibly even for buyers of horses, cannot suffice for the purchaser of products that are too intricate and complex to be subject to anything like an exhaustive and revealing inspection by lay persons. Thus certain rules are needed to guarantee to the consumer that products are indeed fit for their purpose and that they perform as specified. The market alone cannot protect the consumer, as it forms its judgements but slowly and retrospectively, and the cost of learning about a product's quality or fitness for purpose by individual consumers would be very high.

Fitness for purpose implies minimum standards of quality and of safety, as well as social fitness, meaning the minimum interference by any user of a technology with others. Thus certain electrical equipment must be shielded in order not to interfere with radio and television reception; headlights on motor cars must comply with certain standards, including the capability of being dipped; the use of electromagnetic waves is strictly controlled. If unbridled competition were allowed, nobody could use electromagnetic waves for the transmission of information because each message would be likely to interfere with any other message, thus leading to a breakdown of the system. Only by allocating specific wavebands and making very clear rules, is it possible to use electromagnetic waves for broadcasting, for public telecommunications, and for communications of the emergency services or radio-controlled taxis.

Telecommunications, even without electromagnetic transmission, has traditionally been subject to regulation for a number of compelling reasons. First and foremost, to ensure that every subscriber could reach every other subscriber; secondly to ensure that privacy is safeguarded; and thirdly, for reasons of social equity. Some of the regulation can and has been achieved by voluntary arrangements within the telecommunications industry, although not without some involvement by government. Other social objectives, such as social equity, which requires that every subscriber, irrespective of location or intensity of the use of the facility, should have the right of access to a telephone at a reasonable and affordable price, were achieved largely by government regulation.

As consumers cannot protect themselves against possible hazards posed by the use of certain technologies, they need to be protected by the government or its agents. Cars are a good example, although even the most up-to-date regulation cannot protect people from their own folly. Electrical appliances must be designed to avoid electrocuting their users, and certain garments must not be made from easily flammable materials. Without regulations for the construction of furniture upholstery, consumers could not possibly know whether their new expensive furniture could be easily ignited and might then give off lethal fumes. Indeed, even furniture manufacturers did not initially know, and it took a number of fatal accidents before regulations were formulated to protect consumers from this particular hazard. The rapid pace of change makes it impossible for users of new materials to be adequately acquainted with their properties. Some products cannot be made entirely safe without losing their effect – eg paint-brush cleaners or weedkillers. In this case there are regulations to make the products as safe as is consistent with their efficacy, and for labelling the materials adequately to warn users of residual dangers.

Similar regulations are provided in the work environment. Every country has some act laying down the ground rules, and every country has something like a factory inspectorate which enforces the rules. Essentially, these rules make sure that machinery used in production, or even in offices, is as safe as it can be and that production processes do not pose avoidable hazards.

A class of regulations somewhat similar to those related to safety, are those designed to safeguard the health of the users of products – eg the use of lead as a component of paint or as an additive to petrol is controlled. Small quantities of lead in paint are unlikely to lead to fatal accidents, but there is a certain danger that the health of consumers, particularly that of small children, may be impaired. Thus the use of lead in paint has been severely restricted. Similarly, lead in car exhausts is considered a health hazard, and the use of lead as an additive to petrol is gradually being eliminated, largely owing to government action. For the same reason, the use of certain types of asbestos has been banned because the inhalation of some asbestos fibres poses a severe risk to health. As new hazards to health gradually come to light, so new regulations have to be introduced.

A major class of products which is strictly regulated for reasons of hazards to health are pharmaceuticals. As drugs used to cure disease are potential causes of disease, an elaborate machinery to test the safety of drugs and a system of licensing them has been established. Some say that the system is inadequate, as now and again a previously undetected hazard comes to light after a drug had been in use for some time. Others say that the system is too severe and has crippled the innovative potential of pharmaceutical companies because it takes too long and costs too much to get a new drug approved.

The regulation of technology is controversial. The argument is partly about freedom, partly about the efficacy of markets, and partly about the costs and benefits of regulation.

The first argument cannot be resolved, as it touches upon fundamental beliefs that are largely unaffected by rational argument. Although universal agreement might be reached that

> ...there is a large range of such activity where the larger interest – the more general liberty – requires control (and it will certainly always be imperfect control) over the lesser and more specific interest. ...a distinction between wise regulation and unwise regulation must be made (Galbraith: 8–9, in Siegan 1980).

Regarding the costs of compliance with regulation, no universal agreement appears to be in sight either. A recent summary of existing studies comes to the conclusion that

> ...existing studies shed little light on the dispute between those who hold that regulation benefits the regulated and those who hold that regulation is of necessity a burden on those who are regulated (Peacock 1984: 39).

In the absence of hard evidence to the contrary, and with the essential proviso that regulation must be wise, it seems that the arguments in support of a regulative role for technology policy, taken together with historical evidence of the disastrous effects of laissez faire in matters technological, provide a watertight case in favour of a modicum of regulation. The crucial questions of when, how and how much to regulate cannot be answered in a generally helpful way and have to be resolved from case to case and from issue to issue.

Regulation rests upon three pillars:

1. Laws, statutes and by-laws – ie legislation passed by appropriate legislative authorities. The laws themselves can specify regulatory detail, but generally they set the framework for executive authorities to issue specific orders and to make detailed arrangements.

2. Orders specifying details of regulations within the given legal framework. The details flesh out the skeleton provided by legislation and specify actions to be taken in specific cases. The orders are issued by the authorities specified as competent in the relevant laws – eg ministries, local authorities or other statutory bodies.
3. The final pillar consists of the various enforcement agencies. Although the last resort of enforcement and arbitration are the courts, the all-important day-to-day enforcement and detailed supervision rest with regulatory agencies. The institutions created for regulatory supervision are at least as important as the legal framework in which they operate.

Detailed arrangements clearly differ from country to country and from technology to technology. No detailed account can be given here, especially as the matter is further complicated by the fact that some regulatory functions are fulfilled by supra-national organizations, such as the European Community.

A variety of enforcement agencies are set up under either primary or secondary legislation. Many of these agencies operate under approved codes of practice which do not have the force of law, but constitute an important instrument setting down methods by which regulation is enacted in practice. An example of such an agency in the UK is the Health and Safety Executive, which operates under the Health and Safety at Work Act. The Executive controls the work of an inspectorate, which has comprehensive powers. Two further examples are the Office of Telecommunications (OFTEL), which regulates the deregulated telecommunications industry; and the Office of Water Services (OFWAT), which regulates the privatized water and sewage services. The last two do not so much regulate technology as the commercial framework in which these technologies operate.

In many cases of the regulation of technology – eg in the case of road traffic – there is no specific statutory body enforcing legislation and enforcement is in the hands of the general law enforcement agencies – ie the police and the courts.

Technology policy has been described as a separate and distinct activity of government at various levels. We must ask whether the formation of good technology policy requires the use of specific and distinct information inputs. The instrument suggested for this purpose is known as technology assessment.

Technology Assessment as an Input to the Formation of Technology Policy

What is technology assessment (TA) and in what way can it be useful in the process of formulating technology policies? The ultimate question behind this question is, of course, whether TA can help us to use technology to better advantage and with fewer undesirable consequences (for details of TA, see eg Porter et al 1980).

The founding fathers of technology assessment – people within, or close to, the United States Congress in the late Sixties and early Seventies – imagined and hoped that by equipping legislators with an interdisciplinary, all-embracing, objective and forward-looking analysis of the foreseeable and less foreseeable effects that might result from the application of a new technology, it would become possible both to control and support technology in such a way as to provide optimum utility and cause minimum damage to society. The early definitions of technology assessment used phrases such as 'identify affected parties and unanticipated impacts in as broad and long-range fashion as is possible'; 'neutral and objective'; 'total impact on our society'. But they also contained phrases such as 'Technology assessment is intended to aid our political decision-making process become more effective ... in implementing technology in such a manner as to make the maximum contribution to our society's welfare and our individual quality-of-life' (Hetman 1973: 56–7).

Technology assessment was born out of the need of policy-makers to fill a severe deficit in information on technologies under their consideration. The purpose of TA is to provide an interdisciplinary analysis of the full range of consequences which are to be expected from a technology under different circumstances, thus providing an input into the policy-making process. Technology assessment is the activity of describing, analysing and forecasting the likely effects of a technological change on all spheres of society, be it social, economic, environmental or any other.

The division of labour between technology assessors and political decision-makers was clear from the very beginning of TA. The assessor was to describe, forecast, analyse – in short, to provide interdisciplinary and well-ordered information; the decision-maker was to use this and other information to reach decisions in conformity with his or her goals and system of values.

Generally speaking, the 'assessor' consists of a team of experts with different backgrounds; it is impossible, almost by definition, for a single person to carry out an interdisciplinary assessment. The assessor is responsible for the highest possible scientific quality and integrity of the assessment, but not for the decisions taken under the influence of the assessment. Responsibility for decisions must rest firmly with the decision-maker who may, or may not, have used certain aspects of the technology assessment to reach the decision.

The early definitions of technology assessment should be viewed as statements of an ideal. It is obviously beyond human capabilities to achieve objective, all-embracing descriptions of the future impacts of a technology, let alone the effects of a miscellany of combinations of technical and non-technical developments. Objectivity, foresight, omniscience – all these are attributes which the ideal technology assessor should, and cannot, possess. Ideals are useful, however, as beacons guiding us in the desired direction, even if we know that the ultimate real achievement must remain far short of the goal. The quality of TA must be judged by the closeness of its approximation to the ideal, by the reliability of its information, and by its humility in acknowledging uncertainties and gaps in knowledge and understanding.

Technology assessment in its original meaning was, and has remained, part and parcel of the political process. In the meanwhile, however, a certain confusion of terminology has occurred. The term 'applied TA' is sometimes used to describe assessments meant to be used as an aid to decision-making, while studies on the mechanisms of the interaction between science, technology and society, as well as studies in abstract methodologies which might prove useful to TA, are sometimes referred to as 'fundamental TA' (Braun: 1-10, in de Hoo et al 1987, vol 2). Similarly, certain strategic planning exercises in industry that are related to TA are often referred to as industrial technology assessment (Braun 1987; Paul 1987). There are, however, fundamental differences between industrial and public domain TA and we are concentrating mostly on applied technology assessment in the public domain – ie as a source of information in the formulation of public policies, although some of our conclusions are transferable to TA performed in or for industry.

Technology policy may deal with either the support or control of a new technology or new application of a technology – ie with technological innovation; or it may deal with an attempt to solve some societal problem by technological means. Although the two aspects appear very different at first sight, as far as the need for information, and hence technology assessment, is concerned, the differences are not so very great. Indeed, TA must adapt its methods to each individual task and the differences between technologies are at least as great as the difference between technology-oriented and problem-oriented TA.

Technology assessment aims to supply the specific information requirements of technology policy. Each of the two main aspects of technology policy has its own need for information. In order to support technology effectively, and to know when such support is needed from the point of view of public interest, the decision-maker needs to know, as accurately and as reliably as possible:

1. The benefits which the technology, or technological solution to a problem, or new application or combination of technology or technologies, can bestow upon society, now and in the future. The beneficiaries and the extent of their benefits need to be explicitly assessed, as far as this can be foreseen and estimated.
2. Why and in what respects this particular technology (we speak of technology, bearing in mind that in fact we may be assessing a technological solution to a given problem or a new application or combination of technologies) is superior to its rivals.

3. What the full requirements for the successful introduction of the technology are likely to be. The technology may require the development of a whole gamut of complementary technologies to form a system; or it may demand new institutional arrangements, training programmes, and so on.
4. Why a policy of doing nothing would be against the public interest; in other words, why the benefits obtainable from the technology cannot be obtained by market forces alone, without public support or intervention.
5. What negative effects the technology is likely to have. The listing of negative effects and their distribution must be as detailed as that of the benefits, although the question of what is positive and what is negative may often remain open. Whether the disadvantages do or do not outweigh the benefits is clearly a matter of political value judgements, which cannot be provided by TA.
6. What policy measures are available for the support of the technology and what are their likely costs, efficiency, efficacy and acceptance.
7. Finally, the politician needs to know what the various interested parties think, what interests are at stake, what public opinion is and how any policy measures might fit into the general political framework.

All this knowledge needs to be free from special pleading and advocacy so that the politician may form his or her own view. It also needs to go far beyond the obvious and the glossy sales brochures in its assessment of the true benefits now and in the future, as well as its assessment of the direct or indirect hazards and unheralded impacts and influences. Much has been made of the need to discover unexpected and indirect effects. This is, indeed, a central, albeit difficult task of TA which also falls into the category of ideal, only imperfectly achievable goals.

In order to formulate policies for the control of a technology (obviously, one and the same technology may require both support and control measures), the information requirements are, in general, similar. The decision-maker needs to know:

1. What are the hazards associated with the technology, how grave are they, and how well-founded are the fears?
2. How strong is the consensus on the undesirable nature of the effects?
3. Who are the affected, or potentially affected, parties?
4. What modifications to the technology are possible to avoid the unwanted effects?
5. What control measures are possible, how much are they likely to cost and how effective might they be?
6. What benefits does society forgo by controlling this technology in a particular way?

Obviously, all the above requirements for information as an input into technology policy are stated somewhat schematically and do not bring out the full flavour of the complexity of the issues. With this proviso, we can now turn our attention to the main issue under discussion – ie which of the above needs and expectations can technology assessment fulfil and what are the conditions for its successful application.

One of the thorny issues of TA is the expectation of objective, non-partisan, all-embracing analysis. These requirements clearly stretch human resources up, and beyond, their limit, but a competent team of assessors can achieve an acceptable approximation to these goals. Clearly, perfect objectivity is not given to humans who have beliefs and adhere to systems of values. Nevertheless, one of the tenets of faith of scientists is that they should attempt to be as objective as possible and if a diverse group of scientists conscientiously collects information and illuminates a problem from all sides, a reasonable approximation to objectivity may be achieved. In any case, the objectivity of TA should be a great deal better than that of single individuals or advocates of specific causes.

Because of the impossibility of total personal or institutional impartiality, it has been suggested that a number of TA studies on one and the same topic should be carried out in different institutions, each with its own bias. For mainly practical reasons this suggestion has fallen on barren ground. It would seem that to all but the purists the solution of having assessments done by teams of assessors, augmented by teams of advisers, seeking deliberately to incorporate as many points of view as possible and exercising as much care and impartiality as possible, provides adequate safeguards for what, when all is said and done, is only an information input into a political process.

The requirement of illuminating a problem from all sides, to be all-embracing in the treatment of an issue, is equally controversial. Not only is it impossible to consider all aspects of an issue – some may be overlooked or judged insignificant – the requirement also runs counter to traditional recipes for success, which seek clarity by concentration on the essential.

Realistic compromises can be achieved however: for one thing, financial constraints bound the subject matter to be covered, for another, time limits are imposed by political expediency and, last but not least, judgements as to what the essential features of a problem are must inevitably be made to achieve any real comprehension of the issues. The selection of the features of a problem for detailed examination is part and parcel of the study and requires a good deal of insight, iteration, discussion and judgement. There are distinctly diminishing returns on investing too much effort into too much detail.

The ultimate stumbling block on the path to achieving a perfect technology assessment is, of course, the need to look into the future. Technology assessment with hindsight can teach us a lot about the fundamentals of the relationship between technology and society; but only forward-looking technology assessment can be of any utility to decision-makers. Decisions are concerned with the future, not the past. TA invariably contains several elements of forecasting: techno-logical forecasting both for the technology under discussion and its technological rivals and complements; social, economic and political forecasting in an attempt to foresee what sort of world the technology will be interacting with; and, finally, a cross between forecasting, guessing and analysing the relationships between the new technology and the world of the future.

To say that forecasting is prone to error is not only a common-place but also an understatement. Nonetheless, it is an essential aspect of the human condition that we attempt to foresee the future in an effort to shape it. Thus forecasting must be viewed as a tool for shaping the future and as a dynamic, interactive process. Forecasts do not state what the future will be; rather they attempt to glean what it might be and what opportunities for shaping it may offer themselves.

The fact that TA uses forecasting methods as one of its tools would, by itself, suffice to warrant the correctness of the oft-repeated statement that TA is a process, to be repeated at suitable intervals, rather than a once-and-for-all activity. There are two further facets of TA which underline this statement. First, science and technology change so rapid-ly that any activity describing them in their social setting must be repeated as frequently as the dynamic nature of technology and of soci-ety demand. Secondly, the process of performing a technology assessment is not something that is done quietly by mad scientists in a back-room. For a useful TA, it is vital to obtain information from wher-ever it resides, and much of this information is not simply factual but may involve attitudes, interests, fears and hopes of all those involved in, or potentially affected by, the technology. The gathering of information involves interested parties, and thus real people. It also involves a great deal of discussion and dialogue in which the positions of the parties may shift and new light may be shed on likely patterns of future devel-opments. In this very real sense, technology assessment not only gathers information about the world, but actually shapes the world. It has been said that if all the information contained in a TA report has not diffused by the time the report is published, then the process of conducting the technology assessment was faulty. 'The journey, not the arrival, mat-ters' (Leonard Woolf, autobiography).

It is because of this interactive quality of technology assessment that the idea of 'constructive TA' has found so much resonance (see eg Leyten and Smits: 121–31, in de Hoo et al 1987, vol 2). For any interac-tion may cause change, and if the TA is carried out early enough in the life of a technology and unwanted effects are discovered, the technolo-gy may adapt to avoid these effects. If, on the other hand, the TA is carried out on a mature technology, entrenchment will have occurred and all control or adaptation may prove much more difficult. The reverse side of the coin is that the effects of a new, not fully developed and widely diffused, technology are much harder to foresee. Collingridge has called this the dilemma of control (Collingridge 1980).

If a technology assessment is to be of some practical utility to decision-makers, it must deal with a technology, or a societal problem related to technology, which, for some reason, demands the attention of the decision-maker. In other words, the questions raised must form part of the political agenda. It may be possible, of course, for TA to be part of the agenda-setting mechanisms and much use made of its function as a watchdog that provides an early warning of impending problems related to technology. The process of providing early warning is now sometimes separated from TA and institutionalized as technology monitoring, or technology foresight, although this is used mainly as an instrument of innovation support policy. Similarly, some of the early warning functions of TA in environmental matters have shifted elsewhere. Be this as it may, the fact remains that TA can be effective only if it deals with technologies or problems on the political agenda, whether it contributed to the agenda-setting or not.

Obviously, the political agenda contains a large number of very weighty problems to which both technology and TA are irrelevant. But even when technology matters, and at least partial answers as to how it might be fostered or controlled are available, these solutions may still be politically unacceptable. A good example is urban traffic congestion. We all know that more and better public transport and restrictions on the use of private cars would provide the answer, yet this knowledge brings us no nearer to a solution. Just as TA tackles problems which transcend the boundaries of any one science, so politics is confronted with problems which transcend the boundaries of informed decisions.

The first issue to be resolved in attempting any technology assessment is the choice of topic – ie which technology might be a suitable candidate for control or support and should therefore be subject to a technology assessment. The scope of the TA to be undertaken must be resolved at the same time. The preliminary issue, the zeroth question to be answered, is thus: what is to be the topic and the scope of the technology assessment?

The first part of any TA consists of a description of the technology under scrutiny, or of the technologies relevant to the solution of a problem under discussion. In addition to merely describing the technology, a description of alternative, supplementary and rival technologies must be included and some considerable thought should be given to the likely development paths of all the technologies described. Performance as well as costs are regarded as major descriptors, although forecasting the latter often proves misleading in the extreme. The descriptions should be couched in a language accessible to the intelligent layman and thus be truly informative for the politician or the civil servant.

This part of the TA is not simply an exercise in scientific journalism (although the importance of this function should not be underestimated). It contains an element of analysis in that it asks questions about related technologies and the technological system, and it contains an element of forecasting in that it attempts to foresee the future of the technology under scrutiny as well as that of its rivals and complements.

The second part of any TA goes to the core of technology assessment and asks what benefits are to be expected from the technology and what, if any, state support for its development or diffusion is required. The benefits may be purely economic and commercial, or they may be found in environmental improvement, health benefits or, on a more subtle level, improvements in the social, cultural or political fabric of society. The technology may not require any intervention from a public body and may thrive happily in a purely commercial domain; on the other hand it may require help in terms of grants, tax allowances, training or information programmes, legislative or regulatory measures, or administrative and institutional arrangements.

The question of utility is, of course, laden with value. On the assumption that in a capitalist and liberal society the willingness to purchase is a sufficient yardstick for utility, commercially viable technologies are deemed to be useful unless proved otherwise by showing that they cause some harmful effects. On the other hand, some technologies may offer considerable benefits to society, yet are commercially too risky or otherwise too unattractive to become viable without some form of public support. The final arbiter of worthiness for support must be the political decision-maker, although technology assessment can carefully marshal the arguments advanced both in favour and against the beneficial effects of the technology and its dependence on public magnanimity for survival.

The TA analyst provides descriptions of costs and benefits, attempts to quantify them, and assigns both costs and benefits to affected parties. The analyst also describes perceived difficulties in the path of the technology and provides an analysis of available options for supportive action. The analyst does not offer advice such as 'this ought to be done', but rather 'if you wish to achieve this and that, the following instruments are at your disposal and may prove effective'. The strength of TA lies in its humility, in knowing its preserve and in not usurping a role which does not legitimately belong to it. It has often been argued that scientists do, in effect, provide advice in their choice of topics, in their treatment of issues, in ignoring some facets of a problem and in stressing others. All this may be so, but this should merely be the difference between human frailty and ideal achievement, not a deliberate act of using the disguise of TA to become a back-room politician.

Finally, technology assessment must address the question of what unwanted effects or hazards the technology might cause. When such undesirable impacts or dangers are identified, the associated problem of control measures arises. In analogy with the previous point on beneficial effects of a technology – bearing in mind that what appears as a benefit to one may appear as a drawback to another – close attention must be given to all its possible side effects which might prove destructive of the natural environment, dangerous to human health, disruptive of society, or otherwise trigger a chain of events which appears unpredictable and risky. As far as possible, the risks and impacts ought to be described in quantitative terms, although very often these are artificial and meaningless, and it is wiser to stick to qualitative statements. Generally, only the measurable ought to be measured; for the immeasurable, verbal or graphical analysis must not only suffice, it is indeed superior. Often hazards associated with the use of technologies are mere hunches and it is an important task of TA to collect the evidence and show consensus or controversy.

It needs to be emphasized that the scientific answers TA can provide cannot be better than those provided by the individual disciplines concerned, except that the whole of a TA report ought to give better insight than the sum of its parts. If climatology does not know for sure what carbon dioxide in the atmosphere will do to the climate, then neither does TA. If economists and sociologists cannot tell whether microelectronics will cause unemployment or deskilling, then neither does TA. Ignorance does not turn into knowledge, uncertainty into certainty, by merely relabelling the package. What can be expected of TA is a well-documented assessment of the state of all the relevant aspects of the art, neither more nor less.

Finally, an analysis of possible measures for the control of the unwanted effects and risks, and for the likely efficacy and efficiency of such measures, must form an integral part of any technology assessment. The proviso of not making recommendations to politics, but merely furnishing an analysis of the options and their effects, is as valid for control as for support measures.

In summary, TA ought to answer the following questions: What is the technology we are talking about? What benefits does the technology bring with it and what help does it need to be given? What dangers does the technology harbour and what can be done to control them?

For TA to be useful to the decision-maker, certain conditions must be met. The first condition for the effective use of technology assessment in politics is that TA should be concerned with matters which form part of the political agenda. If TA deals with matters politics does not deal with, its results will be ignored. If TA is too late in providing answers to political problems, the problems will be solved without the benefit of TA. There must be effective mechanisms which enable TA institutions to undertake the required studies at the required time.

Technology assessment or similar institutions can fulfil a monitoring role. They can use their many sources of information in a systematic manner to discover the first signs of danger emanating from new discoveries about a technology and, of equal importance, to look for the first signs of promise from new inventions or developments. The role of watchdog, which draws attention to both friend and foe, may be shared out between institutions with tasks of technology foresight, environmental monitoring, TA, and others. Setting the political agenda is by no means a trivial exercise; but even having decided that political attention is required, the question of whether or not the subject is suitable for the 'technology assessment treatment' needs to be decided in collaboration between technology assessors and politicians. Some technological issues may be simple enough to be resolved without much ado; some may be too urgent to be able to wait for the long-winded process of a full technology assessment, although some form of mini-assessment may be suitable for them. The resolution of many socially important questions, whether they involve technology in some way or not, may not be affected by the kind of knowledge which TA can provide. If issues of fact and/or issues of rational analysis are not relevant because the problem is dominated by emotions, value judgements and partisan political stance, then technology assessment might try to steer the debate into more rational channels, although success is by no means a foregone conclusion.

TA can be effective only if a relationship of trust exists between the decision-maker and the technology assessor. Only if such trust exists will the assessor be made privy to the agenda-setting and be given the time and the money to carry out the assessment. Only if trust exists will the politician listen to the assessor and take the analysis seriously into consideration when reaching decisions. In order to establish trust, the assessor must have an impeccable scientific pedigree, must be seen to be independent, must take great care to fulfil the conditions of impartiality, must listen carefully to advice and opinions, and, last but not least, must keep the decision-maker and all interested parties constantly informed.

The model case for the blending of TA into the political process is the case of the Office of Technology Assessment (OTA) in the United States Congress. The fit appears, at least to the outsider, perfect. For here is a parliament equipped with its own civil service, involved directly in the control of government departments, and extremely active in its own right in formulating laws and controlling federal expenditure. Congress, or Congressional committees, in discussion with the OTA, agree on topics for the OTA in time for proper technology assessments to be undertaken, and for the results to be considered in detail as an input into the decision-making process. The essence of US governance is the sharing of power between the executive and the legislative branch. The location of the OTA within Congress acts to restore, at least partially, the equality of information between legislature and executive, for the latter has access to the whole massive machinery of government for the procurement of information.

The sharing of tasks, and power, between governments and parliaments in Europe is very different. The basic principle is that executive government is not under such immediate control of the legislature as in the US, while, on the other hand, the head of the executive can, in effect, be removed by parliament and the whole government with him. Parliament has only the tiniest of an administrative apparatus and individual members have practically no staff. The great majority of proposed legislation emanates from government, which relies on its own sources of information or buys in expertise as required.

The effective political use of technology assessment with these forms of government is possible at three points in the policy-forming process:

1. before and during the first drafting of proposed legislation in the various ministries;
2. during the passage of legislation through parliament;
3. before or during the formulation of policies which do not require legislative action.

Which of these methods is used, singly or in some combination, will depend on details of circumstance.

It took many years of political debate for European governments and parliaments to agree on their own forms of technology assessment, but in most countries it has finally been institutionalized, albeit not on the US scale. A recent publication gives an overview of all European TA establishments (von Berg, 1994), while European parliamentary technology assessment was discussed at a meeting in October 1993, organized by the Austrian Academy of Sciences, and the proceedings are to be published.

If technology policy is to be not only effective but also transparent, technology assessments ought to be publicly available and ought to include as much input from the public as possible. The location of TA in independent institutions may ease the transparency, although government departments and parliaments need not necessarily be secretive about these matters either.

The task of carrying out a major technology assessment is a formidable one and any mutual assistance and international division of labour can be helpful. It is sometimes possible for a TA in one country to consist largely of an up-dating and adjustment to local conditions of a TA carried out elsewhere. By thus not reinventing the wheel, a great deal of effort may be saved and used more constructively. The adjustment to local conditions may still require a lot of work and of insight, because nothing can substitute for local knowledge, local gathering of opinion and information, and analysis of local conditions of politics, values, geography, industrial structure, and so on. The globalization of both the economy and some of the more outstanding problems of humanity – eg climate changes probably caused by the excessive use of energy and other technological abuses of nature – is a further reason for international cooperation on TA. Global problems require global studies as an input to global solutions.

CHAPTER FOUR

TECHNOLOGY AND THE NATURAL ENVIRONMENT

◆

Introduction

The fact that we are stressing our natural environment beyond its probable capacity to withstand the resulting strain, is no longer under serious dispute. As our overwhelming attitude is one of ignoring long-term problems and concentrating entirely on short-term advantage, the problems of the environment are either ignored, or trivialized, or treated by palliatives that are as painless as they are ineffectual. In the current mood of what J K Galbraith has called the Culture of Contentment, short-term comfort and smug self-satisfaction dominate the attitudes of the affluent majorities of voters in the developed countries.

> The larger point is not in doubt: the fortunate and the favored, it is more than evident, do not contemplate and respond to their own longer-run well-being. Rather, they respond, and powerfully, to immediate comfort and contentment (Galbraith: 6).

As the destruction of the natural environment by technology is a gradual and long-term process, rather than a dramatic event with immediate drastically adverse consequences for the contented, the chances of adequate remedial action are remote. Nonetheless, the effort to convince humankind to turn away from the path to disaster must be made and persevered with. The need for action does not stem from romantic notions about an idyllic past, when humans supposedly lived in perfect harmony with benign nature. We need to change our ways in order to survive and in order to find the best possible harmony with nature.

The idyllic notion of nature living in harmony and equitable balance with herself is an illusion, even if we were to conjecture the absence of humans. Strong and dominant species do displace others; to eat or be eaten is a cruel fact of natural life; and temporary overpopulation, followed by destruction of the habitat and resultant reduction of the population is a common occurrence. Nature is neither benign nor free from disaster and disequilibria. Yet several intrinsic properties of nature guarantee its long-term survival, with mostly slow and gradual changes in its overall quasi-equilibrium. Almost all natural processes are cyclic and thus can continue indefinitely. Nature derives its energy from the sun – ie from a source that is inexhaustible on any time-scale except that used to describe the evolution of the universe itself. Most disequilibria right themselves over reasonable periods and may thus be viewed as temporary aberrations. Some species die out as a result of natural causes and without human intervention, the best known among them being the dinosaurs. Because no species generally achieves substantial dominance, nature is characterized by an enormous diversity of living creatures and a multitude of synergetic, predatory, and other interdependent relationships between them (see Knapp et al 1989, Ch 12). Apart from activities by living creatures, there is an awe-inspiring variety of natural processes caused by wind, weather, waves, chemicals, natural radioactivity, and other natural forces. Some of these changes are cyclic, some are slow, some are catastrophic. It is the multifarious beauty and the constant changes of nature that are the source of much of our wonderment and deepest sense of exhilaration. Feeling part of this world, wonderful in its variety despite its cruelty, is one of the basic sources of happiness. When all is said and done, despite all the ill-conceived talk about man's mastery over nature, the natural environment is the only one that can sustain our lives. And yet we destroy the very world that sustains us and that we love.

The history of the infliction of damage by humans onto the environment is a long and inglorious one. As technology developed and – mainly as a result of technological and social civilization – humankind grew in numbers, its effect on the natural environment became more widespread. More agricultural land was provided by the clearance of forests and, undoubtedly, some animal species and wild plants were displaced even in the early stages of agricultural expansion. Medieval and early modern cities had unpleasant problems of pollution, resulting, among other things, in the decimation of the population by infectious diseases. These ills were eventually remedied by civil engineering, which provided sewers and clean water supplies, and by general hygiene. Even in those early days technology made the expansion of humankind possible and was thus the cause of much environmental damage, yet the damage was on a scale and of a kind that technology was able to remedy. We shall not dwell on the problems of early agriculture and of the early cities, as the craft-based technologies used by them are too remote from our modern technologies. Instead, we shall seek the roots of today's problems in the Industrial Revolution, which laid the foundations of our modern industrial society.

With the introduction and expansion of industrial production and with the rapid growth of cities, problems of pollution achieved both a new magnitude and new dimensions. Because British forests had already been decimated, the change from charcoal to coal in the production of iron and steel was hailed as a great leap forward; alas the emission of carbon dioxide, soot and sulphur dioxide increased enormously and began to blight the remaining forests and to blacken the skies and cities of Britain. The smelting of other metals, the production of town gas, and the beginnings of a chemical industry produced both noxious fumes and foul effluents to an extent that led to the first legislation for the protection of the environment. The Lighting and Washing Act (1833) attempted to control effluents, while the Alkali Act (1863) regulated the nuisance of emissions.

The Contemporary Problem of Pollution

The very essence of the pollution problem changed with industrialization. Humans became dependent on non-renewable resources of energy, eg coal. Previously they had depended on timber which, in principle, is a renewable resource; although if it is used faster than it grows, the principle of its renewability has little utility. If we burn fossil fuels, we not only deplete our resources, but also produce carbon dioxide which enters the atmosphere as an addition to the equilibrium concentration. If, on the other hand, we burn only as much wood as we grow, all the carbon dioxide produced in the combustion process is used up by newly growing trees. It is clearly impracticable at the moment to dispense with the use of fossil fuels, but this must be the long-term aim. In the long run we can only use either renewable resources or the virtually inexhaustible solar energy in its various manifestations. This will solve both the problem of limited reserves and of the greenhouse effect, caused mainly by the accumulation of carbon dioxide in the atmosphere.

The second major change in the pollution problem, caused by industrialization, is the enormous increase in the amount, the number and the complexity of chemicals released into the environment.

The third change is associated with the enormous increase in total population and in total consumption. The more people there are and the more they consume, the more waste is produced. This has not only the effect of polluting the earth, but also of depleting its resources for the use of future generations. The only long-term remedies, apart from the imperative end to the increase in population, are in the reduction of waste by recycling; the reduction of consumption by the more efficient use of materials; and in the substitution of rare materials by more common ones.

Nature has not been able to adjust to the presence of this gargantuan and dominant race and the waste we produce cannot be utilized by other creatures in a balanced cycle of natural processes. We have caused nature to get out of equilibrium, both in the short and in the long run. Humans equipped with technology are like giants capable of wreaking terrific havoc in their habitat. They move fast, thus requiring more space and more energy for their movement. They resemble Gargantua in doing everything on a huge scale: they consume and excrete as Gargantua and destroy all that stands in the path of what they call progress.

The modern problem of environmental strain began to receive attention in the early Sixties when the environmental movement was born. The first book that succeeded in drawing attention to the problem was the widely acclaimed *Silent Spring* by Rachel Carson, written in 1962 (Carson 1965). The main thrust of the book was to call attention to the havoc wreaked among wildlife by persistent pesticides. Carson also drew attention to the problems caused by the rapidity of the introduction of new chemicals into the environment, thus bringing the time dimension into the environmental debate:

> *To adjust to these chemicals would require time on the scale that is nature's; it would require not merely the years of a man's life but the life of generations. And even this, were it by some miracle possible, would be futile, for the new chemicals come from our laboratories in an endless stream; almost five hundred annually find their way into actual use in the United States alone ...chemicals totally outside the limits of biological experience* (Carson 1965: 24).

And that was written in the 'good old days' when genetic engineering, with its possibilities of creating new organisms, had not been heard of.

Time enters the pollution problem in three ways:

1. The time that is necessary for an ecological balance to be established and the environment and its organisms to adapt, where possible, to the new chemical substances. Except in the case of very rapid changes of generations, such as in the case of bacteria or certain insects, the time thus required is many orders of magnitude longer than a human generation.
2. Time plays a role in the life-time of goods. The shorter the time between purchase and scrap-heap, the more the environment

suffers. Throw-away goods and packaging, and a fast turnover of models owing to obsolescence, all contribute to the mountains of waste that we produce and that the environment must cope with. If we remember that the production of all these goods requires raw materials, transportation and energy, it is clear that there is something like an inverse relationship between the service life of goods and environmental damage caused by them.

3. The third role time plays is in the rate of introduction of new substances. If we are in a great hurry to innovate, we do not have the time necessary to test and think out all the possible consequences that might follow the release of a new substance. There are many examples of the consequences of the release of substances into the environment becoming known only after long periods of damage, and action being taken only slowly and hesitantly. A little known example is the release of some industrial chemicals with oestrogenic properties that find their way into rivers, lakes and water supplies, causing damage to male reproductive organs and to fertility, both in man and in animals ('Assault on the Male', BBC Horizon Programme, 31 October 1993).

More recently, the release of genetically modified organisms (GMOs) has become subject to a heated debate. The specific risks, associated with any particular release, depend on the nature of the released organism, on the type of genetic modification it has undergone, and on the environment that it is released into. Critics argue that the risks of releasing genetically modified micro-organisms or small animals, that in effect cannot be recalled once they are released, are too great to warrant such experiments, whatever the promise of benefits. The risks associated with the release of large animals and, more particular-ly, plants, is regarded as less severe (Umweltbundesamt 1993). Those in favour of the use of genetically modified organisms point to the large benefits to be expected and argue that all risks can be controlled to the extent that they become negligible. The number of releases is surprisingly large. It is estimated that by 1993 about a thousand release experiments had been carried out. The controls are severe indeed (OECD 1993), although Levidow argues that one of the main functions of the controls is to make genetic engineering appear as a normal, acceptable technological activity (Levidow 1994).

Some Examples of Present Environmental Problems

It took many years before the effect of chlorofluorocarbons (CFC gases) upon the ozone layer was even suspected, let alone established. To allow sufficient time for the environment and its organisms to adjust to new man-made substances is unrealistic; but to ask that the effects of all substances upon the environment be thoroughly investigated before they are released should be a self-evident requirement, and its implementation should not be beyond the wit of humans. Unfortunately, despite official approval and even limited legislation demanding that all substances in human use should be environmentally benign, the pressure of competition and the headlong race toward faster innovation are such as to cause inadequate testing to be carried out and insufficient thought to be given to the destructive potential of newly released substances. Novelty takes precedence over safety. The chance of a profit is more important than the risk of environmental damage.

The use of these potentially murderous chlorofluorocarbons is mostly trivial. Of a total of 43,000 tonnes of CFC gases used as aerosol propellants in the United Kingdom in 1977, 17,500 tonnes were used for hair-sprays, 10,000 for deodorants and 2,100 for Colognes and perfumes. Only 7,500 tonnes were used for industrial aerosols, while 4,500 tonnes were used for household aerosols, such as air-fresheners and insecticides. Within the European Community, 70 per cent of CFCs consumed in 1977 were used in aerosols, 9 per cent as refrigerants, and 19 per cent in foams (Department of the Environment 1979: 22). The fear of misplaced hair or slight body-odour obviously ranks higher than the fear of skin-cancer, caused by a depleted ozone layer. Is a hair out of place truly worse than a destroyed molecule of ozone? Would life be poorer without hair-sprays or deodorants?

There is a great deal of talk about producing environmentally safe substitutes, yet these have been very slow in coming. We have here one further instance which shows that innovation does not necessarily occur readily, even in a case when a need has been articulated and shown to be urgent. It is very hard to innovate to order, to invent what is needed, and much easier to bend demands toward innovations that can be produced. In the case of a replacement for CFC gases, the need is urgent and vital, yet finding a suitable replacement is proving a hard nut to crack. With a very large research effort, ICI have produced a refrigerant, HFA-134a (a hydrofluoroalkane), which appears to fulfil all the requirements of an efficient refrigerant that causes no damage to the ozone layer (Steven and Lindley 1990). For propellants, a partial answer is available in the use of HCFC gases (hydrochlorofluorocarbons), but it appears that these still cause some, albeit less, damage to the ozone layer.

CFC gases are still in widespread use, although there has been endless talk about banning them. The Montreal Protocol of 1987 came into force on 1 January 1989, and required industrial nations to reduce the consumption of CFC gases by 50 per cent by 1999. In view of the truly alarming growth of the ozone hole, a further meeting was held in London in 1990, where it was agreed to phase out the use of CFC gases completely by 1 January 2000 (NSCA 1991: 88). HCFC gases should have been phased out by the year 2005, but recently a group of countries, led by Britain, has forced a postponement of this ban to 2020, while agreeing to accelerate the ban on CFCs. And this at a time when the antarctic ozone hole has reached a record size! (Geoffrey Lean, *The Observer*, 19 October 1992). Some countries have been more active than others in attempting to deal with the problem. The USA, for example, banned the use of CFC aerosols as early as 1978. Unhappily, total world production of CFC gases in the Eighties was as high as it had been in the Seventies (Meadows et al 1992: 144).

One report claims that a benign substitute for CFC gases for refrigerators has been found, but that it is not making much headway because the gases used are ordinary, non-proprietary and cheap compounds. Perhaps this is a case when going back to simple technology is more effective than the investment of billions into sophisticated R&D (John Vidal, *The Guardian*, 19 November 1992).

The tragedy is that the ozone layer is truly essential to life on earth and that its depletion has been shown to be real beyond reasonable doubt. The causation by CFC and other gases may still be doubted by a few extreme sceptics, but the case against them is very strong and the harm done is so life-threatening that the doubts should not weigh heavily and the substances be found guilty. It is much better to err on the safe side, even at the risk of causing some unnecessary economic costs. The protection of life and health must take precedence over small economic losses. The condemnation of chemicals should occur on strong reasonable suspicion and they should be deemed guilty until proved innocent. This is as cautious an approach as the principle of innocence until proved guilty beyond reasonable doubt, which is vital in criminal justice for the protection of the freedom of the individual.

The ozone layer, some 25km above the surface of the earth, was formed at about the same time as the oxygen-rich atmosphere and, it is thought, the protection it afforded against ultra-violet radiation was a vital factor that enabled life to emerge from the oceans on to the surface of the earth, some 300–400 million years ago (Commoner 1972: 30–1). Excessive ultra-violet radiation damages not only human skin and eyes, but is also damaging to animals and plants. By destroying the protective layer of ozone we are thus risking initially an increased incidence of virulent skin cancers and, in the long run, an uncertain future for all life on earth as we know it. The vision that we shall not be able to venture out of doors without wearing protective goggles, protective clothing and protective creams, is very unpleasant, but not at all far-fetched and close to today's reality in some parts of the world. Is it a price worth paying for relatively trivial advantages and the lack of relatively simple technical precautionary measures, such as the careful disposal of worn-out refrigerators?

The most obvious, and yet the most harmless, type of environmental pollution is that by inert trash. Discarded packaging and containers of all kinds, waste from kitchens, worn tyres, unwanted clothing, cigarette stubs, and so on form mountains of rubbish which cause great problems of disposal and, when carelessly discarded, disfigure our cities, towns and countryside. This type of rubbish is environmentally harmless, except that it requires large pits to bury it in, euphemistically called land-fill, and represents a large amount of used resources, including energy. The waste can be reduced by recycling the rubbish and a fraction of the energy can be regained by burning it, although great care is needed not to cause severe air pollution from the combustion processes.

Recycling is making some progress and a great deal of effort by local authorities is going into attempts to recycle glass and plastic bottles, metal cans and paper. Unfortunately, the collection and processing are expensive and the effort pays dividends in terms of saving raw materials and energy, but is not currently economically viable without subsidies from public funds. The economic viability should improve with improved methods of recycling, improved product design, and with higher prices for energy and raw materials. Here are needs for innovation, but will environmental incentives prove sufficient to warrant the emergence of suitable technologies? Without intervention by public bodies, either by regulation or by subsidy, recycling will be slow in becoming universally effective. In an economic regime motivated purely by profit and in a political climate advocating minimum intervention by the state, innovation in environmentally dangerous products is bound to outstrip innovation in methods of safeguarding the environment.

The annual amount of municipal waste produced per head of population rises alarmingly. Between 1975 and 1989 it increased from an average in the OECD countries of 407kg to 518kg. The figures for the USA are 648 to 864 kg; for Japan, 341 to 394 kg; for England and Wales, 323 to 354 kg (OECD 1992: 200). If we were to seek a single measure for progress, the amount of garbage produced per head of population might be as good a measure as any. In this respect, our progress has been monotonous and rapid.

The changing composition of household waste is an indicator of our changing way of life. The declining proportion of screenings in household waste in Britain, for example, shows the declining use of solid fuel for domestic heating (Table 4.1). The average amount of packaging materials per capita rose in the USA from about 183kg in 1958 to about 238kg in 1966 (Hodges 1973: 222). In the same period, the number of non-returnable beer and soft drink containers rose from 10,177 to 25,570 billion (loc cit: 221).

This is not, of course, the full story. A huge amount of waste is not included in these figures – eg cars, refrigerators, washing-machines and other bulk items of domestic refuse. Industrial waste, waste from mines and quarries, sewage sludge and so on, are not included either. The Institution of Water and Environmental Management gives the following figures in Table 4.2 for waste arising in the United Kingdom in 1987 (in million tonnes).

Table 4.1 *The composition of household waste in the UK, in % weight.*

Type of waste	1935	1963	1970	1980
Screenings	57	39	15	14
Putrescible	14	14	24	25
Paper & cardboard	14	23	37	29
Metals	4	8	9	9
Textiles	2	3	3	3
Glass	3	8	9	10
Plastics			1	7
Other	6	5	2	4

Source: Department of the Environment 1992, *Waste Management Paper No 1, A Review of Options*, second edition, HMSO, London: 9, Table 2.2.

Table 4.2 *Total quantities of solid waste arising in the UK in 1987 in million tonnes.*

Industrial	45	Hazardous	3.7
Mining	70	Municipal	26
Quarrying	60	Sewage sludge	25
Special	1.6	Agricultural	250

Source: The Institution of Water and Environmental Management 1989, *An Introduction to Waste Management*, London: 2

According to the Department of the Environment (DoE 1992, Table 7.1: 47), 90 per cent of municipal waste is disposed of as land-fill and 8 per cent is incinerated, with apparently only a small proportion of the heat used. Industrial and commercial waste is also mainly disposed of as land-fill by private contractors. Under a renewables order published in 1990, the Regional Electricity Companies are obliged to obtain 102MW of their net declared capacity from renewable sources. The intention is to increase the amount to 600MW by 1998 (loc cit: 48). Considering that municipal, industrial and commercial waste alone have an estimated energy content sufficient to supply a generating capacity of roughly 25,000MW, these aims may be seen as modest indeed.

The focus of attention must now shift from harmless, although unsightly and wasteful, rubbish to dangerous materials such as batteries, engine oil, paint, medicines, solvents and suchlike. Many of these substances find their way into domestic refuse and, when dumped and used as land-fill, they seep into the soil and, eventually, into the ground-water. As these substances are highly toxic, the quality of the soil and of the water is seriously impaired and real hazards to the long-term health of plants, animals and humans arise. In some countries such waste is separated from harmless household garbage and is disposed off safely, although nobody knows just how safely. In any case, it is better to concentrate toxic materials for disposal rather than to allow them to spread irretrievably into the eco-system.

To deal with the problem of environmental pollution from domestic refuse, two technological and two social innovations are necessary. The social innovations are, first, a reduction in the amount of packaging and, more generally, in the amount of throw-away items that we consume. All sensible argument points in the direction of reducing the amount of packaging to its purely functional level. Functional packaging can be aesthetically pleasing and can consist of materials that lend themselves to easy recycling. Every environmental argument points in the direction of generally using high quality products with a long life, rather than low-quality, throw-away trash. The use of high-quality products gives more pleasure and more satisfaction, and breeds a caring attitude, rather than an attitude of contempt for quality, and a throw-away mentality. It is very likely that the throw-away attitude, the liking for the new and contempt for the old, is readily transferred from matters technological to a general contempt for lasting values and lasting quality, with a resultant deterioration in the quality of life. The argument that large-scale consumption, encouraged by a short life of products, is necessary to maintain a high level of economic activity and employment, is no longer valid. Indeed, low-quality mass-production provides little employment, whereas the production and maintenance of high-quality goods requires more and better qualified labour.

The second social innovation – which is currently making substantial strides forward – is the habit of separating different kinds of waste at source, so that recycling becomes easier. The best way to deal with the problem of separating the components of trash is not to allow them to become mixed in the first place. This is a particular case in point of the general argument that entropy, a measure of disorder, has a natural tendency to rise and should be kept as low as possible at all stages of a process, as its reduction from a high level requires much effort and energy.

The technological innovations that are required are: first, better methods of recycling and better design for recyclability, particularly for items that contain obnoxious substances; secondly, it should become increasingly possible to substitute less hazardous and more bountiful materials for toxic, dangerous and rare substances.

Some progress is being made in both these spheres, but much more needs to be done. Unhappily, the economic argument in favour of such innovations is much stronger on the macro-level than on the micro-level. In other words, although public interest demands such innovations and the economy at large can greatly benefit from them, it is very difficult for individual firms to make a profit from such innovations. The reason for this is well known. The cost of the disposal of rubbish and the cost of pollution are largely borne by the general public rather than by firms manufacturing or distributing polluting items. The cost of pollution is externalized and thus manufacturers and people in general have little economic incentive to try to reduce it and are unlikely to pay high prices for innovations designed to reduce pollution. With regard to hazards, the consumer is helpless to recognize the dangers arising out of the use of exotic materials and complex designs. Only careful assessment of all innovations in advance of their introduction, careful government supervision, and a much reduced and more responsible pace of innovation can prevent the repeated occurrence of hazards faced by an unsuspecting public. With the current pace of innovation and the reluctance of governments to intervene, innovations run far ahead of the assessment of either their utility or their safety.

Clearly, this situation can only be improved by policy intervention. Policies can be designed to prevent the externalization of pollution costs on the principle that the polluter must pay. He who causes environmental degradation must pay to put matters right – an admirable principle, often enunciated, although rarely enforced. Alternatively, policies can enforce higher standards of environmental care by proscribing the use of dangerous substances and enforcing the separate treatment and recycling of potentially toxic and/or scarce materials. And certainly technology assessment and environmental impact assessment should be widely used to recognize the costs, dangers and benefits of innovations long before any damage is actually done.

There are fashions even in environmental dangers. If the toxicity of some substance becomes fashionable, it receives priority in being replaced. Sometimes the replacement is by insufficiently tried new substances that might, in the long run, prove as damaging as the hazard they are designed to eliminate. Currently, mercury in batteries has had a very bad press and manufacturers are anxious to stress that their products do not contain the offensive substance. They are less anxious to tell us what obnoxious substances modern batteries contain instead of mercury, let alone tell us what they know and what they do not know about the environmental hazards caused by modern batteries. It is a game of hide-and-seek between committed scientists and environmental pressure groups and manufacturers. As soon as a substance has been branded as dangerous with sufficient force and sufficient publicity, it is replaced by some other substance. The pressure groups then face the task of finding out how harmless or risky the new substances are. As manufacturers have far better research facilities and can hide behind a cloak of commercial secrecy, the struggle is an unequal one. On the other hand, it is very difficult, if not impossible, to prove beyond doubt that a substance is truly safe. Even if nothing adverse is known about it, the possibility that some danger might be discovered later exists for all but the simplest and best understood uses for the simplest and best understood materials. Asbestos is a good case in point: who would have thought some thirty years ago that this seemingly inert and harmless substance might eventually prove a killer?

Industrial production may be seen, in the most general terms, as a chain of processes in which raw materials are first extracted from natural sources and then converted into products. At each stage of the chain, energy is invested and waste is ejected. Manufacture consists of 'mixing' raw materials with energy to produce the desired product and, inevitably, waste.

Sooner or later and, unhappily, often rather sooner, the product itself is discarded and also becomes waste. Many products, such as cars, produce a great deal of waste during their lifetime. The waste can be gaseous, liquid and solid, in addition to the inevitably rejected thermal energy. The final desired product may require many individual stages of manufacture – eg the extraction of ores and their refinement and shaping into usable metals; machining of parts; assembly; finishing; packaging and dispatch, and so on. The principle that energy needs to be added and waste needs to be removed applies to each and every stage.

The principle is inescapable, but the quantity of energy used and the amounts and nature of waste can be changed. Process innovations generally affect the nature of the waste produced, as the manufacturing process determines what materials and methods are used and thus also what waste occurs. Innovations in the control of manufacturing processes, on the other hand, essentially leave the process, and thus the type of waste, unchanged, but affect the quantities of wastes and of energy used. Firms have varying incentives to introduce process innovations. They may aim to reduce costs by reducing waste and by reducing inputs of factors of production – ie materials, labour and energy. They may aim to improve the quality of production by reducing the number of rejects and thus reducing waste and the need for reworking. They may need to introduce a new process in order to be able to produce a new product. Product innovation is frequently linked to an associated process innovation. Finally, firms may be forced to change their processes, or at least their controls, in order to comply with rules regulating the amount and type of pollution they are allowed to discharge into the environment. In the more fortunate cases, cost savings and the reduction of pollution go hand-in-hand. It stands to reason that the reduction of waste saves costs and spares the environment, although the constellation of circumstances is not always that favourable and the cost savings are often insufficient to justify the necessary investment. Worse still, the substitution of obnoxious substances by benign ones may add to costs and the removal of pollutants may save little or nothing. To remove sulphur dioxide from the chimney stacks of power stations may save the flora of the near and not so near surroundings, but it saves no money to the operator of the power station. The introduction of more efficient methods of combustion, on the other hand, may reduce both costs and pollution.

The reduction of pollution often adds costs and this calls for one of two remedies. The first remedy lies in state intervention. The state must achieve, by regulation or by artificial incentive, what cannot be achieved by economic incentive. In the case of sulphur dioxide, an artificial incentive can be achieved by levying a tax on the sulphur content of coal or oil, thus pushing the operator in the direction of using fuel with a low content of sulphur. The operator of the power station can also be forced to pay for the damage caused to the environment, although this is not a desirable method on the grounds that prevention is not only better than cure, but a cure may not exist. Alternatively, or additionally, the state can set, control and enforce strict limits on the amount of sulphur dioxide that the power station is permitted to emit into the air.

Artificial incentives create an illusion of the operation of market forces and are therefore preferred by those who believe in the sanctity of the market. However, even the most ardent opponents of regulation realize that artificial incentives have limited effects and that often there is no alternative to regulation.

The second remedy that is needed is technological innovation: new, more efficient and cheaper filters; new uses for the residues collected in the filters; new processes for the preparation of cleaner fuels; more efficient methods of combustion and generation of electricity. Moving away from the example of power stations, we can generalize to conclude that technological innovations are needed that will prevent, or alleviate, the stress caused to the natural environment.

If the factory is considered as a system inside its walls, then, roughly speaking, everything that leaves the factory, other than its products or people, must be regarded as waste. The word waste has two meanings and both apply: we waste energy, effort and raw materials on unwanted byproducts, and the byproducts themselves are waste that needs to be disposed of. We are wasteful and we produce waste.

An interesting concept on the path toward environmentally benign products is that of 'product stewardship'.

> This considers a product from the first development of a
> specification, through the research and development phases to
> manufacture and marketing, and beyond to the obsolescence of
> the product including plant shut down and decommissioning.
> At each stage the implications for humans and the environment
> are considered and it is ensured that satisfactory procedures are
> developed (Felton: 34, in Roberts and Weale 1991).

These thoughts are very close to the spirit of technology assessment and must become the norm for industrial behaviour and not remain the domain of the rare pioneer. We might add that this thought includes the consideration of the energy requirements and the production of waste throughout the life and use of the product. The concept of 'environmentally benign', or 'green', must include such considerations if it is to acquire real meaning.

The thermal equilibrium of the planet is determined by the amount of radiation absorbed from the sun, less the amount reradiated into space. As the amount of thermal energy radiated into space depends on the average temperature of the earth's surface, the equilibrium temperature must rise if we need to dissipate more heat than has been created in the course of our activities. Fremlin shows that the thermal output required to supply an increasing population puts an ultimate limit on the number of people the earth can support (Fremlin 1972: 126–56). Long before such ultimate limits were achieved, the rising average temperature on earth would wreak havoc with our way of life. The climate would get warmer; the polar ice-caps would melt and many an island or low-lying coastal region would be flooded unless it was protected by high sea-walls. What would happen to rainfall is somewhat unpredictable, but certainly the agricultural use of land in different regions would have to undergo substantial change. Some currently arable land with a moderate climate might turn into a blazing desert, other land lying in moderate zones with well-distributed rainfall might get monsoon-like rain instead.

The amount of heat reradiated into space also depends upon the composition of the atmosphere: introducing carbon dioxide and some other so-called greenhouse gases into the atmosphere has the same effect as covering the earth with a blanket. We speak of the greenhouse effect, because greenhouses owe their warmth to the fact that their glass cover allows more radiant heat to enter than to escape. Thus the more fossil fuels we burn, the more carbon dioxide we produce and the hotter the surface of the earth will become. This particular danger – and it is a very serious danger indeed – shows that it is not sufficient to control pollution by obnoxious substances, for what can be more harmless than the inert gas carbon dioxide? And yet the excessive use of fossil fuels puts the future of the earth in real peril.

Table 4.3 shows that total energy consumption is rising inexorably and that the differences in energy consumption between rich and poor have by no means been eliminated. The mind boggles at the thought that consumption of energy throughout the world might rise to North American levels. On the other hand, the table shows very clearly that people can live very comfortable lives without indulging in the prolific waste of North American energy consumption.

The rising energy consumption not only depletes finite reserves, but contributes to the dangerous greenhouse effect. There are two possible remedies:

1. energy saving by the use of better insulation, better methods of combustion, better controls, lower speeds for motor cars and more efficient processes;
2. substitution of fossil fuels by renewable resources, such as biomass, solar energy, windmills or wave power.

Table 4.3 *World energy consumption MT oil equivalent (toe)*

1970–100	1988	% of total 1988	per capita toe
North America	123	27.2	8.05
Western Europe	131	16.3	3.85
China	284	9.0	1.49
Japan	159	5.0	3.30
South-East Asia	396	3.0	0.65
Latin America	233	5.3	1.14
Africa	236	2.5	0.36
World	164	100	1.61

Source: S Simpson (1990) *The Times Guide to the Environment*, Times Books, London, Table 7.1: 95

Burning hydrogen instead of carbon would also reduce the greenhouse effect, as the result of such combustion is water rather than carbon dioxide. If hydrogen could be extracted from water with the aid of solar energy, then a completely renewable carrier of mobile energy would be available, albeit with plenty of problems of safety yet to be resolved.

The use of so-called biomass as fuel also permits a renewable operation, essentially driven by the sun. Some successful experiments of either burning it or producing alcohol or diesel fuel from it have been carried out. It is to be hoped that if and when oil and natural gas become truly scarce and, hence, expensive, these alternative fuels and technologies will be available to take over on a massive scale. In the meantime, more research and development work ought to be carried out under government sponsorship in order to be prepared for the long-term future. R&D work on improved batteries and fuel cells also seems very important, even if success in these areas has been hard to come by in the past. Indeed, such research is being carried out by a consortium of US automobile manufacturers under the auspices of the US government. Solar energy is available in a variety of manifestations: direct sunlight that can be used in photo-voltaic applications or as heat; wind with its long history of technological use that should not be regarded as overtaken by events; and possibly wave-power, that is also ultimately driven by the sun. Even the moon can help us to obtain energy if we use the large potential of tidal estuaries, although the major civil engineering constructions that would be necessary to harness that energy might prove detrimental to sites of natural beauty and to wildlife. Nuclear sources of energy, although they do not produce carbon dioxide, have terrifying problems of safety and of long-term storage of radioactive waste associated with them, and it is highly questionable whether more money ought to be invested in their further development.

Our total use of energy must decrease; we must shift towards low-energy consumption if we are to survive in the long term. The Brundtland Report suggests that effort should be diverted from fur-

ther development of primary energy sources towards the development and application of energy efficient technologies.

> By using the most energy-efficient technologies and processes
> now available in all sectors of the economy, annual global
> per capita GDP growth rates of around 3 per cent can be
> achieved. ... Fundamental political and institutional shifts
> are required to restructure investment potential in order to
> move along these lower, more energy-efficient paths (World
> Commission on Environment and Development: 173).

Modern agriculture poses extremely serious environmental problems.
One of them is the extensive use of mineral fertilizers. The annual
nitrate application in areas of intensive farming is about 100kg per
hectare. Much of this nitrate finds its way into the ground-water and
it is becoming increasingly difficult to supply city dwellers with water
that contains less than the recommended maximum levels of nitrates.
At the same time, it is extremely difficult to return all the natural fertility to the soil without the use of mineral fertilizers, as most of the
crops grown are consumed in large cities and it is hard to see how all
the waste products can be returned to the land. City sewers are so
contaminated by industrial waste that the use of sewage sludge as fertilizers is impossible. One possible answer is to use more cover crops
and so-called green manuring by ploughing in crops such as alfalfa or
mustard. A much greater scientific effort is required to make modern
farming as organic as possible by combining technology with biology,
rather than by attempting to substitute technology for biology
(Seymour and Girardet 1986: 108–12).

Much discussion centres around the question whether modern
farming methods not only destroy the ground-water, the lakes and the
rivers, but also whether the soil can stand intensive agriculture in the
long run. A further doubt arises as to the quality of the food produced. Are the vegetables grown by modern farming methods
healthy? Is modern fruit healthy? Is the grain used for modern bread
wholesome? Or do we need to go back to organic farming in order to
avoid chemical fertilizers, chemical pesticides and chemical fungicides? Is the air so polluted that anything growing near industrial
centres or near roads is too contaminated to be fit for human consumption? It is extremely difficult to obtain definitive and certain
answers to these questions. The systems being dealt with are exceedingly complex and chains of cause-and-effect in such systems are very
hard to trace. It is known that any radioactive contamination is bad,
but even here the amount of damage done by small doses of radiation
can only be stated in statistical terms and these are meaningless to the
individual. Similarly, it is known that lead is poisonous, but how
much harm is done to an individual by very small doses of lead is
impossible to ascertain. Where humans are concerned, clear-cut

155

experiments cannot be carried out, varying one variable at a time and observing the results over many years on a large number of individuals. Thus we are reduced to experiments on cells, to dubious experiments on animals, to epidemiological observations, and to reasoning, speculation and extrapolation. The epidemiological differences are often striking. Thus, for example, the death rate from breast cancer per 100,000 females aged 14 and over varied in 1960 from 55.66 in Boston, Massachusets, to 24.07 in El Paso, Texas (Berry and Horton 1974: 320). But it is extremely difficult to know, with any degree of certainty, what conclusion to draw from such data.

One of the great worries of recent years is the destruction of forests. So much has been written about the destruction of tropical rain forests that very little can be added here, except to say that this destruction is a conscious and deliberate act and not a result of accidental or incidental environmental damage caused by some other activity. It is thus purely a political, economic and social question on a grand scale. Although the issue was addressed by the Rio summit, it is doubtful whether much has been achieved in real terms (United Nations 1992). The destruction of the tropical rain forests may yet prove to be one of the main causes of a final decline of humankind on earth, but the possible ways of solving the problem are only indirectly related to technology.

What is closer to our interests is the continuing damage to the forests of Europe and North America, caused by air pollution, by monocultures, by large populations of deer, and possibly by other causes. These causes are closely related to our quest for increased economic activity, improved technology and increased wealth, without taking the time or giving sufficient thought or care to the environmental damage caused in the course of such quest. Even in the UK, a country that lost most of its indigenous forests a long time ago, the health of the relatively few existing forests has become problematic. In merely two years, from 1987 to 1989, the proportion of trees that is very badly affected by a reduction in crown density has increased from 4 per cent to 6 per cent, the proportion somewhat less affected has increased from 18 per cent to 22 per cent and the proportion least affected has decreased from 44 per cent to 41 per cent (Central Statistical Office 1992: 171).

However, 'the search for a simple cause-and-effect relationship between a given air pollutant and a specific disease breaks down in a hopeless morass of complex interactions' (Commoner 1972: 77).

Some writers are less cautious and more willing to assign causes to certain harmful effects. *The Times Guide to the Environment*, (Simpson 1990: 56–7) for example, lists a great number of air pollutants, their sources and their effects. A few of these are shown in Table 4.4.

It is very obvious that many harmful pollutants are emitted by road vehicles. These not only damage human health, but they also damage vital parts of the eco-system in causing fatal stress to trees and forests. Vehicle exhausts are a good example of how end-of-pipe technologies are used as palliatives. Although catalyst converters have been introduced into vehicle exhausts, nothing is being done to curb vehicular traffic and very little attempt has been made to curb its speed and the fuel consumption of engines. There are plenty of so-called green cars on drawing-boards or at motor shows, yet the media concentrate their attention on the almost criminal creations of the motor industry, such as vehicles of 500 horsepower and speeds of three times the legal speed limits. The green cars remain firmly on the drawing-boards, traffic jams and road accidents get worse, the railways and other public transport decline further and the environment suffers irreparable damage. (For detail on green cars, see Nieuwenhuis et al 1992).

Table 4.4 *Some air pollutants, their sources and their health effects.*

Chemical	Source	Health effect
Benzene	Oil refining, vehicle exhausts	Leukaemia
Carbon monoxide	Combustion, vehicle exhausts	Heart disease
Hydrocarbons	Vehicle exhausts	Carcinogens
Hydrogen chloride	Waste combustion	Eye and lung damage
Nickel	Combustion, smelting	Lung cancer
Nitrogen oxides	Combustion, vehicle exhausts	Respiratory disorders
Ozone	Photochemically from nitrogen oxides	Eye and lung irritant
Sulphur dioxide	Combustion, smelting	Eye and lung damage
Methane	Sewage, wastes, rotting vegetation, cattle	Lung irritant

Source: Simpson (1990) *The Times Guide to the Environment*: 56–7

The contribution of road vehicles to air pollution is very considerable. In the United Kingdom, 88 per cent of carbon monoxide emissions, 39 per cent of black smoke, 48 per cent of nitrogen oxides, 19 per cent of carbon dioxide and 37 per cent of volatile organic compounds emanate from road transport. Only power stations are equally potent polluters. They contribute 71 per cent of all sulphur dioxide, 29 per cent of nitrogen oxides and 33 per cent of carbon dioxide. Industry (other than power stations and refineries) comes a poor third. It contributes 'only' 16 per cent of sulphur dioxide, 17 per cent of black smoke, 10 per cent of nitrogen oxides and 23 per cent of carbon dioxide (Central Statistical Office 1992: 161).

Table 4.5 compares the carbon dioxide emissions of some European countries in the years 1980 and 1989 and shows very clearly that some countries have been more successful than others in reducing their emissions, and thus their contribution to the greenhouse effect. It is arguable that some of the most dramatic reductions, eg in

France, were achieved by a shift to nuclear power generation and this might be equivalent to jumping from the frying-pan into the fire. As carbon dioxide contributes 61 per cent to the greenhouse effect, the reduction in its emission is crucial.

Table 4.5 *Carbon dioxide emissions in million tonnes.*

	1980	1989
United Kingdom	528.7	530.1
Belgium	120.0	99.1
France	459.2	360.6
Germany (Fed Rep)	767.5	647.9
Italy	355.6	386.1
The Netherlands	151.0	148.7
European Community	2,747.1	2,562.9

Source: Central Statistical Office (1992) *Social Trends* 22: 162

Environmental Problems and the Market

In a world in which innovation is driven purely by the profit-motive, only two basic types of innovation can thrive: those aimed at kindling new needs and/or at producing more competitive products; and those aimed at reducing production costs. The market thus caters for certain types of product innovations – those that enhance the size of the market for the innovating firm – and at certain process innovations – those that reduce costs. The environment, alas, is not a force in the market. It cannot speak for itself and even less can it purchase goods or services. Thus the environment is endangered not only by the speed of innovation, but even more by its direction. Only political will can create a market for environmentally sound technologies, only political will can create the environmentally benign forces that markets, by their very nature, cannot create. Power in the market is achieved either by purchasing power or by political clout; as the former does not favour the environment, the latter must be tilted in its favour.

The very best the market can do is to ensure that a wide range of goods and services is available to consumers at favourable prices. A clean environment, however, is neither a marketable good nor a service in the ordinary sense. The environment is a public good and thus a government responsibility. We all enjoy a clean and safe environment and we all suffer from its degradation. None of us is prepared, or able, to buy a clean environment, except in the limited sense of buying a house in a nice area and keeping the garden tidy. A share of a clean atmosphere, of clean ground-water or of unimpaired soil cannot be bought. Neither can we buy a share of the ozone layer in the upper atmosphere to give us personal protection from damaging ultra-violet radiation. Nature has no purchasing power either, and interests not backed by cash are ignored by markets.

Some people feel that environmental awareness has reached such a pitch that it has become the self-interest of firms to produce environmentally friendly products and to use environmentally benign processes. This is a very doubtful proposition. First, there is the danger that only substances which receive a bad press will be dealt with. Too large a role is thus given to pressure groups: they must seek out the hazards, they must arouse public opinion and get the media on their side. Pressure groups suffer from lack of resources and cannot wage war on too many fronts at any one time. They must concentrate their efforts and in this way 'fashionable hazards' arise as the preferred targets of publicity campaigns. Mercury has been mentioned as an example; other examples are lead in petrol or phosphates in washing powders. The elimination of phosphates from washing powders has become a promotional advantage; if Brand X is free of phosphates this is a distinct point in its favour. Yet whether the substitutes for phosphates are environmentally more benign remains to be seen. The lay consumer has no way of knowing and no reason to trust the purveyors of public relations whitewash. And the voluntary watchdogs are unable to be on guard everywhere at all times.

It is not easy to distinguish clearly between reality and publicity. Products have become extremely complex; environmental interactions are beyond the grasp of most of us. We therefore fall easy prey to claims of environmental friendliness which may or may not have any substance in ecological or toxicological terms. Environmental friendliness has become yet another device for creating a favourable image for firms and their products. The public can but hope that there is some substance to such claims. There is a real danger that the label 'environmentally friendly' might be grist to the mills of smug self-satisfaction of contented citizens. Who can blame them for destroying the environment if they buy, for preference, environmentally friendly goods? Who can claim that their prolific consumption puts intolerable strains on the environment if they always buy the latest, environmentally friendly products? Indeed, they feel obliged, for the sake of the environment, to discard old machinery in favour of new, environmentally more benign models.

Just as the state controls medicines and puts limits on the claims that can be made for their potency, so the state ought to control the content of claims for environmental friendliness. The trend in the direction of environmentally friendly products is a positive one; the state must ensure that the positive effect is not dissipated by claims that prove vacuous and misleading. Currently the EC is attempting to define and award green labels for goods and it is to be hoped that these efforts will continue and will be crowned with substantive success, although the issue is not without its problems (Potter and Hinnells 1994).

The great innovative potential of firms can be of tremendous benefit to the environment. If a systematic search were made for environmental hazards and if innovative effort were then directed toward replacing hazardous substances by harmless ones, a great service could be rendered to nature. To use innovative potential in this way requires conscious effort at environmental research – funded largely by the state – and great effort by firms to find benign substitutes for those products found wanting. Cooperation between environmental researchers and innovators in testing the substitutes is necessary, as the whole process makes sense only if the substitutes for obnoxious substances are thoroughly and exhaustively tested. We cannot eliminate all hazards, as future surprises can never be ruled out, but we can greatly improve on our present performance. Innovation used in the service of a healthier environment can only be applauded.

Manufacturing processes are more problematic. The glare of publicity hits them only very occasionally and pressure groups cannot hope to monitor all that goes on. The best hope is in the setting of rigorous standards for every kind of emission in whatever form. These standards are invariably vigorously opposed by industry and the dual argument of international competition and domestic prices often proves powerful. The argument, in a nutshell, runs thus: if domestic producers have to adhere to more rigorous emission standards than their foreign competitors, and thus face higher costs, their competitive position will deteriorate. Furthermore, added costs will force manufacturers to raise their prices at the expense of their domestic and international customers alike. The first argument is unassailable for goods dominated wholly by price competition and in a world in which the price of goods is the only thing that matters. In a world which cares about its own future as much as it does about the price of goods, the argument should have no validity at all. To buy cheaply at the expense of the natural environment is, in the long run, folly. And we need not all be dead in the long run – humans can and should think beyond their individual graves.

In the hard world of international trade there are only two ways of achieving globally high environmental standards. One way is to incorporate environmental standards as conditions in all trade agreements. The other way is for pressure groups to try to pillory firms that offend gravely against the environment and achieve international boycotts of such firms. To organize the latter in a fair and widespread manner is almost impossible, whereas the former should not be beyond the wit of humans. The domestic price argument shows the paucity of our values. If the cheap purchase of goods is all that people care about, then nobody should be surprised that the environment is allowed to deteriorate. If enlightened self-interest has given way to pure self-interest and if long-term thought and care have been supplanted by the quest for novelty and short-term monetary advantage, then the chances of long-term survival are dim indeed.

The care for the environment must take precedence over arguments of short-term price advantage and governments must recognize that pure market mechanisms are – in principle as well as in reality – incapable of taking care of precious common goods. No sane firm will voluntarily bear costs internally if it can legitimately externalize them; indeed, a manager who is willing to bear unnecessary costs for the purest of altruistic reasons would be guilty of disregarding the interests of the firm. A limited amount of green sentiment may do the image of the firm a lot of good and its costs may be justified in terms of publicity, but serious efforts to modify manufacturing practice in favour of the environment, out of the firm's free will and at its own expense, is extremely unlikely. Only in those fortunate cases when acting in the interest of the environment brings tangible benefits to the firm will such action be taken.

There is no practicable alternative to regulation. We must set strict limits on the amount of pollutants that any firm may discharge into the environment, be it in solid, liquid or gaseous form. Limits must be set and reviewed in the light of scientific information and in the light of what is regarded as technically possible. The latter statement is a risky one. Whenever governments try to set mandatory low levels for emissions, industry raises a cry of impossible. The claim that the achievement of such a standard is impossible or, at best, is achievable only at horrendous and ruinous cost, is made as a reflex action. As Pavlov's dogs produced saliva when a bell rang, so modern industry shouts 'impossible' when environmental standards are to be raised. Although this involuntary reaction occurs no matter how feasible or impossible the standards may be, it is true that not all things are technically achievable, at least at reasonable cost. Standards must be set at the best level that can be achieved with reasonable effort. A reasonable time span must be given before the standards are enforced, although what is regarded as reasonable is a matter of values and of power and, thus, of politics.

Enforcement must be convincing and effective, backed by an adequate inspection system and adequate penalties. What is reasonable can only be determined if industrial and government, or independent, experts thrash out the issue. Government, aided by good expert advice and after serious consultations with all concerned, must be able to gauge how far standards can be pushed and how much time is needed before enforcement can commence. Standards are only as good as their enforcement, but the enforcement is only as good as available methods of measurement and detection. Innovations in measuring instruments may be a necessary part of an environmentally benign innovation. Consideration of the methods of measurement and detection must form an integral part of the setting of standards. The standard must inevitably be a compromise; indeed, all technological solutions to problems are compromises and truly zero emissions cannot normally be achieved. There is no such thing as absolutely pure air or absolutely clean water. Nature knows no absolute purity.

The full innovative potential of industry ought to be harnessed to the service of the environment. What can be achieved easily by today's technology is not good enough. If it is possible to innovate in the pursuit of trivial wants, it should be possible to innovate in the pursuit of the survival of our planet and of life as we know it.

Whether or not government supports the achievement of environmental standards with financial subsidies, technical advice or any other means, must be a matter of judgement in individual cases. There can be no objection in principle to such help. Indeed, the more the care of the environment is seen as a collaborative rather than an adversarial process between government and industry, the more likely it is to succeed – provided, of course, that government is not lulled into thinking that industry's main task is to look after the public interest, which it is not. That is strictly a task for government.

There may be those who argue that the setting of rigorous environmental standards distorts the operation of the free market. This is a disingenuous argument. All transactions in a market (or, indeed, in society) are carried out within a legal framework. Bargains are struck according to certain rules, financial arrangements are regulated, and goods and services must comply with certain standards. Why should the degree of the fouling of the environment be an exception to the general rule and be left free from regulation? Civilized existence is subject to certain rules and what rules can be more important than those safeguarding public health and the continued existence of the planet in a state in which it can support the life of civilized society? Of course, it would suit the convenience of some to be allowed to discharge any pollution into the nearest river; but would it not also suit some to be allowed to print as much money as they wish? The latter is not permitted because it would destroy the legal framework within which market operations can thrive; the former should not be allowed because it would destroy the framework within which life itself can thrive.

Sustainable Growth

Ever since the publication of *Limits to Growth* (Meadows et al 1974), there has been no excuse for not realizing that exponential growth in consumption, population and pollution cannot be sustained in a world with finite resources and a finite capacity to digest the waste products of our civilization. Yet people desperately want growth and are not content to reach a steady state at current levels of consumption or population. Thus the concept of sustainable growth was born.

There can be no doubt that the poorer countries of the world do, indeed, need economic growth in order to establish standards of living that are sufficient to prevent acute hardship and to develop the full cultural potential of the people concerned. Even the simplest sense of equity must be offended by the crass differences in consumption between rich and poor countries, not to mention between the rich and poor people in any one country. That the problem of population growth needs to be solved before we can talk meaningfully of raising standards of living and of reaching a sustainable level of activity, let alone growth, is generally realized. However, reproduction is so close to the very essence of life that it takes a great deal of civilization and development to achieve acceptable birth rates. Unfortunately, there are very potent cultural forces at work to undermine efforts at reaching stable levels of population. These efforts must continue if hope for a sustainable world without poverty and with a civilization that does not destroy its own habitat is to have any chance of being realized.

The concept of sustainable development is simple and the necessity to achieve it is unassailable. It is only by sticking our heads in the sand, ostrich fashion, that we manage collectively to ignore the simple logic and pretend that we can go on much as before. The World Commission on Environment and Development (popularly known by the name of its chair-person as the Brundtland Commission) defines sustainable development as follows: 'Sustainable development is development that meets the needs of the present without compromising the ability of future generations to meet their own needs' (World Commission on Environment and Development 1987: 43).

The report sees the problem of sustainable development – and by development it means mainly the development of the Third World, or 'the South' – in terms of several interlocking crises: an environmental crisis, a development crisis and an energy crisis. The crises are made that much harder to solve because of the enormous growth in population, with estimates of a stable global population, some time in the next century, of between 8 and 14 billion people. It is also made more difficult by the enormous increase in world industrial production, contributing both to the depletion of natural resources and to the increase in pollution. Most developing countries face substantial problems in supplying their energy needs: they need either to spend valuable hard currency or to deplete what slender reserves in timber they have, leading to severe loss of forest areas. (For a more detailed discussion see eg Smith, ch 6: 244–85, in Smith and Warr 1991.)

One of the facets of the new world order that the report is concerned about is a shift of the so-called 'smokestack industries' into the developing world. As industrialization proceeds, it concentrates on the older industries, such as iron and steel, that require fewer infrastructural conditions to be fulfilled to work effectively. These industries are heavy consumers of raw materials and energy and are heavy polluters. It is to be feared that the developing countries try to acquire price advantages over the rich countries by not being too fussy about environmental degradation, in addition to using the availability of cheap labour (Braun and Wield 1994). Thus a new division of world activities arises, with the poorer countries producing the simpler and less differentiated products, which add little to their economies but cause a great deal of damage to the environment, while the advanced countries concentrate on high-technology industries and on services. Pollution and excessive use of resources, however, know no boundaries and the world as a whole suffers. The specific destruction of the environment in the Third World is so severe that further economic development is put in serious jeopardy.

> *We have in the past been concerned about the impact of economic growth upon the environment. We are now forced to concern ourselves with the impacts of ecological stress – degradation of soils, water regimes, atmosphere and forests – upon our economic prospects* (World Commission 1987: 5).

One of the reasons for attempting to innovate as rapidly as possible in the rich countries is the wish to keep ahead of the developing countries. This attempt has been highly successful and the newly industrialized countries (NICs) have not gained substantial market shares in the developed countries. Although enough industrial production has been established in the NICs and in developing countries to cause – in conjunction with the growth in population and, most important, with the use of new 'Western' methods of farming – catastrophic environmental degradation, the dominant pattern of trade in manufactured goods is still overwhelmingly in favour of the developed countries. Indeed, the less developed countries' (LDCs) share in world manufacturing value added has only risen from about 10 per cent in 1960 to under 13 per cent in 1985 (Jenkins: 20, in Hewitt et al 1992). The developed countries import only a very small fraction of their total consumption of manufactured goods from the less developed countries – on average, only 2.8 per cent! On the other hand, it is estimated that as many as 2 million jobs in Japan are sustained by trade with the less developed countries (Jenkins: 34, in Hewitt et al 1992).

Sustainable development is only possible if our activities rely entirely on cyclic processes and on the use of virtually inexhaustible resources. Only under these conditions can we hope to proceed for ever, without exhausting either scarce resources or causing irreversibly detrimental changes to our habitat. Currently, none of these conditions are met. They are not met in the developed world, which still plunders scarce reserves and pollutes the soil, the water and the atmosphere in intolerable fashion. They are met even less in developing countries which, despite their overall tiny consumption and because of their poverty, live on what has been called their environmental capital.

> *In many countries economic growth depends principally upon their stocks of environmental resources, or environmental capital: soils, forests, fisheries, species, water.*

164

...some developing countries have depleted virtually all of their ecological capital and are on the verge of environmental bankruptcy... (Smith: 251, in Smith and Warr 1991)

Agenda 21, a programme prepared for, and adopted at, the UN Conference on Environment and Development, held in Rio de Janeiro in June 1992 (United Nations 1992), sets out the issues involved in obtaining sustainable development, and the steps necessary to achieve it, unexceptionably, comprehensively and clearly. Unfortunately, these types of document appear to be processed by a high-tech text-blander that removes all traces of controversy and thus hides the real political problems behind bland and clever words. Nevertheless, as a summary of the issues, this is an admirable document that sets out the complex intertwined problems of poverty, population growth, world trade, patterns of consumption and environmental degradation.

> *The combined forces of poverty, wasteful consumption and rapidly-growing population must be brought under control to make sustainable development a reality* (loc cit: 3). *Countries can no longer afford to make decisions without considering environment and development issues at every step of the planning process* (loc cit: 7). *Agenda 21 proposals include: – Promoting sustainable energy development. – Promoting safe and environmentally sound transport systems. – Promoting industrial development that does not adversely impact the atmosphere. – Promoting agricultural (and forestry) development that does not adversely impact the atmosphere [promoting sustainable resource development and land use]. – Promoting sustainable energy consumption patterns and lifestyles. – Addressing uncertainties [becoming assured of the scientific basis for decision making]. – Preventing stratospheric ozone depletion* (loc cit: 8).

This is all highly laudable, except that the requirement of becoming assured of the scientific basis could be used as an excuse for virtually indefinite procrastination. Ecological problems are so complex that answers that may be regarded as certain are elusive and reasonable suspicions must be acted on. In any case, scientific theories are on permanent probation: what is correct today may prove false tomorrow; but we must act on what is correct, or even only probably correct, today.

A final quote from Agenda 21 gives some of the flavour of the complexity of apparently simple problems, in this case forest preservation:

> *A holistic approach to forest conservation and development*

must address other issues: population pressures,
unsustainable agricultural and industrial practices, land
ownership, employment opportunities and external debt.
Policies to address these problems must be coordinated
internationally and regionally (loc cit: 11).

Some types of consumption and pollution must stop and give way to
a sustainable regime. This can be achieved in part by more sensible
technological innovation, but to a greater extent by more sensible
social organization. This, however, is much easier said, or written,
than done. For example, world fertiliser consumption is now fifteen
times greater than it was at the end of World War II. The increase was
exponential with an initial doubling time of 10 years, which from 1970
slowed down to a doubling time of 15 years and recently has shown
signs of slowing down further (Meadows et al 1992: 15). The atmos-
pheric concentration of the greenhouse gases, particularly carbon
dioxide, methane and nitrous oxide, has been increasing exponential-
ly since the late 18th century. The concentration of carbon dioxide
has increased from about 270ppm (parts per million) to close to
360ppm; nitrous oxide has increased from about 285ppm to nearly
310ppm; and methane has increased from 0.7 to 1.8ppm. If we take
the average global temperature between 1951 and 1980 as our reference, then the five-year average in 1880 was about −0.4°C below
average, while the 1985 five-year average was about 0.25°C above average. The average global temperature has risen fairly steadily by an
alarming 0.6°C in the hundred years from 1880 to 1980 (op cit: 95).

Between 1970 and 1990, in just 20 years, the world's human population increased from 3.6 billion to 5.3 billion; the number of
automobiles increased from 250 million to 560 million; oil consumption increased from 17 billion barrels per annum to 24 billion barrels;
and electric generating capacity went up from 1.1 billion kW to 2.6
billion kW (op cit: 7).

Herring catches in the North Sea were 1.4 million tons in 1965
and this rapidly declined owing to over-fishing to only 0.7 million
tons in 1970. After a further period of decline, a ban was imposed in
1977. It is estimated that the maximum sustainable catch is 0.75 million tonnes a year (Smith: 50, in Smith and Warr 1991).

How many species of fauna and flora and how many habitats have
been irretrievably lost during the last few decades is a matter of conjecture. It is estimated that between 10 and 100 species per day are
lost. In Madagascar more than 90 per cent of the forest has been eliminated and it is estimated that only half of the 12,000 plant species
and 190,000 animal species have survived this carnage. In Western
Ecuador, the forests were converted to human settlements, banana
plantations and oil wells. As a result, 50,000 species of plants and animals have disappeared in a 25-year period. Nobody knows how many
species are left, although 1.4 million species have been classified

166

(Meadows et al 1992: 64–6). Neither does anybody know what valuable natural resources may be lost for ever with the loss of some forms of life. But more important than the loss of resources for human use is the destruction of natural equilibria and forms of life which we, as the unquestionably dominant species on earth, have a duty to protect rather than to destroy. Even those who believe that we have been given dominion over the earth must accept that dominion means a duty to preserve the planet, not a licence to destroy it. In order both to preserve the planet and to maintain human long-term self-interest, we must change our ways to make continued human existence on earth possible.

When proper policies are introduced, success can be achieved and in many cases has been achieved. Although the economies of the seven richest nations grew by almost 60 per cent between 1970 and 1988, their emissions of carbon dioxide and nitrogen oxides grew only very little because the previous link between economic activity and energy consumption has been successfully broken by measures to increase the efficiency of energy use. Emissions of the extremely harmful sulphur oxides actually decreased by 40 per cent, mostly because of the successful application of control policies (op cit: 90). It is on this optimistic note that we turn to a brief discussion of environmental policies.

CHAPTER FIVE

ENVIRONMENTAL POLICIES

◆

Attitudes and the Political Agenda

Environmental policies are shaped, decided upon and executed in a general framework of a given society and its system of governance. The principal initial steps of policy formation are analysis and choice (Mann 1981: 2). Analysis of the problem that requires a remedy and a choice of action or inaction. Both steps are fraught with difficulty. The analysis rarely, if ever, gives a very clear picture of the nature of the problem or of the available remedies. More often than not the analysis is controversial and distorted by value systems and ideologies. To compound the difficulties, unexpected events, especially actions taken by a multiplicity of actors within or without the social system under consideration, may change the situation and invalidate the results of the analysis even before policy decisions are taken. Worse still, policies in place may become inappropriate by the occurrence of such surprise events, rather like verdicts of a court may need to be reviewed in the light of new evidence not available at the time of the initial trial.

Policy formation is influenced by innumerable actors: government at all levels, pressure groups, public and private institutions, economic interests and interest groups, the media. Each group and each institution pursue their own interests, have their vision of problems coloured by their own ideology, have their own value systems, and their own incentive structure.

In the late Sixties the environment became part of the political agenda. Under the influence of scientists, publicists, pressure groups and the media, the feeling that the environment was posing a problem and that something ought to be done about it gathered ground, particularly in the United States. It was a time when people felt sufficiently affluent not to be too scared that environmental policies might endanger their standard of living. It was also a time when the starry-eyed belief in the potency of science and technology to solve all problems – prevalent since the end of World War II – had given way to scepticism and to the realization that the application of science and technology can cause as many problems as it can solve. How problems become part of a political agenda and how views undergo radical change is a complex issue. But undoubtedly various manifestations of environmental degradation – the disappearance of birds and butterflies, brooks covered in foam from detergents, the disappearance of fish from rivers and lakes, the prevalence of smog – contributed greatly to alarming both the public at large and the influential elites. The Three Mile Island incident and other major technological failures contributed greatly to shaking public trust in science.

Three conditions must be fulfilled to put matters on the political agenda in a democratic country:

1. there must be a stirring of awareness and an initial analysis of a problem among scientists and activists;
2. publications must appear, followed by meetings and the formation of pressure groups. These groups must then succeed in drawing attention to the problem among influential members of the elite, such as politicians, civil servants, media people and leading scientists;
3. a sufficient number of ordinary people must become convinced by the mounting evidence and mounting publicity to impress politicians and officials that indeed there is a groundswell of public opinion demanding action.

Once a problem becomes part of the political agenda, further analysis proceeds and discussion of possible remedies becomes widespread. Normally, controversies ensue, but the balance of attitudes changes.

The political embodiment of this change of attitude is the National Environmental Policy Act, passed by the US Congress in 1969. The act 'imposes a substantive burden on federal agencies to protect and defend the environment' (Mann 1981: 7). The act sets up a new federal institution, the Environmental Protection Agency (EPA), and requires that all major projects that might have implications for the environment should submit an environmental impact statement. Only if the EPA approves the statement can such projects proceed.

169

The National Environmental Policy Act did not resolve the inherent conflict between free economic activity and unhampered growth on the one hand, and environmental protection on the other, but at least it has tilted the balance slightly away from unbridled development toward environmental protection.

> *Private economic power is very much in evidence,*
> *challenging unwanted regulations, ignoring some strictures*
> *of the law, ...and endeavoring to convince the public of the*
> *costs and foolishness of much environmental policy.*
> However, *They can no longer count on arguments for*
> *unbridled economic growth to gain acceptance without*
> *careful assessment of the attendant costs of that growth.*
> *Public officials and the public alike are sensitive to such*
> *costs* (Mann 1981: 7).

The perception of an environmental problem is one thing, the attitude toward solutions quite another. Milbrath reports on a study conducted in the USA, England and Germany to elicit attitudes to various aspects of change related to environmental issues (Milbrath: 43–61, in Mann 1981). Table 5.1 shows the percentage of people who answered as shown when asked how much change was necessary in the social, economic and political system in order to solve environmental problems.

Table 5.1 *Perceived need for social change*

	no basic change needed	*considerable change needed*	*completely new system*
United States			
General public	10	65	16
Environmentalists	4	80	10
Business leaders	34	50	5
Labour leaders	16	62	10
Appointed officials	21	63	6
Elected officials	24	62	10
Media gatekeepers	27	61	2
England			
General public	11	52	25
Conservation Society	5	67	24
Nature Conservationists	12	64	14
Business leaders	26	53	12
Labour leaders	9	50	34
Public officials	34	54	5
Germany			
General public	16	59	9

Source: Milbrath: 47, in Mann 1981

When asked to rank the importance of environmental protection in relation to the importance of economic growth, using a scale of 1 to 7, with 7 meaning pre-eminence of economic growth and 1 meaning the pre-eminence of environmental protection, the mean scores of different groups of actors were as shown in Table 5.2.

Table 5.2 *Preference for economic growth (score 7) or environmental protection (score 1).*

	mean score
USA	
General public	2.99
Environmentalists	1.97
Business leaders	4.16
England	
General public	2.80
Conservation society	1.48
Business leaders	3.38
Germany	
General public	2.99

Source: Milbrath: 57, in Mann 1981

More recent enquiries confirm the trend. On a scale of zero for not being concerned at all, 1 for not being very concerned and 2 for showing a fair amount of concern, public opinion in the EC scored close to 2.5 for concerns about climate change, loss of natural resources, extinction of plant and animal species, disposal of industrial waste, air pollution, damage to sea life and pollution of inland waters. The degree of concern on all counts increased between 1986 and 1988 (Central Statistical Office 1992: 160). This trend in public opinion is reflected, to some extent, in actions. Thus, although total petrol consumption in the UK increased from 100 per cent in 1975 to 150 per cent in 1989, emissions of lead decreased in the same period from 100 per cent to about 35 per cent. Sales of unleaded petrol increased by 40 per cent between 1988 and 1991 (loc cit: 168). The total percentage contribution of recycled paper remained fairly static, around 20 per cent, between 1974 and 1989, but the contribution of recycled glass rose from about 10 per cent in 1983 to about 20 per cent in 1989. The total tonnage of glass collected in bottlebanks is an impressive 132,700 tonnes (loc cit: 169).

Some writers discuss the growth versus environment debate in terms of fundamental political-philosophical stance (see eg Humphrey and Buttel: 125–35, in Mann 1981). In these terms, those who adhere to the conservative point of view, which considers that markets can take care of everything and that the benefits of economic growth do diffuse to all members of society, see relatively little need to intervene in the operations of the market. Yet the more enlightened among them accept that environmental damage can be done and that social institutions must be alert to signals received from the scientific community and others regarding environmental problems or other market failures, and be prepared to apply remedies when necessary. Conservatives may be reluctant to accept such evidence and are reluctant to apply remedies other than attempts to improve the operation of the market, but even they do see the need for some legislative and regulatory intervention. Radicals, on the other hand, see the capitalist social order (a term rarely used in these days dominated by public relations and euphemisms – market economies being the preferred term) as one that systematically exploits both humans and nature. In principle, it might be argued, the only way to save the environment is by overthrowing the capitalist system. But, radicals too, do compromise. The more enlightened among them see that the capitalist system can be modified and reformed to accommodate some concerns of social equity and, more important in the current context, some environmental concerns. Thus there is a middle ground where all philosophical stances can meet (and not only the ones mentioned here) and can agree that something can and should be done about saving the environment. They may see it as enlightened self-interest, as an imperative of not fouling your own nest, as a moral obligation to take care of the environment that has been entrusted to us, or as simply trying to ensure the future of humankind on earth. Whichever way people look upon the issues, and from whatever corner of the political spectrum they come, they can achieve some sort of consensus on the need to act to preserve the environment. It is on this premise that virtually all the discourse in this book is based.

It does not matter whether people believe in the fundamental benefits or the fundamental evil of the capitalist system or whether they believe that markets are benign or wicked. They can all agree that markets do operate in all countries to a greater or lesser extent, that most countries are capitalist, and that markets can and must be regulated and modified to safeguard some social and environmental interests. There are very few anarchists who believe that all regulation by the state is evil. It may be noted that, contrary to expectations, there is no correlation between the degree of market orientation and the degree of environmental protection in a country.

Examples of Environmental Policies

The question arises how much can be done to safeguard the environment within a market economy and what measures are best suited for particular situations. In particular, the question of whether market incentives, ie pricing policies, are more effective than prohibitions is hotly debated and must be faced. The likely answer is that different problems require different solutions, but we must try and be more specific. As there is little empirical evidence on the efficacy of various policies, some of the answers will remain speculative and controversial.

One success story for pricing policies is the Dutch case of effluent charges (Bressers: 5–39, in Dietz and Heijman 1988). The case study described deals only with industrial effluents in the Netherlands. The policy, which aimed at cleaning up the surface waters, consists of three components:

1. The 'backstop principle', aimed at reducing the total amount of existing pollution, without accepting a pollution increase anywhere.
2. The principle of attempting to stop pollution at source, rather than concentrating on cleaning up contaminated water.
3. In order to pay for large investments in the treatment plant required to clean up existing pollution, despite the second principle, the principle of 'polluter pays' was introduced in the form of effluent charges. Each firm pays for the amount of effluent it discharges.

The efficacy of these policies was tested by observing the amounts of oxygen-consuming organic wastes and heavy metal pollution discharged into the sewers. This study, like virtually all others, suffers in that there is no parallel case study of an equivalent situation without effluent charges; the conclusions that may be drawn legitimately concern, therefore, only the effectiveness of the package of policies on the basis of the situation before and after they had become operational.

The reductions in pollution achieved are impressive. In the five years between 1975 and 1980 the levels of heavy metals in industrial waste water were reduced as follows: mercury by 83 per cent, chromium by 64 per cent, cadmium and nickel by 50 per cent. The smallest reduction was in lead, which came down by only 20 per cent. The reduction in oxygen-consuming organic pollution is equally impressive. Between 1970 and 1983 it dropped to about 30 per cent, whereas industrial production rose to 130 per cent (loc cit: 9–10).

The authors go to a great deal of trouble to answer the two related questions: were these reductions in pollution caused by the Pollution of Surface Waters Act and, if so, which of its three policy component was the most effective? The conclusions they reach, on the basis of statistical analysis and assessments by experts, are that the great reduction in pollution was caused by policy and that the most effective part of the policy were the effluent charges. The particularly favourable outcome can be attributed to several factors. The charging authority was strongly motivated to raise the charges effectively, as this was their only means of funding their large investments in new sewage treatment plant. In order to reduce the amount of information required for the implementation of the charges, householders and other small polluters were not included in the system of charges per unit of pollution. Medium-sized polluters are charged on the basis of the amount of water they consume, using a table of coefficients worked out by experts for different industrial processes. Actual measurements of pollutants thus needed to be carried out only for large polluters. Although pragmatic adjustments and appeals are possible and are used, no legal loopholes have been discovered in the act and the courts have upheld all the decisions made by the water authorities. Thus the charges proved an easily administered and enforced system and the only way for individual firms to reduce their costs is to reduce the amount of waste they discharge.

It is difficult to draw a general conclusion from this case, except to say that charging policies have to be carefully thought out and implemented. They can probably only work in conjunction with other measures, so that the overall efficacy of the whole package of measures becomes plausible. It is also necessary that there should be strong general support for the desirability of the aims pursued by the policy and full trust that the charges are not diverted from their purpose to line private pockets or augment general government revenue. Charges imposed by private companies, operated for profit, can never gain this trust as the public always suspects, undoubtedly rightly, that despite all the public service rhetoric of such companies, their true aims are to enrich their shareholders and their directors. A further conclusion must be that charges can work only if what is charged for is accessible to reliable measurement or assessment, and that the quantities are truly under the control of the firm or person that pays. It is futile to use charges as an incentive to reduce pollution or consumption if the body paying the charges cannot actually control the amounts it uses or discharges. A further condition is that the firm must operate under conditions that make it impossible to pass on the charges to the customer. Private monopolistic utilities, as they operate in Britain, are immune to incentive charges as they can simply pass them on to their captive customers.

The final and most important condition is that the price to be paid for pollution should not be such as to cripple the firm and that the abatement technology available should be cheap enough to make it possible for the firm to make savings which cover, or nearly cover, the price it pays for pollution. Only under these conditions will the firm really try to solve the pollution problem. If the technology to abate the pollution is more expensive than the price to be paid for pollution, then clearly the firm will not invest in technology. Instead, it will try to pass on the cost or, if this is not possible, it will make other savings or go bankrupt. In other words, the charges must be such as to make cost effective abatement measures possible.

If the principle of 'polluter pays' is to be effective in terms of reducing pollution rather than just raising revenue, the cost of abatement must be less than the cost of continued pollution. This creates opportunities for technological innovation: if technological innovation in abatement technologies can reduce the cost of abatement, a reduction in pollution is more likely. Those who produce such technologies may reap the economic benefits of their innovation, while society reaps the benefits of reduced pollution. This type of innovation is worthy of every support it needs.

Unless all the above conditions are fulfilled, any attempt to protect the environment by charges is futile and the belief that it can work falls into the category of wishful thinking. Dietz and Vollebergh discuss the theoretical problem of market incentives as an instrument of environmental policy (Dietz and Vollebergh: 40–60, in Dietz and Heijman 1988). They point out that economists, in general, feel that the optimum balance between various economic activities can be achieved by proper pricing. This applies even to public goods, such as the environment. Thus the environment can be safeguarded if the proper price is charged for its use or abuse. Non-economists do not find this point of view very convincing. The price argument is based on the theory of the rational behaviour of economic man, which Dietz and Vollebergh regard as a 'thin theory' because it assumes a fully informed and fully rational calculus as the basis of all human behaviour. This is acceptable as an assumption for the development of economic theory, but less useful as a guide to real human behaviour.

> *The thin theory of rationality is a rather weak foundation. Its universality does not do sufficient justice to the complexity of all environmental problems. Acid rain, the pollution of rivers and oceans, the degradation of soils and forests, noise pollution in the vicinity of airports or in transformers differ in cause, seriousness and extent. We do not want to suggest that there should be no room for pricing in environmental policy. A dynamic world full of uncertainties about future events causes severe problems for every policy instrument. There is no a priori ground for a rock-bottom belief in the working of pricing. To be very optimistic about the effect of using market instruments seems more or less the result of wishful thinking* (loc cit: 53).

Environmental Policies in the EC and in the UK

One of the most fundamental concepts in UK environmental policy is best practicable means (BPM). It was first introduced in 1842 and was formally embodied in the Alkali Act of 1863. As applied to air pollution, BPM has been defined as follows:

– no emission could be tolerated which constituted a recognised health hazard, either short or long term; – emissions in terms of both concentration and mass, had to be reduced to the lowest practicable amount taking into account local conditions and circumstances, current state of knowledge on control technology and effects of substance emitted, financial considerations, and the means to be employed; – having secured the minimum practicable emission, the height of discharge should be arranged so that the residual emission was rendered harmless and inoffensive by dilution and dispersion (NSCA 1991: 4).

The first of the three statements is simply not true in this stark form. Although the discharge of many obnoxious substances is truly prohibited, many others are tolerated up to certain levels. Or are sulphur dioxide, lead, nitrogen oxides, carbon monoxide, or even the ubiquitous carbon dioxide defined as harmless because their emission is deemed to be unavoidable? We should speak of a principle of best practicable prohibition, rather than pretend that the emission of all harmful substances is prohibited. The advantage of replacing complacency by honesty is that the matter would need to be kept under review more obviously in the light of new knowledge about the effects of the emissions and the new technologies becoming available for reducing further emissions that are falsely claimed to be prohibited.

But the principle of best practicable means is an excellent concept that enshrines the need for compromise in all matters of environmental pollution. It should be interpreted as meaning that we must achieve the best possible solution at any given time, that we must seek constantly to improve the best solution by new technical means and, if necessary, devote more resources to the protection of the environment. If the best practicable solution is not good enough, then we should stop the polluting activity. The whole concept must be dynamic and must be subject to negotiation between a technically competent and decisive inspectorate and the polluter. For what is best available, what is a reasonable cost and what is safe enough, are all matters that are not clear-cut and need to be enforced with reason. Clearly, technological innovation has plenty of scope in all this as it can improve both manufacturing processes and pollution abatement techniques.

The third statement defining BPM contains an altogether dubious proposition. Although it is true that whether a substance is beneficial, harmless or harmful may depend on its concentration, it is also true that dispersal may mean getting rid of something nasty by sending it across the water to somebody else. Dilution obviously must be one of the means of dealing with all kinds of emissions, but dispersal ought to be used, if at all, with a great deal of caution and only as an aspect of dilution.

The EC and the British Environmental Protection Act 1990 use a concept similar to BPM, known as best available techniques not entailing excessive cost (BATNEEC):

> 'Best' must be taken to mean most effective in preventing, minimising or rendering harmless polluting emissions. ...'Not entailing excessive cost' needs to be taken in two contexts, depending on whether it is applied to new processes or to existing processes. The presumption will be that best available techniques will be used, but that presumption can be modified by economic considerations where it can be shown that the costs of applying BAT would be excessive in relation to the environmental protection to be achieved. (NSCA, 1991: 11 and 12)

The acronym is longer, but the sentiments are much the same as in BPM.

The most recent concept in pollution control is integrated pollution control, also embodied in the Environmental Protection Act 1990. It was suggested as early as 1976 by the Royal Commission on Environmental Pollution that pollutants cross the boundaries between air, water and soil and that unified control would be much more effective than separate controls. Thus HM Inspectorate of Pollution (HMIP) came into being in 1991. Integrated pollution control gave rise to the new concept of best practicable environmental option (BPEO): 'This specifies the pollution control technology which is the best practicable for the environment as a whole – considering the total impact on water, land and air pathways together' (NSCA 1991: 10–11). Certain industrial processes and installations will require authorization and monitoring by HMIP. Firms will have to pay for this service, on the polluter pays principle, but there is very little indication that the charging system has been devised so as to reduce pollution; its only aim appears to be to recover the costs of control.

The processes that fall under the act are those that previously fell under the regulations for air emissions under the Health and Safety at Work Act 1974; processes giving rise to 'significant quantities of special waste', and processes giving rise to emissions to sewers or controlled waters of substances with particularly noxious effects (NSCA 1991: 5). HM Inspectorate of Pollution has the task of dealing with large-scale and complex industrial pollution; the more ordinary, though not less important, pollution remains under the control of local authorities, with the National Rivers Authority and the Health and Safety Executive playing more specialized roles.

The Environmental Protection Act 1991 constitutes a real legislative advance on the previous acts in force in that it gives local authorities the power and duty to control a large number of processes that were previously controlled only in cases of complaint. Processes scheduled for local authority control will now require authorization, and among the conditions to be attached to such authorization will be the use of best available techniques not entailing excessive cost. Whether, and how quickly, environmental improvement will follow remains to be seen. Effective action is generally taken if, and only if, there is a public outcry. Although the Public Health (Smoke Abatement) Act of 1926 enabled the Alkali Inspectorate to control industrial smoke, nothing was done to control smoke from non-industrial sources in Britain until the public outcry that followed the great London smog of 1952 forced the issue. About 4,000 additional deaths were directly attributed to the smog and after a great deal of enquiry and argument the Clean Air Act 1956 was enacted. 'The legislation also prohibited the emission of "dark" smoke from any chimney, provided for Government funding for the conversion of domestic grates to smokeless operation, and regulated the fuels that could be burned on them' (NSCA 1991: 26-7). The effect of the Clean Air Act and the actions and amendments that followed was a social revolution in that the cherished British coal-fire was eliminated. The success of the act in completely abolishing the infamous British pea-soup smog verges on the miraculous.

The Single European Act 1986, which establishes the Single European Market with effect from 1 January 1993, explicitly states several principles of environmental policy. The objectives of Community actions with regard to the environment shall be:

- to preserve, protect and improve the quality of the environment;
- to contribute towards protecting human health;
- to ensure a prudent and rational utilization of natural resources.

> *Action by the Community relating to the environment shall be based on the principles that preventive action should be taken, that environmental damage should as a priority be rectified at source, and that the polluter should pay. Environmental protection requirements shall be a component of the Community's other policies* (NSCA 1991: 288).

These are noble sentiments and sensible principles, but to achieve real improvement is a long and arduous process with environmental actors doing battle with entrenched political and economic interests.

One example is the friction between environmental standards set by the EC and British standards concerning drinking water. Nitrate levels in certain regions of the UK are higher than EC standards permit. The EC standards were supposed to come into force in 1989, but the British government has only agreed to comply by 1995 and the dispute continues (Taylor and Press 1990: 11). A low level of nitrates is not only relevant to drinking water, but is also of great importance for the prevention of the growth of algae and, hence, the capability of water to sustain fish. In 1988, the Commission of the European

Communities (CEC) issued a proposal aimed at reducing nitrate levels in all waters. The proposal includes, among other measures, a reduction in the amount of fertilizer spread on agricultural land. A proposal is not a directive and nobody knows if and when action will follow this undoubtedly important proposal. Bearing in mind that the water companies in Britain have recently been privatized and that they are motivated by profit-making, it can be appreciated how difficult it will be to get EC standards accepted and enforced.

It is clear that only a very small proportion of environmental control relies on pricing incentives. This is not surprising, as such incentives can work only under a restricted set of favourable circumstances, as discussed above. In general, there is no alternative to setting standards, supervising and enforcing them rigorously, and revising them constantly in the light of experience and of new technology. This calls for considerable technical expertise among the inspectorate and for support of technological innovation in environmental control and environmentally benign technologies. The term benign is, of course, relative. Cleaner and more benign would be appropriate terms. For controls to be effective, they must be acceptable to public and industrial opinion. Enforcement should not be confrontational but should include elements of advice and cooperation. The inspectors should be equipped with considerable negotiating skills in addition to their technical expertise.

The days of confrontation ought to be over, as many industrialists now realize that the tide is moving in favour of the environment. Industrialists are beginning, albeit hesitantly and with some reluctance, to supplement rhetoric with deeds and money. In a paper entitled *Acceptance of Innovation: An Industry View of Environmental Aspects*, J C Felton writes:

> *Equally, a healthy industry depends on a healthy*
> *environment, one in which industry can carry out its*
> *operations and which is acceptable to society as a*
> *whole...Public expectations with respect to environmental*
> *conservation are increasing...an increasing demand for*
> *consumer products must be compatible with the maintenance*
> *of clean rivers and beaches.* (Felton: 31, in Roberts and
> Weale 1991).

Felton may be an avant-garde thinker in industry, but the realization that things cannot go on as they were is beginning to dawn on everybody. Unhappily, however, as we said at the outset, the measures taken are nowhere near sufficient to deal with the seriousness of the situation and people still see a choice between affluence and environmental protection, rather than seeing the choice between squalor and death on the one hand and environmental protection on the other. It is to be hoped that, with increasing experience of environmental protection, both legislators and inspectors will become bolder, and industrialists and the public will gradually accept more serious protective measures. So far, we are still only at the stage of dealing with relatively obvious and relatively painless measures and are not tackling the root causes of the problem either deeply enough or fast enough.

Currently the European Community operates its fifth programme of environmental policy: *Towards Sustainability, A European Community Programme of Policy Action in Relation to the Environment and Sustainable Development* (CEC 1992). The four previous programmes (which expired at the end of 1992) enacted some 200 pieces of environmental legislation, yet the Commission acknowledges that environmental deterioration in the Community continued. The pressures on the environment from international competition and economic growth were so strong that environmental legislation succeeded only in slowing down deterioration, not in halting or reversing it.

The Treaty on European Union, signed in February 1992, introduced as a principal objective 'the promotion of sustainable growth respecting the environment'. It also acknowledges the need for 'integration of environmental considerations in the formulation and implementation of economic and sectoral policies'. This is a most welcome recognition of the importance of the environment at the highest political level, although environmental considerations have not been accorded the supremacy they deserve. The principle that environmental considerations should form part and parcel of all policy formation has been accepted and this is of the greatest importance.

The fifth programme departs from the previous programmes in some important respects. First, the view is now accepted that the environmental problem is an extremely serious global issue that cannot be solved by merely looking inwards and tackling individual symptoms of the malaise. Hence, the new focus is on activities and agents that damage the environment and on attempts to change the trends in society's patterns of behaviour and consumption.

Secondly, more attention will be paid to the involvement of as many actors as possible so that environmental action will not be seen as top-down, but as participative. To this end several new consultative bodies have been created: a Consultative Forum, an Implementation Network, and an Environmental Policy Review Group. It is only to be hoped that the environmental policy will not get bogged down by the application of the principle of subsidiarity. This principle states that decisions should be taken as far away from the centre as practicable. This makes the Commission and the central Community institutions more or less a back-stop for actions not taken at a more local level. This is admirable from the point of view of democracy and of devolution of power, but dangerous because of the risks of inaction and delay on matters as vital as environmental protection. Some European governments are keener than others to do something toward a solution of environmental problems. Some indulge in wishful thinking in believing that the market will solve these problems or that they will simply go away. Alas, they will not go away and neither will the market solve them. Real urgent action is needed by all governments, not merely beautifully written documents that everybody is happy to sign but not to act upon.

The new policy acknowledges the need for better information and education. The public needs to be better informed and better educated in order to make environmentally sound individual decisions. Institutions, whether governmental, industrial, commercial or whatever, all need reliable information. Finally, we need better information and education for environmental professionals: consultants, academics, engineers, inspectors. A new European Environment Agency is to play an important role in providing information and attempts at disseminating such information are to form part of the policy action.

The environmental problems that are to be given priority are:

- sustainable development of natural resources: soil, water, natural areas and coastal zones;
- integrated pollution control and prevention of waste;
- reduction in the consumption of non-renewable energy;
- improved mobility management, including more efficient and environmentally rational location decisions and transport modes;
- coherent packages of measures to achieve improvements in environmental quality in urban areas;
- improvement of public health and safety, with special emphasis on industrial risk assessment and management, nuclear safety and radiation protection.

The document describing the policy (CEC 1992) has some very well informed and thoughtful things to say about the environmental problem – for example: 'Present trends in the Community's transport sector are all leading towards greater inefficiency, congestion, pollution, wastage of time and value, damage to health, danger to life and general economic loss' (loc cit: 6).

The main target sectors for the policy are: industry, energy, transport, agriculture, and tourism.

The Commission will attempt to form a partnership with industry to achieve improved resource management, improved use of environmental information, and to set Community standards for environmentally sound production processes and products.

In the energy sector, the Community will attempt to achieve an overall improvement in energy efficiency and will develop a strategic technology programme towards less carbon intensity and towards the development and deployment of renewable energy options.

On transport, the emphasis is on better planning to reduce transport need; on the development of public transport; on the technical improvement of vehicles; and on the promotion of a more rational use of cars.

In the field of agriculture, it is realized that environmental policy and agricultural policy must act together; thus the reform of the Common Agricultural Policy (CAP), which has run into such enormous difficulties and has produced such vast surplus production, is seen as part of the answer to the environmental problem. No doubt the problem is largely caused by incentives towards more intensive agriculture, and the removal of such incentives might be highly beneficial to the environment. However, advances in achieving fertile soils and in controlling weeds, pests and disease by more benign means will also have to be made.

The fifth programme intends to broaden its mix of instruments:

1. legislative instruments to set fundamental levels of protection;
2. market-based instruments through the application of economic and fiscal incentives and disincentives, through the use of civil liability for damage caused to the environment, and through attempting to get price mechanisms to operate in favour of environmentally benign products and processes;
3. horizontal supporting instruments, such as better data, more relevant research, improved planning, and public, consumer and professional information and education;
4. financial support mechanisms through the use of a variety of Community funding in favour of environmental projects.

Environmental Impact Assessment

The solution of environmental problems depends on two things in almost equal measure: the political will to solve them, and the technical and scientific knowledge to recognize problems and to find feasible solutions. Will and knowledge are the father and mother of solutions. Knowledge needs to encompass knowledge of the problems, knowledge of possible solutions, and knowledge of how society operates in the implementation of solutions. The tasks are truly interdisciplinary and information from many disciplines is needed. We have previously dealt with these questions for technology in general, under the heading of technology assessment, and shall now turn to the more specialized task of assessing environmental impacts of individual projects.

The first step in dealing with the environmental impact of any technology or any project is to give these impacts some thought before the technology or the project are put into operation and it becomes too late to do anything about the environmental consequences. The attempt to discover the effects of using a technology prior to its full deployment is technology assessment in the general sense. Environmental impact statements are the equivalent of TA for the more special case of physical developments, such as major civil engineering projects, the erection of a factory, of a power station, and so on. The US National Environmental Policy Act demands an environmental impact statement for all major developments of this kind. The European Commission Directive (85/337) on environmental assessment introduces a somewhat similar scheme in Europe, and indeed most, or possibly all, European countries use some variant of environmental impact assessment in their planning process. The so-called Brundtland Report is also explicit in demanding environmental impact assessments. 'States shall make or require prior environmental assessments of proposed activities which may significantly affect the environment or use of natural resource' (World Commission on Environment and Development 1987: 349).

The environmental impact statement bears considerable resemblance to a technology assessment, but is limited to environmental impacts of a particular project and is thus limited not only in scope but also is confined to a specific location. It could be said, therefore, that TA is a generic class of studies and environmental impact statements form a specific group within this class.

Environmental impact statements are a direct and formal part of the decision-making process, whereas TA only occasionally serves as a direct aid, and very often merely forms part of the background information on which decisions are based. In the US, an environmental impact statement is mandatory for any major project that might impact the environment and in which the Federal government plays a role. The role may vary from direct sponsor to mere regulator. Thus all projects sponsored by a Federal agency or requiring a licence or permission from the Federal government, as well as projects that involve Federal funding, must provide a satisfactory environmental impact statement before they can proceed. Federal states have similar legislation in place and thus the environmental impact statement is part of the planning process for virtually all major developments. In Europe, different states handle the statements differently but, by and large, some form of assessment of likely environmental impacts is a mandatory part of the process of planning permission for major projects.

What environmental impact statements cannot do is to consider the question of whether the development in question is needed at all; it is only a method of asking what damage, if any, it will cause to the environment. This damage will then be weighed up against the benefits of the project by the authorities entrusted with licensing or permitting the project. However, even they would exceed their authority if they were to ask whether, for example, additional power stations are needed at all. They can only answer the question whether a given power station, of a given design, will damage a given site unduly in relation to the benefits that it is assumed to bestow, taking into account best available techniques not entailing excessive cost. It has therefore been variously proposed to institute a generic environmental impact statement (GEIS), which would be tantamount to a technology assessment and could ask all the fundamental questions about the generic technology. Individual project appraisals could then base their decision on the generic EIS as well as on the specific one for a given project.

Among the many difficult questions with regard to the practice of environmental impact statements are questions of 'scoping' – ie what is and what is not to be included as possible impacts; who should prepare the statement; and the question of who should be allowed to make representations. These problems are common to all planning regulations, but they become more acute with the magnitude of the project under consideration. Unfortunately, nature cannot be represented directly at any hearings. The environmental interest of people can be represented by neighbours and political groupings. The interests of plants and animals must be represented by proxy and this can only be done by pressure groups, preferably well equipped with expertise. Governments should either recognize the vital role of such groups and support their activities, or else accept the responsibility for representing nature themselves through some designated agency. In other words, nature should be given a recognized expert and committed voice. As long as we regard such pressure groups as marginal and cranky, we shall not make much progress in safeguarding nature. Obviously, the big issues, such as the ozone hole or the greenhouse effect, are far beyond the local scope of environmental impact assessments. However, whether the problem is a major global one or a small local one, we must create a respected, sane, well-informed voice to speak for nature. Until this voice becomes the voice of government and part of the normal processes of governance, the special pleading by committed groups is vital.

CHAPTER SIX

SUMMARY AND
CONCLUSIONS

◆

It has been shown how the present quest for the fastest possible rate of technological innovation, without regard for the environmental impact of technology or for the real needs of society, has many serious drawbacks and is not sustainable in the long run. To expect sustainable advance from random rapid technological progress is futile. This futility is summed up under four headings.

The Four Dimensions of Futility

The Irrelevance of New Technologies to Real Needs

What society really needs are technologies and attitudes that help to solve, or alleviate, societary problems. What we do not need are technologies designed merely to stimulate flagging demand by making products of technology subject to fashion and by producing ever new toys and gadgets.

We need technologies that solve environmental problems, urban problems, health and safety problems; that help to provide meaningful employment; and those that help developing countries to overcome barriers to development. This sounds simple and unassailable in principle, but is of no practical use unless we can answer two questions: what might these technologies actually be; how do we make sure that they become available and achieve widespread use?

185

Examples of useful technologies that already exist or can readily be imagined as feasible might be:

- Cars that use far less energy and produce far fewer harmful emissions, without sacrifice of safety. It is likely that the performance of such cars would be much reduced, but this is a small price to pay for saving the environment and, at the same time, also saving life and limb.
- Public transport could be much enhanced. This would not only save energy and reduce pollution, it would also increase safety and improve the quality of life in congested cities. The private car is probably the one item that destroys cities more than any other. A major change of heart and of policy is required to achieve both of the above improvements; the technical obstacles can be readily overcome.
- Heating of homes and other buildings could be much improved to increase its efficiency, and thus reduce both energy consumption and pollution. Such improvement includes better thermal efficiency both of buildings and of heating systems, and is not beyond the wit of engineers and architects. Improved building regulations and some support policies would be needed to give a boost to such developments.
- Renewable energy resources could be much further developed and used. These include biomass, wind power in all its guises, tidal power, and solar energy in a variety of forms. The development of fuels produced from biomass, or of hydrogen produced from water, needs to be pursued. Much more development work needs to be done and the policies required to get renewable energy off the ground need to be formulated and vigorously pursued.
- Major changes in agricultural practice are required to reduce pollution from fertilizers, weedkillers and pesticides, while maintaining, or reinstating, a greater variety of wildlife and of landscape. As with other desirable technologies, a judicious mix of R&D and of technology and agricultural policies is required.
- Technologies for dealing with oil and other spillages need to be developed, in addition to improving the safety of transportation of hazardous materials.
- Artificial spare parts for use in human surgery need to be developed much further. The development of artificial blood for transfusions would be a major benefit.

The list could be extended almost indefinitely, but this would not serve my purpose of illustrating the thinking that should be the motive for technological innovations and for technology policy.

These required technologies are all possible, some are even available, but currently what has been termed the 'selection environment for technologies' does not favour them. The selection environment consists of markets, albeit manipulated by extensive salesmanship; of government policies; and of public opinion, albeit manipulated by the mass media.

It is obvious that our current selection procedures do not give us the technologies we need. What we get is technological innovation that aims at the fastest possible rate of obsolescence in order to increase the markets for technological products. This is done by making all goods subject to fashion and by adding an ever-increasing number of trivial features to all products.

Sometimes even the present selection mechanisms produce desirable results. In cars, for example, marketing has now understood that safety can sell and the public has been made aware of the fact that cars designed for the protection of their occupants are more desirable than those that merely stress speed, comfort and performance. Despite this highly laudable recent trend towards safety, the speed merchants are still marketing cars on the basis of higher performance, greater speed and more powerful engines, despite the fact that a study by the British Department of Transport shows that 'high-performance cars are nearly twice as likely to be involved in fatal accidents than standard models' (*The Guardian*, 13 May 1992). The Department has recently taken the positive step of publishing statistical evidence on car safety, which will, hopefully, help to slant the market towards demands for greater safety (Department of Transport 1994).

Cars and roads have moulded our thinking to the extent that we are now talking about super-highways of information when we mean an all-embracing network of optical fibres to carry the maximum possible amount of information. This will mean further advantages for so-called networked organizations – ie large global firms that already dominate much of the economy of the world. For the private person it will mostly mean an added choice of entertainment, in all likelihood more of the same trash at a higher price. Our new dependence on telecommunications and multi-media presentations will probably mean that the slick, spectacular, superficial statement, supported by visual images, will become the dominant form of communication, and thoughtful in-depth analysis will be replaced by manipulative superficial half-truths.

The latest innovation in IT is mobile communications for all. Huge sums are being invested into making portable telephones smaller and soon we shall all be persuaded that to be unreachable, wherever we may be, is a sign of being an unimportant, and hence inferior, person. If you want to be somebody, you had better carry your portable phone with you at all times. PCN (personal communications network) is the latest in the infinite series of incomprehensible acronyms that everybody needs to know. The new technology is being hailed as a saviour from many social ills: if you get stuck in a traffic jam, you can telephone to say that you will be late for your appointment. If your car breaks down and you dare not get out for fear of being attacked, you can summon help without leaving your vehicle. And if accident statistics are unsatisfactory, you can add to the casualty figures by driving along while holding your telephone in one hand and concentrating on your interesting conversation, instead of on the boring traffic. The slogan 'telephones for people' will soon become irresistible, but did anybody know that they needed it, other than as an inadequate surrogate for real solutions to the intractable problems of overloaded roads and high crime rates? Is it not futile to provide such poor technological surrogates for real solutions? Do we really prefer to have mobile telephones and sophisticated burglar alarms, rather than eliminate the virulent and widespread social diseases of robbery and burglary?

The list of trivial innovations is infinite. If we compare subsequent models of almost any major household equipment, the differences between them are trivial. Real improvements are discernible only infrequently, and often the consumer is unaware of what really matters. What is the consumer told about substitutes for greenhouse gases in refrigerators or about the quality of their thermal insulation and their power consumption? What do house purchasers know about the insulating qualities or the efficiency of the heating system of the house they are buying?

Environmental awareness has, to an extent, taken root among the general public, and business has learned to pander to it. It has become fashionable to attach 'environmentally friendly' or 'bio' labels to many goods. But these labels are not well controlled and many of them are entirely meaningless, and thus fraudulent. The label 'green' does not signify much more than the infamous 'whiter than white'. Governments ought to insist on meaningful environmental labelling, but this runs counter to their free market philosophies and is advancing very slowly, although the Commission of the European Communities and the US authorities are attempting to tackle this difficult issue (Potter and Hinnells 1994). Competition is powerless to give meaning to these labels, as the consumer is unable to test their real content. Competition can produce socially beneficial results only within a circumscribed set of circumstances, and one of the conditions that must be fulfilled is the consumer's knowledge and understanding of the properties of the goods the market has to offer. Thus social or environmental compatibility of products cannot be left to the market, as the purchaser is unable to judge products by social or environmental criteria in the absence of full information and in a climate in which crass egotism so often prevails. To achieve social or environmental compatibility of products, institutions must be created which provide full unbiased information about the products and, in addition, governments must assume responsibility for creating a regulatory regime which ensures that only correct information is given and only environmentally acceptable products are offered on the market.

Far from supplying what the consumer needs, technology supplies what it is able to produce, in the hope that consumers can be persuaded that this is precisely what they need. Sometimes these efforts meet fierce resistance, particularly if the product on offer seriously threatens the interests of some social group. A case in point is bovine somatropin (BST), produced by the marvels of genetic engineering and designed to increase milk yields by some 15–40 per cent. Farmers, especially small farmers, resist it fiercely, as yet further increases in their productivity are a threat to the livelihood of many of their number. In a market in which consumption cannot increase, higher productivity means the removal of some producers. Yet farmers are crying out, in vain, for some innovations, as, for example, methods of straw utilization or the production of silage without effluent (Jones, *Farmers Weekly*, 1 May 1987). This issue highlights one of the obscenities of our age: while the advanced countries make strenuous efforts to find the political means of dealing with excessive food production, and technologies add to their problems by following their normal trend of increasing the efficiency of production, millions of people in the poorer countries starve, often to death. The sheer irrelevance of technological innovation to the solution of the gravest problems of humankind strikes one with blinding obviousness and induces a feeling of helplessness in the face of so much human misery. The rich indulge in ever more trivial pursuits, while the poor suffer and die, with anger in their hearts. What William Keegan calls 'bourgeois triumphalism' (*The Observer*, 10 May 1992) knows no pity in its smug ways.

Indeed, much new technology has made a major contribution to the steady growth in unemployment and poverty in the rich nations. Despite all the arguments to the contrary, labour-saving technology has displaced workers faster than new products, new services and new markets could re-employ them. The net effect in recent years is a relentless growth in unemployment in most advanced countries. Official figures hide a considerable amount of this unemployment by clever manipulation of definitions, and much lack of employment finds expression in poorly paid and insecure part-time jobs that replace proper full-time careers. Even if a dozen sophisticated computer models, supposed to describe the employment effect of information technology, show only small effects or claim that the benefits are not quantified, the unemployed know full well what has happened to them. And even though unemployment is the net result of a myriad of factors, it is unlikely that the massive introduction of labour-saving technologies has had a beneficial effect upon it. It may be true, of course, that unemployment in those industries that could not afford to, or would not, introduce advanced technologies is worse than in more 'progressive' enterprises; nevertheless, the net effect of new technology is a reduction in employment opportunities, especially for the less skilled (Matzner et al 1988).

The successful young of the world buy Porsches, the less successful either steal them or, more often, make do with public transport.
The successful are tremendously busy and important and chase
about with their mobile phones, while the less successful desperately
try to kill time with no money to spend, sometimes turn to crime
and, surprisingly infrequently, indulge in violent protest. George
Carey, the Archbishop of Canterbury, is reported to have questioned
whether industry is fulfilling its purpose when 'prolonged bursts of
private sector led economic growth' in advanced countries left more
people than ever 'hungry, thirsty, ill, naked or in prison' (*The
Guardian*, 13 May 1992). However, 'It is not in the nature of the politics of contentment to expect or plan counteracting action for
misfortune...' (Galbraith 1992: 40).

Is it not futile to abolish jobs at a terrifying rate by introducing
new process technology and rationalizing all processes to their ultimate limit; only to find that there is insufficient demand for the goods
and services thus produced in abundance? The logical consequence is
to try to create new demands for new goods and services, in the futile
effort to compensate for the job losses incurred. Frantic technologists
and workers produce ever more goods and services; frantic salesmen
try to sell them; a frantic public tries to earn enough to be able to buy
these luxuries; and in the end none of this adds up and a large residue
of bitterness remains.

Yet there is no shortage of work to be done. Public transport is
overloaded and underdeveloped. Cities are decaying. Housing is largely poor. The health service is overloaded. Culture is underfunded.
Science is starved of basic funding. The old, the poor and the jobless
have no support. Schools, education and training are in decline. All
public services are constantly trimmed and forced to reduce both the
quality and the range of their services. Yet the unemployed go idle and
massive real need remains unsatisfied. Markets are capable of satisfying only some demands; needs in the public domain, needs without
the backing of sufficient private cash, remain unsatisfied. An economy based on pure market forces, with no consideration for real needs,
leaves large parts of the population in distress. Fast technological
innovation exacerbates the problems, rather than alleviating them.

We are told constantly that innovation occurs only in response to
human needs, that the desires for improved technology are the desires
of the great buying public. In my view, these statements are humbug.
The desires are those of the engineers and scientists, ambitious to
achieve ever more elegant solutions to self-imposed problems. The
desires are also those of the entrepreneurs, eager to carve out a niche
for themselves and make a good profit. The desires are those of manufacturers, eager to stimulate new waves of purchases for new products
when markets are saturated. The desires are often shared by politicians,
keen to be seen as champions of modernity and progress, and eager to
see their country in the forefront of innovation.

I have argued repeatedly that innovation is rarely a result of market demands, let alone of real needs. In most cases innovation is based on technological feasibility, coupled with a wishful hunch that the market might be persuaded to buy the new product or process. Time and again one hears remarks made by disappointed engineers: 'We have the technology – where is the market? We have to break this deadlock!' 'Industry does not need anything that does not exist.' 'We are chasing that elusive animal, market take-up.'

Technology-push is the dominant mode of innovation, although market-pull does exist in a limited number of situations. In particular, assembling manufacturers know fairly accurately what improvement innovations they want from their suppliers.

Similarly, once a radically new technology has obtained a foothold in the market, early purchasers do help the innovator to find its weaknesses and make suggestions for improvements. In general, the market can signal needed improvements, but radically new technologies arise from ideas by engineers and scientists who bear marketing possibilities in a hopeful mind.

The Cost of Rapid Change

There is a price to pay for speed. If we wish to produce technological innovations as fast as possible, we must invest very large sums into research and development, much larger than if we were prepared to accept a more sedate pace of technological change. The need for high expenditure is aggravated if we are unwilling to wait for one step of development to be completed before taking the next step; instead, in our haste to innovate faster, we wish to explore several avenues simultaneously. As, by definition, the outcome of R&D is uncertain, high speed of innovation requires that we should try all conceivable approaches at once, knowing full well that some of the effort will be wasted. Indeed, we must often conjecture the outcome of any particular step in any one of the avenues being explored, in order to take the next step sooner than the outcome of the logically preceding step is known. We must act on mere hints, hunches and preliminary results, thus wasting valuable resources, but gaining more highly valued time. The parallel approach to R&D is certainly more expensive than the linear one, but it is faster and, hence, is now often preferred.

Because of the tremendous pressures of time, most R&D is conducted hastily and mistakes are likely to be made. These have to be rectified later, at high cost. Sometimes the cost of mistakes is borne, in part, by the customer, as early models of a new product are likely to display any number of faults. If there is insufficient time for testing the new products, the customer is assigned the role of guinea-pig. Neither customers nor, for that matter, four-legged guinea-pigs, take on this role willingly. However, playing involuntary guinea-pigs is only a minor part of the cost of rapid technological change that we all bear, for if rapid technological development is substantially more expensive than more sedate progress, this expense must be reflected in the cost of the products. Although the manufacturer bears the cost in the first place, he must achieve repayment of these costs if he wishes to remain in business. Innovation without pay-back is clearly not an acceptable business proposition.

It is often said that the fast imitator is likely to reap greater benefits than the original innovator. To be second is often more lucrative than to be first. This may be so, but even to be second requires very great effort and expenditure. The risk of being third or fourth is great, and the fruits of an innovation are often entirely consumed by the fastest imitators. If progress were more sedate, the window of opportunity open to firms on any product would be much more extensive and the risks of failing to retrieve the cost of R&D and the investment in new production facilities would be lessened. As the cost of R&D and the investments associated with the introduction of new products are very substantial and increase with increased speed of innovation, the consumer ultimately pays a surcharge for rapid innovation.

If technological progress were more sedate, it would be possible to assess the market for new products more accurately, and thus the very large over-investments now commonly made in production facilities for new products could be avoided. Over-investments are caused not only by inaccurate assessments of total markets, but also by the fear that the next innovation will make the product obsolete; hence there is a perceived urgency to make hay while the sun shines. As more production facilities for a new product come on stream, competition becomes more severe and prices fall. The good times, when monopoly profits can be made on a new, desirable and scarce product, are very short.

Rapid innovation carries an increased risk of total failure. Many inventions never reach the market and the costs associated with their R&D must be written off. Even many technically successful innovations are failures in the market and their costs must also be written off. Innovating is a gamble, and gamblers often lose their stakes. Whereas many innovators lose money and many innovating firms go bust, by and large innovating firms, especially the large ones that manage to spread their risks over a wide portfolio of innovations, do manage to make profits. The invariable losers are the customers, who pay for the innovations; or the economy at large, which pays the price of inordinately rapid and risky innovation. In fairness, it ought to be added that firms that rest on their laurels and stop innovating altogether, usually run into severe difficulties. We do acknowledge that individual firms have to try to keep up with the general pace of innovation. Our argument is that this pace is too fast, that firms collectively should do nothing to accelerate it, and that governments should avoid attempting to promote innovation at an ever-faster pace.

We also acknowledge that technological innovation, albeit at a more sedate pace, brings benefits, though slower and better thought out and planned innovation would be more beneficial than the present unseemly rush in all technologically feasible directions.

The fact that innovation has become compulsive, that we cannot leave well alone, means that, time and again, we come up against the law of diminishing returns. Trying to improve an already highly developed technology imposes ever-higher costs. While progress on an entirely new technology is comparatively easy, rapid and cheap at first, it becomes increasingly difficult as the technology approaches its limits of perfection. Once the figure of performance for a given technology approaches the limits set for it by the laws of nature, or by constraints imposed by ancillary technologies, it becomes more and more difficult to achieve further improvements. Sometimes the constraints are removed by technological developments in another sphere altogether, and improvement becomes possible again. Indeed, the use of a technique in a novel setting is a common process in innovation. By and large, however, the law of diminishing returns operates without pity and without regard for human desire. Our insistence on improving some aspects of the performance of highly developed products has to be paid for dearly, as the law of diminishing returns increases the cost of each tiny step forward.

The rapid pace of innovation poses dilemmas for the setting of technical standards. Standardize too soon, and you are likely to settle on a poor technology which will be constrained by the standards as if by a strait-jacket. Standardize too late, and there will be a proliferation of technological solutions, each having cost a great deal to develop, and a large proportion of these costs will have to be written off.

The reverse side of the coin of rapid innovation is rapid obsolescence. The purchaser of the new technology is barely given time to learn how to use it to best advantage before he is told that the technology is obsolete. For the private individual this may be galling, but not catastrophic and, in any case, resistible. For the organization that has made a large investment in production or information technology, this is much more serious. Not only does it mean the premature writing off of the equipment, it also means that all the costs associated with adjusting to it are not given time to be amortized. And costs of adjustment are very high indeed: employees have to be trained, sometimes extensively, to use the new equipment. The organization often has to change its structure and its procedures to obtain the full benefit of the new technology. This is a notoriously expensive process. There is much learning associated both with making a reorganization function and with making the best use of new machinery. If both become obsolete rapidly, if indeed they are obsolescent at the time of introduction, then the optimum learning and adjustment will never be achieved. The technology will never be used to its full potential, the optimum on the learning curve will never be reached.

Individual firms and, as a result, the economy at large will use existing technology less effectively than they might otherwise do. It is a moot point whether the advantages of the successor technology can compensate for the disadvantages of the poor utilization of the predecessor technology. The point, however, is rarely made or debated, as everybody seems to cheer innovation and the excitement drowns the voices of the ordinary workers who feel constantly frustrated and ill-at-ease with what they are doing. I am not suggesting that the old lady was right who wrote a letter to *The Times* when the British currency became decimal, arguing that 'they could have waited for the old folk to die before making the change'. I am suggesting, however, that change ought to be gradual, to give time to adjust to it and make optimum use of technology for at least a while before replacing it with the latest marvels of science. At any given time some technology used in an organization will always be new and adjustment has to be permanent, but the pace of adjustment should not be too fast as this imposes very large costs both in terms of investment and in terms of inefficient use; not to mention the permanent unease of the members of the organization.

Most writers about information technology now concede that traditional cost-benefit analysis, or analysis in terms of return on investment, or pay-back period, is impracticable, meaning that the tangible and measurable benefits are too small to yield an acceptable cost to benefit ratio. But far from advocating that less should be invested in IT, it is suggested that the traditional accounting methods should be ignored and investment in IT should be regarded as a strategic investment with largely intangible and immeasurable benefits. New information technology must be bought, and if accepted methods of assessment do not produce this conclusion, ignore the results of the assessment. If the facts do not fit the theory, ignore the facts!

IT equipment is bought sometimes to justify organizational changes desired for other reasons, using flimsy calculations to justify the purchase. The hoped-for increase in efficiency often proves elusive, yet organizational changes and shifts inevitably follow in the wake of the investment in an attempt to make the best use of the new technology. The result is much dislocation, many shifts in the distribution of power, much dissatisfaction, and generally further purchases that are deemed necessary to cure the deficiencies of the first purchase. Overall satisfaction with new IT is the exception, rather than the rule.

The answer to these problems is now deemed to be a different introduction strategy for IT: a so-called bottom-up instead of the traditional top-down approach. This means that it is now recommended that more people within the organization should have a say in what is purchased and how the new technology is introduced, that more consultation with actual users should take place before an order is placed and while the software is being developed. This is all for the good and, hopefully, will slow down the precipitate pace of introducing IT that nobody really wants, although whether this approach will be taken so far as to reduce the redundancies caused by IT, is doubtful. It seems that the trend to increase the apparent labour productivity of organizations will continue, albeit at the expense of their ability to deal with exceptional cases. Real problems need solutions by real people. Despite all the lip-service to flexibility, no computer has the adaptability, imagination and empathy needed for true flexibility.

The Uncoupling of Technical Progress from Social Advance

All this frantic effort at innovation – new products, new processes, new services, changing organizations – certainly does not create the greatest amount of happiness for the greatest number of people. It creates a new elite of the very busy, very rich, very successful, although for every successful fast mover there are hundreds of unsuccessful ones. The majority of citizens are somewhat bemused; older people especially feel more than ever that 'things are not what they used to be'. Change, of course, has happened throughout the ages, yet now change is so fast that the bewilderment comes at a relatively young age and is more thorough than ever before. Finally, it leaves vast numbers of people outside; outside this self-indulgent consuming society, trapped in poverty, bewildered by their own uselessness, alienated and either apathetic or angry.

All the new technologies, all the tremendous effort at innovation, show very few signs of actually improving the lot of humanity. Egotism without enlightenment, self-indulgence and thoughtlessness for everything except the most immediate self-interest, bring no happiness in their wake. It all seems like a Faustian deal, like a frantic march towards societies without conscience and a ruined planet.

Of late, the rich have been getting richer and the poor poorer. Rapid technical progress has helped only very few of the developing countries, and it has certainly made the task of catching up with the developed world even more difficult. To the poor of the world – and they form a large majority – all the glittering new technologies are but a dream. Although advances in agriculture have made it possible to feed a growing population and starvation is not as widespread as had been predicted, the predicament of the poor has, by and large, not been lessened by advancing technology.

Some well-meaning advocates of technological innovation argue that innovation leads to growth, and growth leads to a reduction in poverty. Yet this argument is false, because growth in recent years has not led to a reduction in poverty. Stark poverty has increased in the less enlightened capitalist countries; poverty has increased in all the former socialist countries; and the gap in wealth between the developed and the developing world has increased even further. Poverty, deprivation and real hunger have become worse and economic growth, whether induced by technological innovation or not, has proved irrelevant to the elimination of poverty.

Shops are extremely well stocked and are cunningly arranged to induce the unwary to buy more than they ever intended. But the discerning buyer still finds choice very limited, and real choices not very easy to make. With so many new models of everything on the market at any given time, the few testing organizations are struggling to keep up and, generally, the consumer finds that the models described in consumers' magazines are obsolete. The sales assistants usually are not much help either. They know little or nothing about the technical intricacies of the products they sell and can offer only very limited, and probably not very objective, advice about the quality, safety, and reliability of the products they sell. Consumers are reduced to choosing by pure guesswork, or simply are guided by the pocket, as the real differences between products on offer are largely hidden. The technical jargon of the specifications is not normally intelligible and does not allow differentiation between different models. So, in the end, consumers choose on price without knowing whether they are getting good value for money; they choose on appearance, which is about all they can judge, and they choose according to what advertising proved the most persuasive or the most recent.

Fashion is a very powerful influence. This statement is obvious in clothing, where it is virtually impossible to buy anything that is not currently fashionable. But even technical goods are subject to powerful fashions. All television sets of a given period look alike, all cars, all cameras, all those technically sophisticated products look very nearly the same. Technical specifications and features also spread like wildfire. It is a pity that models are never allowed to continue to full maturity, until all the bugs are removed, and the product achieves the full performance it is designed to achieve. It is also a pity that most consumers not only do not need most of the sophisticated features, but are, in fact, never able to master their use. If change were slower, there would be time for tests to be published and for reputations to be established. People would be able to choose with more discrimination, particularly if products of different specifications, possibly of different vintages, were allowed to be on the market side by side. But such real choice for buyers who intend to keep their goods for a long time goes against the current trend of moving goods fast, making people buy the latest and making shops stock only the newest. Novelty, not quality, is the motto.

The dominant political doctrine of recent years has been capitalism without the encumbrance of more than the minimum social safety net, the minimum provision of public services, and the maximum reliance on pure self-interest as a driving force for all action. It is a time that has seen the replacement of public monopolies by private monopolies, as apparently vast private profits are morally superior to profits made by the state – ie by the public at large. It is also a time that has seen the growth of financially unsound speculative investment, with resultant massive fraud and massive bankruptcies. Crime has soared and most of the wealthy cities of the world have become unsafe. Business in security equipment is brisk. The essential meaning of civilization, enabling members of civilized societies to live in peace and security, has been eroded. The law of the jungle reigns supreme, except that in the human jungle, unlike the real one, people accumulate riches far beyond their needs. The word culture has become a vacuous description of the ambience of even the most trivial organization, while Culture itself has been largely left to the vagaries of commercial life. The results, with a few notable exceptions, are a general decline. Competition in matters of Culture leads either to a levelling down to the lowest common denominator, or to Darwinian attempts at differentiation with scant regard to quality – to be different and novel is all that matters. The desperate urge to innovate has spilled from technology into the arts.

Yet the relentless pursuit of wealth and worldly success does not lead to personal happiness. The purchase of more and more technological gadgets, possessing the latest model of stereo equipment, video recorder, or washing-machine, having a double-glazed greenhouse full of exotic plants, watching unbridled brutality on television – none of these appear to give meaning to life. Very few people can derive meaning, or deep satisfaction, from technological innovation. This is not to deny the sense of wonderment at technological marvels and the great comfort and convenience they provide – the great liberation from physical hard labour, the beneficial effects on health, and generally the many marvellously positive and by now indispensable achievements of technology. The main argument is that technology by itself is incapable of guaranteeing social progress, or of giving meaning to life. It is also arguable that the fastest rate of technological innovation without direction is not the best, nor the most valuable, nor the one that makes the greatest contribution to human happiness.

The sense of bewilderment caused by very rapid technological change, in fact, contributes greatly to the sense of disorientation, of not understanding the meaning of it all, that so many people suffer from. People feel bewildered in rapidly changing environments and lose their sense of belonging and of personal familiarity, as well as their sense of security that stems from it. Happiness is obtained by feeling at home in familiar surroundings, by knowing how to go about things, by feeling a mastery over one's job and daily tasks, by the feeling of being a useful member of society, by making a positive contribution to the well-being of society and, last but certainly not least, by living in harmony with nature, society, family and friends. A happy life is a delicate balance between challenge, struggle and change on the one hand, and well-mastered routine on the other. Different people need a different equilibrium, but the majority of people at the moment are overwhelmed by the rapidity of change.

Is not technological progress ultimately futile if it does nothing to improve the lot of the greatest part of humanity? Is it not also futile to struggle so hard to achieve rapid technological innovation if neither society nor individuals gain happiness or wisdom from it? Is it not futile to create and pander to more and more trivial wants, while real and essential needs are not catered for? We lavish funds on trivia, while education and training, health, public transport, housing for the poor, social services, public buildings and Culture languish. We create more and more toys for wealthy grown-up children, while real children do not even find nursery places and are poorly educated in schools starved of facilities.

Technological Progress and Environmental Destruction

Potentially the most fatal futility of technological development is its failure to ease the pressure exerted by humankind on the natural environment. Instead of preventing or, at least, slowing down the destruction of the natural environment, rapid technological progress exacerbates the problem. In our greed to extract the last ounce of profit, the last ounce of pleasure, the last ounce of comfort and convenience from nature, we barely spare a thought for the future. Our greed is matched only by our lack of wisdom in destroying that which sustains us.

We create new technologies at breakneck speed, discarding old machinery long before it becomes irredeemably decrepit. Thus we impose additional burdens on nature to deal with our discarded artefacts, and have to extract ever more raw materials and invest more energy to create new ones. By accelerating the cycle of obsolescence, we accelerate the cycle of extraction and waste disposal. Our increased sophistication and restless quest for novelty lead us to ever more exotic materials, to ever more toxic chemicals, to ever more dangerous processes. And we do not allow ourselves time to think about the consequences before we use all these complex marvels.

Scientists and activists have been arguing for years now that nature is being overloaded by human activities. We multiply at a most alarming rate and swarm over the planet like locusts, leaving behind us a trail of destruction which it is beyond the power of nature to heal. We have already caused innumerable species of animals and plants to disappear from the Earth for ever. We have poisoned many lakes and rivers; we have overloaded the sea and ruined many beaches; we have poisoned the soil and the ground-water; we have created innumerable waste-sites, many of them containing dangerous toxic materials; we have caused radioactive radiation levels to rise and are sitting on several time-bombs of potentially lethal nuclear reactors and chemical plants; we kill and maim daily thousands on our roads, not to mention the fact that we torture, imprison and kill in innumerable minor and major wars and other criminal activities.

SUMMARY AND CONCLUSIONS

We have now even managed to destroy parts of the ozone layer which protects us from harmful ultraviolet radiation and are in danger of destroying it to the point when life on earth might become unsustainable. We are causing the greenhouse effect by releasing greenhouse gases, particularly carbon dioxide, into the atmosphere, thus causing an imbalance between the radiation absorbed by the earth and that re-emitted into space. Most scientists believe that this effect will cause a warming of the Earth with somewhat unpredictable, but possibly catastrophic consequences. We may lose much arable land, our rainfall may be diminished in many places, and the polar ice-caps may melt, causing widespread flooding and the possible disappearance of many low-lying regions and cities.

We have destroyed most of our forests, and are busily destroying the few remaining ones, thus removing a vital source of oxygen and an equally vital sink for carbon dioxide. We are thus depriving ourselves of a life-sustaining atmosphere, as well as depriving untold species of animals, and many humans with their own unique lifestyles and cultures, of their home. We are rapidly and irretrievably depleting natural resources that took millions of years to accumulate, such as oil, natural gas and coal.

Life as we know it can be sustained only within very narrow limits of certain parameters. Raise or lower the average temperature of the planet a little, change the composition of the atmosphere, change the level of radioactivity, remove the cover of the forests, add a few toxic substances, and life becomes unsustainable. If we carry on as before – and the omens do not augur well for any substantial change of heart – humanity is doomed. It is possible, of course, that when things become utterly insufferable, there will be a slow turning back, which may rescue humanity from the brink, although not without a great deal of suffering. It is equally likely that by then it will be too late, and humankind will either wither away or be destroyed in some apocalyptic catastrophe.

But why rehearse these well-known arguments in a book dealing with technological innovation and technology policy? Because, in my view, innovation should be directed toward saving the natural environment. Obviously, problems of social injustice, and even problems of underdevelopment, cannot be addressed by technological innovation alone. But technology, if correctly harnessed, can contribute to the elimination of poverty, of suffering and of environmental destruction.

Technological innovation is relevant to saving the natural environment. It is possible to develop technologies that are more benign to the environment than present technologies. It is possible to curb the use of environmentally harmful technologies. Even if the case of harm is not proven, technologies can be deemed guilty until proven innocent. It is better to eliminate potential hazards than to discover hazards when much damage has already been done.

To the extent that governments support innovation, they should support it only if the new technologies show promise to cause environmental improvement. This innovation policy in favour of environmentally benign technologies, to the exclusion of all others, constitutes our only hope for survival. I am not suggesting that all other innovation should be discouraged, or even forbidden, but government support should be concentrated on innovations which promise to be beneficial to the environment. Governments are the only organizations that can, and therefore must, act as protectors of the environment, as the selfish and ill-informed interests catered for by untrammelled market forces cannot protect and safeguard nature.

It is futile to support technological innovation, which may or may not make some of us richer, which may or may not produce some fascinating toys, while our house is on fire. The first priority must be to safeguard life on earth; everything else is secondary and ultimately futile.

Even the protection of the environment cannot be left to technological innovation or to technologists. As the Rio Earth Summit showed very clearly, the countries of the Third World are not willing to do their part towards protection unless they are compensated for their costs by the rich countries of the world. As the rich countries are the major consumers of energy and raw materials, as the rich countries are the main polluters, it is the rich countries who ought to help the poor to overcome their poverty without imposing further hardship on the environment.

Technological innovation that does nothing to safeguard the natural environment, that does nothing to address social injustice, that does not address real needs but destabilizes society by constant rapid change, is not the saviour of humanity and is not deserving of public support.

Policy Recommendations

Technology has become too important to be left to technologists or, worse still, to the market. Indeed, leaving it to the market is a euphemism, as the rules of the market are made by government and the phrase 'leave it to the market' simply signals contentment with the existing rules. One major aspect of the present rules of the market is that the common interest is ignored and pure self-interest is the only factor considered by all participants in the exchange mechanisms of the market. Thus the public interest, including safeguarding the natural environment, is neglected and is taken into account only if specific regulations force the actors in the market to consider such interests.

We can divide the activities required by government in matters of technology into four spheres: indirect actions; environmental policy; and technology policy proper, consisting of control and of support. For our purposes, we shall somewhat blur the distinctions between different policy spheres, as it is often a combination of policies from different spheres that is most effective.

Indirect action includes primarily education and training, regulation of labour markets, macro-economic management, and industrial, agricultural, defence and health policies. It is quite possible that the total influence of indirect policies on technology is greater than that of technology policy, but despite this, our focus is firmly on technology policy and indirect policy influences will be dealt with in the briefest possible way.

Education and training policy, regarded narrowly from the point of view of technology, must ensure a sufficient supply of people who are qualified in all spheres and at all levels required by industry. This does not mean manpower planning, but it does mean providing adequate educational facilities and resources, ensuring that education and training keep abreast of changing technologies, and coordinating efforts by industry itself to provide on-the-job training. A complex web of apprenticeships, educational establishments at all levels, and a system of formal qualifications are all part and parcel of a thriving industry and of an effective national innovative capability.

Industrial policies must ensure that industry has all the right conditions to thrive in. An adequate, efficient and reasonably priced network of transport, adequate and reasonably priced power, effective protection of intellectual property rights, are, among others, all preconditions for success.

Government creates the conditions under which investment in industry takes place. One way or another, government must try to safeguard sufficient investment for industry, probably by making purely speculative and unproductive investments and financial manipulations less attractive. Under certain circumstances, it is necessary for government to help industrial firms out of temporary difficulties, provided the help may reasonably be expected to enable the industry to prosper again in the foreseeable future. This may be particularly necessary in industries that have to face major structural change. Although it is not possible, even for government, to halt certain developments, it is possible to ease the transition.

All the help that government can give by way of information and advisory services, especially to SMEs, and by way of coordination of industrial cooperation, may be useful aspects of a generally supportive industrial policy. Regional policies and spatial planning may also be important, and thus local as well as central government has a role to play.

We shall leave the indirect policies influencing technology in this sketchy and incomplete form and concentrate on direct technology and environmental policy.

Technology policy in its supportive role should provide all the help it can for the technologies society requires and the market cannot adequately support. No exhaustive and all-embracing prescription can be offered; all we can do is state the principle and give a few examples. Anything more would be out-of-date very quickly and could not possibly apply to all situations encountered in practice, for technology policy, as any other policy, must not only be timely, it must also suit local circumstances. These may consist of existing strengths and weaknesses in industry, in the economy and in natural resources. Circumstances also include the nature of the available workforce, existing trading patterns, existing investment patterns, institutional settings, R&D capabilities, prevailing attitudes and opinions, geographic and climatic conditions, and many more peculiarities of a given economic region or entity.

The following examples may serve our purpose to illustrate the principles that ought to guide decisions on public support for technologies.

Public Transport
Public transport has become the victim of a vicious circle: the more cars there are, the fewer people use public transport; thus public transport declines and causes more people to buy and use cars. This in turn reduces the utility of the car and the quality of life in cities, and imposes a heavy burden on the environment. Despite this, without policy intervention, public transport is apparently unable to regain lost ground. Depending upon local circumstances, the solution to this intractable problem requires a cleverly chosen combination of several measures:

1. Improvements in public transport by a combination of technological improvements and investment into known technologies.
2. Improvements in the environmental compatibility of cars, vans, lorries and public service vehicles, including taxis.
3. Improvements in the combination of long-distance goods haulage with local distribution by lorry or van.
4. Rationing of road space and provision of parking spaces in suitable locations. Whether rationing is by price or by licence is both a political and a practical issue.
5. Planning of urban regions to reduce the necessity for travel.
6. Reinstatement of shopping deliveries, possibly aided by home-shopping and secure delivery ports to make the presence of the recipient unnecessary.
7. Home or local centre distance working may provide some help, but the full social and psychological, as well as the technical and economic, implications ought to be considered very carefully.

This example shows how a major social problem might be tackled by an judicious mix of a large range of policy measures; some technical, and some from several other spheres of public policy. Although technological innovations are necessary, social innovations are equally important. The new technologies may range from improved home shopping and tele-working, improved road space rationing, new or improved forms of transport, such as monorails, trams and electric vehicles, and train-to-van loading, right down to mundane facilities such as delivery ports in homes. Some of these technologies and systems might be commercially viable without government assistance, but government assistance is required on some aspects and government (central and local) coordination is required throughout. R&D support may be necessary for some of the technologies to be developed, but this is not the most important aspect of policy requirements. To reverse the entrenchment of the car and the neglect of public transport, substantial support in the introduction of the new systems will be needed.

Clean technologies
Clean technologies cover a whole range of widely differing technologies. These include metal-plating processes; paper-making; fertilizers, pesticides or herbicides; washing powders and liquids; industrial degreasing processes; the clean burning of fossil fuels; clean car exhausts or zero emission cars; and any number of other technologies. Clean technologies can be developed under three circumstances:

1. If they are genuinely cheaper than their dirty counterparts.
2. If the public is fully and credibly informed about their environmental superiority and is willing and able to pay any surcharge that might be necessary.
3. If government regulation forces their development and use.

Under the first of these circumstances, the government may be required to provide help with R&D, as the economic superiority of the clean products need not be instantly apparent. Once it is established, the market can do the rest, although the government may provide some help with information and coordination. The second set of circumstances requires the government to be active in making sure that reliable and trustworthy information about the environmental performance of products is obtained and disseminated. Labelling of products can work, but it must be done with credibility and intelligence if it is to provide the right market signals. Rules of advertising may be necessary that force manufacturers to disclose environmentally desirable, as well as undesirable, properties of their products. The third set of circumstances requires technology policy in the regulatory mode, but it may also require policy in the supportive mode in order to enable firms to comply with regulations. Regulation is only as good as the possibility (and the enforcement) of compliance. Clean technologies may require support in the form of help with R&D and help with information and coordination. Occasionally, launching aid may be needed, and some form of independent and authoritative eco-labelling may be very helpful. Regulations are vital and must be worked out with the aid of independent government advisers and representatives from the relevant industries. Policies for clean technology can only succeed by a judicious mix of carrot, stick and information.

Energy
Research into new ways of energy production has been receiving substantial government aid ever since the heady days of hope for cheap, clean, inexhaustible energy from nuclear fission and, even better, nuclear fusion. Much money has been spent, somewhat less is being spent, and much of the hope has been dissipated. Although nuclear power generation has become a well-established industry, the power it produces is not cheap and many people have serious misgivings about both the operational safety of the power stations and about the safety implications of the long-term storage of radioactive waste, not to mention the dangers of radioactive materials falling into irresponsible hands. The economic misgivings are such that even the British government, bent upon privatizing everything in sight, has so far not found a way of privatizing nuclear power generation! Considering the principle of better safe than sorry, and the even more important principle of not leaving a troublesome legacy to future generations, we doubt very much whether more public investment into nuclear energy can be justified, even if nuclear power generation does have the great advantage of not contributing to the greenhouse effect.

Substantial progress has been made in de-coupling economic growth from increases in energy consumption, but even more progress could be made. Some countries still consume much more energy per capita than others, despite similar standards of living. Government can help greatly by providing aid to reduce energy consumption. This can take the form of advice, tax incentives, direct grants, building and other regulations, publicly funded R&D, and launching aid for energy-efficient products.

Of equal importance is government policy for alternative energy sources. Substantial support is needed in R&D for such resources. Help is also needed in overcoming institutional obstacles. Why, for example, should private monopoly electricity generators bother to choose any form of primary energy supply other than the one that optimizes their immediate profits? Price mechanisms do not reflect the long-term interests of the global resource position; they merely reflect a short-term balance between supply and demand and the relative power of various suppliers and users. Thus reliance on price mechanisms is not enough to secure the long-term future; only active government policy can do that.

It is remarkable that simple solar energy water-heaters are much more widespread in some southern countries than in others. The reason must be the relationship between the cost of such devices and the cost of other energy sources, although building regulations may also exert an influence. It is necessary for governments to tilt the balance in favour of solar energy water-heaters, even if initial aid might be required to reduce the costs of production and installation.

There are many avenues of research to be explored and international cooperation and coordination may be needed. But there are also relatively simple policies available to boost the cause of sustainable energy production and energy saving (Elliott: 1994).

Information Technology
It is debatable whether government support for this family of technologies was required in their infancy, but by now they are well established, entrenched, profitable and environmentally largely irrelevant. Thus there is no good reason why government should support them. The support they receive is given merely to enhance international competitiveness and accelerate innovation of socially doubtful benefit. This is not, in my view, what governments should do.

Telecommunications, on the other hand, although often operated privately, does form part and parcel of the technical infrastructure of the state and is thus a government responsibility. Because telecommunications, by and large, is a highly profitable industry, this responsibility extends only to providing suitable regulation and supervision to ensure social utility and equity of the network. Where a telecommunications network is in public ownership, there is the added responsibility of government to ensure that it receives sufficient investment.

Government is responsible for regulating the industry. This is necessary to ensure equity of access, fairness in tariffs, and to find a locally suitable and politically desired mix between regulated monopoly and publicly moderated competition. It has to be moderated, for equitable access and unbridled competition are incompatible demands. The regulation and institutional arrangements may affect technological developments, but that is not their primary purpose (Pisjak 1994). Part of the regulation involves the setting of standards. These are particularly important in this industry, as otherwise networks and their parts could not function and certain requirements, such as privacy and security of information, could not be guaranteed.

The recent trend of telecommunications, information technology services and mass media all growing together, calls for government regulation but not for government support. Issues of the monopoly of provision and issues of the content of the entertainment and information services do arise. The British and US governments wish to be seen as supporting the idea of information highways (with or without added superlatives), but in reality the development of these networks is a matter of private investment within a regulatory setting. In the US, where the industry is highly decentralized, the presidential rhetoric will probably make little difference (Sawhney: 1993). In Britain, the regulatory regime will determine whether much of the network will be built by British Telecom (by far the largest telecommunications operator and successor to the telecommunications activities of the Post Office), or by cable television operators, often in US ownership (*The Observer*, 31 July 1994). The true benefits of the much heralded information highways are subject to some doubt (Blackman: 1994) and the benefits of high-definition TV must be doubted even more.

Although government cannot escape its role as provider or regulator of the extremely important telecommunications infrastructure, by and large information technology is an example of a technology that does not need intervention by government technology policy, other than the creation of a regulatory framework. Indeed, IT provides one example of the majority of instances when technological innovation may safely be left to commercial interests. Technological progress is quite fast enough without being accelerated by government intervention.

Government intervention in technology is necessary only in the following circumstances:

1. Long-term national interests are at stake. A good example is provided by the energy sector, discussed above.
2. Vital interests that have no markets are at stake. We have repeatedly argued that governments must intervene on behalf of those interests that cannot be represented by purchasing decisions in the market. The protection of the natural environment is a prime example of this situation. A balance between regulation and support for environmentally beneficial technological innovations must be sought.
3. Provision of infrastructure. Examples are public transport, which needs support, and telecommunications which merely needs to be regulated.

The overall aims of technology policy may be summed up as follows:

1. To secure that technological solutions are found for problems that are of major social interest, yet are not adequately signalled by market forces. Sometimes markets provide signals for the seeking out of short-term solutions, whereas the long-term interest of the nation (or the world) poses quite different problems. It is a task for technology policy to seek out the long-term interest and support solutions for it.
2. Research into health care cannot be left to markets alone. While pharmaceutical firms and medical-instrument makers are very able to develop drugs or equipment, it must be doubted whether they can cater for the interests of very small minorities and, more to the point, whether they can carry out medical research as well as public health research. Some medical technologies, such as artificial organs, involve too much cost and too much risk, and are ethically too sensitive, to be developed without government aid.

3. Technology policy must attempt to bring about innovations that improve the general standards of safety and health, improve standards and efficiency of government activity, and, finally, improve the quality of life of the community. Examples are safety of all products, refuse treatment, sea defences, protection of landscape and forests.
4. Government technology policy should not attempt to accelerate commercially produced and socially indifferent technologies. Although the welfare of the population may require economic intervention in the interest of employment and growth, this should be aimed at industrial and macro-economic policy, or at technologies and infrastructure in the sense discussed above.

All attempts by the government to intervene directly in favour of specific market-oriented innovations are both unnecessary and likely to be ineffectual. Market-oriented innovation requires intimate and detailed knowledge that is available only within the firms concerned and it requires swift responses which government machinery is incapable of achieving. On the other hand, badly needed socially and environmentally oriented technologies cannot thrive without government help.

A technology policy designed to foster sustainable development, as any technology policy, must consist of a blend of regulation and support. It goes without saying that regulation should be kept to a necessary minimum, that it should not impose unnecessary burdens, that it should be readily enforceable and that it should be seen to be fair.

Regulation of technology by some branch of government is necessary in the following situations:

1. The use of a certain technology imposes hazards to health and/or safety. Market forces operate either too slowly or not at all to eliminate such hazards.
2. The use of a certain technology by one user may interfere with the use of the same technology by others, or may generally cause a nuisance to the public. Market forces alone are incapable of preventing such cases of interference; in fact, it is one of the essential tasks delegated to the governing bodies of any civilized society to do just that. The protection of citizens from nuisance and hazard, in whatever shape or form, is at the core of governance.
3. Protection of the natural environment. The obvious cases in point are controls of emissions and effluents; the less obvious, but equally important, cases are concerned with the control of gases damaging to the ozone layer or contributing to the greenhouse effect; control of the use of fertilizers, pesticides and fungicides; control of oil-spills; protection of forests; protection of areas of outstanding natural beauty; protecting the habitat of wildlife. A further major area of protection is the preservation of

scarce raw materials, either by encouraging firms to be sparing in their use or by encouraging recycling.

Direct regulation of technology can operate by three means: proscription; prescription (specification); incentive.

In a sense, prescription or specification also involves prohibition, for it means that the use of devices falling outside the prescribed specifications is prohibited. Prescription can be specific, as, for example, the use of a certain wavelengh for a specified purpose; or it can be general, such as the requirement that all cars used on public roads should comply with certain design specifications. Similarly, it is prescribed that effluents or emissions should not exceed certain general limits, although for large and specialist polluters, these limits may be specifically prescribed for a particular operation or manufacturing plant.

Finally, we may attempt to control technology by incentives, such as raising taxes on fuel to encourage the efficient use of energy; reducing the price of public transport to encourage its widespread use; imposing charges for effluents instead of, or in addition to, prescribing levels of pollution.

The advantage of incentives is, of course, that they need far less bureaucratic control, but the disadvantages are that they do only work to a limited extent under special circumstances and they are not equitable. Imposing charges on fuel will certainly not deter the rich from using as much energy as they please, while it may condemn the poor to suffer acute discomfort.

The Future of Technological Innovation

The rising costs of R&D and the increasing sophistication of technological developments have the effect of causing more and more cooperation between firms. They also cause mergers, takeovers and business failures, so that the tendency in the older branches of high technology is for very few world firms to dominate the markets. This has happened in the aircraft industry, the automobile industry, in telecommunications equipment, large computers, microelectronics, steel, chemicals, pharmaceuticals, and to some extent even in food processing. This continuing tendency toward oligopolies is likely to decelerate the pace of innovation. More and more giant firms may reach the conclusion that the rapid pace of innovation is too costly and is not worth the likely gains in terms of reviving stagnant markets. Although the escape from stagnation will remain a goal of innovators, they might attempt to reach this goal more slowly and be content for longer periods with large market shares of relatively saturated markets before launching new products.

The cost of innovation and the risk of not recouping these costs are rising and this is a self-limiting factor on the pace of innovation. Firms, even very large firms, can neither spend the money nor can they afford to take the risks which fast innovation entails. If governments gradually withdraw their support for commercial innovation, which they are likely to do because they are increasingly short of cash, then firms might be naturally inclined to slow down the pace.

Finally, as innovation becomes more and more centred on large firms, it becomes increasingly inhibited by their bureaucratic apparatus. Large firms, just as governments, are incapable of swift responses. They suffer from complex decision mechanisms and are as difficult to steer as large ships.

Although large firms try to reduce costs and risks by cooperation with other firms and – an important tendency – by passing them on to their suppliers, there are limits to these processes. The main limit is the willingness and ability of suppliers to take on development tasks at their own cost and risk. The second limit is the difficulty of maintaining control over the technology if the number of independent players becomes too large.

At present rates of unemployment and with the strong tendency of process innovations to be labour-saving, the hope of finding salvation in innovation looks increasingly forlorn. Although there is no a priori reason to think that advances in technology will lead to a tendency of capital investment to be labour-saving, there are good empirical grounds for believing that this is the case. High technology does not offer much choice in the mix of factors of production. It is impossible to produce a microelectronic circuit element (microchip) without extensive capital equipment. No amount of labour can substitute for precision machinery; it is entirely impossible to manufacture this type of technology in a labour-intensive way. The same is true for most products of high technology. Even if managers wanted to increase the labour content of their production, which is not likely, they are not able to do so in cases of high technology. This is tragic for the labour forces in developed countries. It is also tragic for developing countries, because their advantage of cheap labour operates in a diminishing sphere of economic activity.

On balance, we are unlikely to solve most of our economic problems by increasing the rate of unnecessary innovation. We are much more likely to solve them by addressing technological innovation to real needs, by developing the sadly neglected infrastructure, by finding ways of financing much-needed labour-intensive services, and by sharing out the work there is – eg by reducing the working week and increasing leisure time.

Some of the most successful industrial firms respond to the risk of losing market shares not by introducing pointless innovations at the fastest possible rate, but by producing products of high quality and innovating only when such innovation is justified by the achievement of true improvements. To hold market shares by a high reputation for quality may be a better response than the attempt to hold on to market shares by a fast flow of trivial innovations.

The challenge to society is not how to innovate faster, but how to find the financial means to develop public transport, health services, educational facilities, and so on. What people need most are these services, not high-definition television, digital sound recording, broadband communications, or more television channels dispensing the same trash as the existing ones. If our cities are to be pleasant places to live in, we must solve the problems of congestion, waste disposal, public cleansing, and, last but not least, poverty-stricken and decaying areas.

If our society is to become civilized, we do not need faster cars and better mousetraps. What we need is to get rid of crime, which is closely related to social alienation, and to get rid of drug abuse, which is closely related to total disillusionment with the way society lives. No amount of technological innovation will solve these problems; it is social innovation that is needed.

We are clutching at straws if we believe that the wave of technological innovations related to information and communication technologies (ICT) will herald the beginning of a new economic upswing, a new Kondratiev wave in economic activity. Despite all that has been said about the difficulty of knowing whether ICT creates or destroys jobs, the view that, on balance, it is a destroyer of jobs appears much more plausible. ICT leads to increased capital and decreased labour intensity in manufacture and, infinitely worse, it has the same effect in the service sector. It is no accident that in Britain services are shedding labour at as alarming a rate as manufacturing industries. Indeed, banks are currently justifying their labour-shedding programmes by saying bluntly that the introduction of information technology has caused their activities to require less labour.

The large-scale unemployment in the developed countries has, of course, reduced the purchasing power of the population and the fear of unemployment has reduced their willingness to part with their money. But even the wealthy do not spend much of their income on industrial goods. They purchase positional goods, eg antiques, or they spend money on exotic travel and on similar services. Often they indulge in speculative financial machinations which can only have detrimental effects on the real economy. It is unlikely that ordinary economic growth will lead to such demand for goods or services as to compensate for labour-saving effects of ICT and no amount of innovation is likely to solve the problem of unemployment.

What is required is not more innovation, but a change of direction. Public support should not be given to innovation as such, but only to innovations that are necessary for the protection of those public interests, eg the natural environment, that markets cannot protect. What is needed is not growth as such, but a new emphasis on cures for social ills: unemployment, alienation, crime, drug abuse, traffic congestion, decay of the inner cities, environmental degradation. The question is not whether we become a little richer and have a few more 'toys', but whether civilization, or indeed life on earth, can survive. What is needed is innovation in the interests of environmental protection, of health and safety, and of infrastructures that can secure a civilized existence. Some leading politicians are well aware of the need for new departures (see eg Lafontaine 1989), but unfortunately not enough of those who are in power.

It is obscene to indulge in technological frills while half the world is starving or living in sub-human conditions. It is obscene that governments should lend support to speculations about making Mars habitable while not giving much thought to maintaining life on earth. We must turn our attention to real issues and away from the twin illusions that random technological innovation can achieve economic growth and that growth can solve all our problems. Let the market cater for technological innovation and let governments get on with their task of securing the public interest that markets cannot secure. Civilized survival is at stake.

REFERENCES

$\blacklozenge$

Aichholzer, G and G Schienstock (editors) (1994) *Technology Policy – Toward an Integration of Social and Ecological Concerns*, De Gruyter, Berlin & New York

Basalla, G (1988) *The Evolution of Technology*, Cambridge University Press, Cambridge

Bentham, J (1970) *An Introduction to the Principles of Morals and Legislation, The Collected Works of Jeremy Bentham*, edited by J H Burns and H L A Hart, University of London Athlone Press, London

Berg von, I (1994) *Technology Assessment in Europe*, AFAS, Kernforschungszentrum, Karlsruhe

Berry, B J L and F E Horton (1974) *Urban Environmental Management*, Prentice-Hall, Englewood Cliffs, New Jersey

Bessant, J (1991) *Managing Advanced Manufacturing Technology : Fifth Wave*, NCC Blackwell, Oxford

Blackman, C (1994), 'Editorial' *Telecommunications Policy*, vol 18, p3

Braun, E (1984a) *Wayward Technology*, Frances Pinter, London

Braun, E (1984b) 'Science and Technology as Partners in Technological Innovation' *Physics in Technology*, vol 15, pp80–5

Braun, E (1987) 'Technology Assessment in Industry' *International Journal of Technology Management*, vol 2, pp515–23

Braun, E and S Macdonald (1982) *Revolution in Miniature*, Cambridge University Press, Cambridge, 2nd edition

Braun, E and D Wield (1994) 'Regulation as a Means for the Social Control of Technology' *Technology Analysis & Strategic Management*, vol 6, pp259–72

Bruce, A and T Buck (1994) 'State Promotion of High-definition Television', *Technology Analysis & Strategic Management*, vol 6, pp161–76

Bundesminister für Forschung und Technologie & Bundesminister für Wirtschaft (1989) *Zukunftskonzept Informationstechnik*, Pressereferat, Bonn

Cabinet Office (1993a) White Paper Cm 2250, *Realising Our Potential*, HMSO, London

Cabinet Office (1993b) *Research Foresight and the Exploitation of the Science Base*, HMSO, London

Carson, R (1965) *Silent Spring*, Penguin Books, Harmondsworth (first published in USA in 1962)

Central Statistical Office (1992) *Social Trends 22*, HMSO, London

Collingridge, D (1980) *The Social Control of Technology*, Open University Press, Milton Keynes

Collingridge, D (1987) *Criticism – its Philosophical Structure*, University Press of America, Lanham

Collingridge, D (1990) 'Technology Organizations and Incrementalism: the Space Shuttle' *Technology Analysis & Strategic Management*, vol 2, pp181–200

Collingridge, D (1992) *The Management of Scale*, Routledge, London

Commission of the European Communities (1992) *Towards Sustainability, A European Community Programme of Policy Action in Relation to the Environment and Sustainable Development*, CEC, Brussels

REFERENCES

Commission of the European Communities (1993) *Growth, Competitiveness, Employment – The Challenges and Ways Forward into the 21st Century*, White Paper, Part C, Contributions by Member States, Office for Official Publications of the European Communities, Luxembourg

Commission of the European Communities (1994) *Proposals for Council Decisions Concerning the Specific Programmes Implementing the Fourth European Community Framework Programme for Research, Technological Development and Demonstration* (1994–1998), Office for Official Publications of the European Communities, Luxembourg

Commoner, B (1972) *The Closing Circle: confronting the environmental crisis*, Jonathan Cape, London

Coombs, R, P Saviotti, V Walsh (1987) *Economics and Technological Change*, Macmillan, London

Daly, H (1991) *Steady-State Economics*, Island Press, Washington DC

de Hoo, S C, R E H M Smits, R Petrella (1987) *Technology Assessment – an Opportunity for Europe*, NOTA, The Hague

Department of the Environment (1979) *Chlorofluorocarbons and their Effect on Stratospheric Ozone*, Pollution Paper No 15, HMSO, London

Department of the Environment (1992) *Waste Management Paper No 1 – A Review of Options*, second edition, HMSO, London

Department of Transport (1994) *Choosing Safety*, HMSO, London

Dietz, F J and W J M Heijman (editors) (1988) *Environmental Policy in a Market Economy*, Pudoc, Wageningen

Dodson, E N (1985) 'Measurement of State of the Art and Technological Advance' *Technological Forecasting and Social Change*, vol 27, pp129–46

Dosi, G, C Freeman, R Nelson, G Silverberg, L Soete (editors) (1988) *Technical Change and Economic Theory*, Pinter Publishers, London

Douthwaite, R (1992) *The Growth Illusion*, Green Books, Bideford

Elliott, D A (1985) *Defence Conversion – a review of options for product diversification and the redeployment of labour in the defence industries*, Open University, Milton Keynes

Elliott, D A (1994) 'Regulation, Technology Strategy and Energy Policy: the missing link' *Technology Analysis & Strategic Management*, vol 6, pp305–15

European Commission (1994) *Growth, Competitiveness, Employment – The Challenges and Ways Forward into the 21st Century*, Office for Official Publications of the European Communities, Luxembourg

Freeman, C (1974) *The Economics of Industrial Innovation*, Penguin Books, Harmondsworth

Freeman, C and L Soete (1991) *Macro-Economic and Sectoral Analysis of Future Employment and Training Perspectives in the New Information Technologies in the European Community*, Executive Summary, EC Conference, Brussels

Freeman, C, J Clark, L Soete (1982) *Unemployment and Technical Innovation*, Frances Pinter, London

Fremlin, J (1972) *Be Fruitful and Multiply*, Rupert Hart-Davis, London

Galbraith, J K (1992) *The Culture of Contentment*, Sinclair-Stevenson, London

Giarini, O and H Loubergé (1978) *The Diminishing Returns of Technology*, Pergamon Press, Oxford

Grabowski, H (1991) *Centre for Medicines Research Annual Lecture*, Duke University, North Carolina

Henderson, H (1980) *Creating Alternative Futures – The End of Economics*, Pedigree Books, New York

Hetman, F (1973) *Society and the Assessment of Technology*, OECD, Paris

Hewitt, T, H Johnson, D Wield (editors) (1992) *Industrialization and Development*, Oxford University Press, Oxford

Hill, S (1988) *The Tragedy of Technology*, Pluto Press, London

Hirsch, F (1977) *Social Limits to Growth*, Routledge & Kegan Paul, London

Hodges, L (1973) *Environmental Pollution*, Holt Rinehart & Winston, New York

References

Houston, J P (1981) *The Pursuit of Happiness*, Scott, Foresman and Company, Glenview
Hübner, H (editor) (1986) *The Art and Science of Innovation Management*, Elsevier, Amsterdam
Knapp, B, S Ross, D McCrae (1989) *Challenge of the Natural Environment*, Longman, Harlow
Krieger-Mytelka, L (editor) (1991) *Strategic Partnerships and the World Economy*, Pinter Publishers, London and New York
Kuhn, T (1970) *The Structure of Scientific Revolutions*, University of Chicago Press, Chicago, 2nd edition
Lafontaine, O (1989) *Die Gesellschaft der Zukunft*, Wilhelm Heyne Verlag, München
Levidow, L (1994) 'Biotechnology Regulation as Symbolic Normalization' *Technology Analysis & Strategic Management*, vol 6, pp273–88
Lippmann, W (1943) *The Good Society*, Grosset & Dunlap, New York (first published 1936)
Mann, D E (editor) (1981) *Environmental Policy Formation*, Lexington Books, Lexington
Martino, J P (1985) 'Measurement of Technology using Tradeoff Surfaces' *Technological Forecasting and Social Change*, vol 27, pp147–60
Massey, D, P Quintas, D Wield (1992) *High Tech Fantasies*, Routledge, London
Matzner, E, R Schettkat, M Wagner (1988) *Beschäftigungsrisiko Innovation?* Rainer Bohn Verlag, Berlin
Matzner, E and W Streeck (editors) (1991) *Beyond Keynesianism – The Socio-Economics of Production and Full Employment*, Edward Elgar, Aldershot
Meadows, D H, D L Meadows, J Randers, W Behrens (1974) *Limits to Growth*, Pan Books, London
Meadows, D H, D L Meadows, J Randers (1992) *Beyond the Limits: g;obal collapse or a sustainable future*, Earthscan, London
Mill, J S (1985) *On Liberty*, Penguin Books, Harmondsworth (first published in 1859)
Mowery, D C and N Rosenberg (1989) *Technology and the Pursuit of Economic Growth*, Cambridge University Press, Cambridge
National Society for Clean Air and Environmental Protection (NSCA) (1991) *1991 Pollution Handbook*, NSCA, Brighton
Nelson, R R and S G Winter (1982) *An Evolutionary Theory of Economic Change*, Harvard University Press, Boston
Nieuwenhuis, P, P Cope, J Armstrong (1992) *The Green Car Guide*, Green Print, London
OECD (1988) *New Technologies in the 1990s*, OECD, Paris
OECD (1989) *International Seminar on Science, Technology and Economic Growth*, OECD, Paris
OECD (1992) *Technology and the Economy*, OECD, Paris
OECD (1993) *Safety Considerations for Biotechnology: Scale-up of Crop Plants*, OECD, Paris
Parliamentary Office of Science and Technology (POST) (1991) *Relationships Between Defence & Civil Science and Technology*, London
Paul, I (1987) *Technikfolgen-Abschätzung als Aufgabe für Staat und Unternehmen*, Peter Lang Verlag, Frankfurt am Main
Peacock, A (editor) (1984) *The Regulation Game*, Blackwell, Oxford
Peissl, W (1989) *Lokale innerbetriebliche Telekommunikationsnetze*, Austrian Academy of Sciences, Vienna
Pisjak, P (1994) 'The Interdependence Between Regulation and Technological Innovation in the Telecommunications Sector' *Technology Analysis & Strategic Management*, vol 6, pp289–303
Popper, K (1966) *The Open Society and its Enemies*, vols 1 & 2, Routledge & Kegan Paul, London, 5th edition
Popper, K (1969) *Conjectures and Refutations*, Routledge and Kegan Paul, London, 3rd edition

References

Popper, K (1992) *In Search of a Better World*, Routledge, London

Porter, A L, F Rossini, R A Carpenter, G Roper (1980) *A Guidebook for Technology Assessment and Impact Analysis*, North Holland, New York

Potter, S and M Hinnells (1994) 'Whither the Eco-Label' *Technology Analysis & Strategic Management*, vol 6, pp317–28

Roberts, E B (editor) (1987) *Generating Technological Innovation*, Oxford University Press, New York

Roberts, L and A Weale (editors) (1991) *Innovation and Environmental Risk*, Belhaven Press, London and New York

Rosenberg, N (1994) *Exploring the Black Box*, Cambridge University Press, Cambridge

Rothman, H (1972) *Murderous Providence*, Rupert Hart-Davis, London

Rothwell, R (1992) 'Development Towards the Fifth Generation Model of Innovation' *Technology Analysis & Strategic Management*, vol 4, pp73–5

Russell, B (1961) *The Conquest of Happiness*, George Allen & Unwin, London (first published 1930)

Sawhney, H (1993) 'Circumventing the Centre – The realities of creating a telecommunications infrastructure in the USA' *Telecommunications Policy*, vol 17, pp504–16

Scarbrough, H and J M Corbett (1992) *Technology and Organisation*, Routledge, London

Schumacher, E F (1974) *Small is Beautiful*, Sphere Books, London

Science and Technology Agency, Japanese Government (1989) *White Paper on Science and Technology 1989*, Tokyo

Seymour, J and H Girardet (1986) *Far From Paradise, The Story of Man's Impact on the Environment*, British Broadcasting Corporation, London

Siegan, B H (editor) (1980) *Government Regulation and the Economy*, Lexington Books, Lexington

Simpson, S (1990) *The Times Guide to the Environment*, Times Books, London

Smith, P M and K Warr (editors) (1991) *Global Environmental Issues*, Hodder & Stoughton, London

Steven, H and A Lindley (16 June 1990) *New Scientist*, vol 126, pp 48–51

Steward, F and G Wibberley (1991) European Institute for Advanced Studies in Management, First Workshop on Strategy for the European Pharmaceutical Industry, Brussels

Street, J (1992) *Politics and Technology*, Macmillan, London

Szalai, A and F M Andrews (editors) (1980) *The Quality of Life*, Sage, London

Tawney, R H (1924) *The Acquisitive Society*, G Bell & Sons, London (first published in 1921)

Tawney, R H (1964) *Equality*, George Allen and Unwin, London (first published in 1931)

Taylor, C and A Press (1990) *Europe and the Environment*, The Industrial Society, London

Townsend, P (1979) *Poverty in the United Kingdom*, Allen Lane, London

Townsend, P (1991) *The Poor are Poorer: a Statistical Report on Changes in the Living Standards of Rich and Poor in the United Kingdom 1979–89*, Department of Social Policy and Social Planning, University of Bristol

Twiss, B and M Goodridge (1989) *Managing Technology for Competitive Advantage*, Pitman, London

Umweltbundesamt (1993) *Beurteilungskriterien für Freisetzungen gentechnisch veränderter Organismen*, Bundesministerium für Umwelt, Vienna

United Nations (1992), *Agenda 21 Press Summary, United Nations Conference on Environment and Development*, Rio de Janeiro, June 1992, Department of Public Information, United Nations, New York

Ward, B and R Dubos (1972) *Only One Earth*, Pelican Books, Harmondsworth

Webster, A (1991) *Science, Technology and Society*, Macmillan, London

Winner, L (1977) *Autonomous Technology*, MIT Press, Cambridge, Mass

Womack, J P, D T Jones, D Roos (1990) *The Machine That Changed The World*, Rawson Associates, New York

World Commission on Environment and Development (1987) *Our Common Future*, Oxford University Press, Oxford

INDEX

◆

217

For Product Safety Concerns and Information please contact our EU representative GPSR@taylorandfrancis.com Taylor & Francis Verlag GmbH, Kaufingerstraße 24, 80331 München, Germany

Printed and bound by CPI Group (UK) Ltd, Croydon, CR0 4YY

08/05/2025

01864366-0012